D1571109

SMART
and *Sassy*

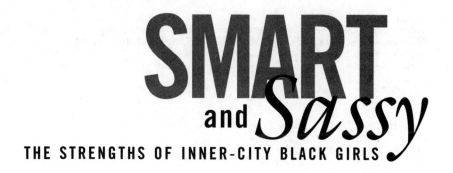

SMART
and *Sassy*
THE STRENGTHS OF INNER-CITY BLACK GIRLS

JOYCE WEST STEVENS

Boston University

New York • Oxford

OXFORD UNIVERSITY PRESS

2002

Oxford University Press

Oxford   New York
Athens   Auckland   Bangkok   Bogotá   Buenos Aires   Cape Town
Chennai   Dar es Salaam   Delhi Florence   Hong Kong   Istanbul   Karachi
Kolkata   Kuala Lumpur   Madrid   Melbourne   Mexico City   Mumbai   Nairobi
Paris   São Paulo   Shanghai   Singapore   Taipei   Tokyo   Toronto   Warsaw

and associated companies in
Berlin   Ibadan

Copyright © 2002 by Oxford University Press, Inc.

Published by Oxford University Press, Inc.
198 Madison Avenue, New York, New York, 10016
http://www.oup-usa.org

Oxford is a registered trademark of Oxford University Press

Library of Congress Cataloging-in-Publication Date
West Stevens, Joyce, 1936–
    Smart and sassy : the strengths of inner-city Black girls / by Joyce West Stevens.
        p. cm.
    Includes bibliographical references and index.
    ISBN 0-19-512164-3 (alk. paper) — ISBN 0-19-512165-1 (pbk. : alk. paper)
    1. African American teenage girls—Attitudes. 2. African American teenage
girls—Psychology. 3. African American teenage girls—Social conditions. 4.
Adolescence—United States.   I. Title.

E185.86 . W4386 2002
305.235—dc21   2001034650

Printing number: 9 8 7 6 5 4 3 2 1
Printed in the United States of America
on acid-free paper

Contents

FOREWORD

Social scientists and interventionists have a history of viewing individuals and communities of color through a deficit lens. In the past, not enough attention was given to understanding the strengths of those who lived in a separate racial or class sphere. During the sixties and early seventies, African American practitioners and scholars began to push their colleagues to think more in terms of a strengths perspective when intervening or doing research in communities of color. Much of this emphasis from the African American scholar was engendered by reactions to Daniel Patrick Moynihan's *The Negro Family in America: The Case for National Action* (1965) or what became popularly know as *The Moynihan Report*. *The Moynihan Report* was heavily criticized by African American and other scholars because of a focus on what Moynihan defined as a deteriorating African American family with a disorganized, matriarchal family structure and a web of pathology. Moynihan's thinking was conventional among scholars of the sixties who tended to focus on deficits in the African American community, which were then accepted by scholars as rooted in a history of enslavement, social and economic injustice, discrimination, and oppression.

More recently, social work scholars have begun to include resiliency theory in their teachings and scholarship. Scholars such as Cowger (1994), DeJong and Miller (1995) and Saleebey (1992,1996) have developed conceptual frameworks and assessments for a strengths perspective which are very different from the conventional thinking guiding the interventions of the sixties and early seventies. This current volume, *Smart and Sassy: The Strengths of Inner-City Black Girls* by Joyce West Stevens advances our knowledge and understanding of resiliency theory even further. Her work takes into account the ability of low-income urban adolescent girls to overcome obstacles in their living situation, seize opportunities, and maximize their internal resources and utilize group affiliations for mastery. *Smart and Sassy* characterizes the potential for positive developmental outcomes for young African American teenage girls growing up in disadvantaged urban communities. Our understanding of the associated developmental tasks is enriched by the combination of theoretical application, anecdotes, and vivid case examples. The introduction of Dr. West Stevens' person-process-context model provides the scholarly community and practitioners with an innovative way of thinking about African American female adolescent development. The concepts of care protective sensibility, self-efficacy, role model formation, and opportunity mobility give us a new paradigm for understanding, assessing, and intervening with low-income African American adolescent girls.

Smart and Sassy is an original conceptualization, which stems from Dr. West Stevens' own research with African American adolescents in the inner city. Disciplined inquiry, clinical acumen from a rich background of health care practice, and a deep understanding of psychodynamic theory and its application combine to produce a culturally sensitive explanatory model about African American female adolescent development. There is no doubt in my mind that this volume will be as widely used as the works of notables in human development such as Irene Josselyn and Leontine Young.

Wilma Peebles-Wilkins, Dean
Boston University
School of Social Work

ACKNOWLEDGMENTS

Sarah's nickname "Sassy" was apt. She was quite impertinent, very pointed. Whatever she had to say, she would say it right out. She didn't hold things back; she was very forward. If there was anything she wanted to do, she would keep that in mind and go forth and try to do it. And that's why she was so successful.

(Gourse, 1993, p. 13)

She had a voice of fascinating quality, which enveloped any group that she sang with. And she could sing any kind of music, because she knew harmony from her piano playing, and she understood the unusual harmonies that the accompanists were playing for her. She could sing in tune with the most complex figures; she could change keys with ease. Dizzy Gillespie, who was playing in the Hines band when Sarah joined told people, "Sarah can sing notes that other people can't even hear."

(Gourse, 1993, p. 20)

When I initially decided to use "sassy" to describe black adolescent girls' behavior, I had not thought of jazz singer Sarah Vaughan. My thoughts at the time were mostly centered on the bold, determined, and courageous stance of the young black women that I was fortunate enough to study. It was later that I thought of Vaughan, for whom the term was used as a nickname. Indeed, for me the jazz musician was a person of heroic dimensions, representing achievements despite all possible odds. My secret fantasy was to be a jazz pianist, despite the fact that I had no talent or ambition for such a career. At the time, it brought me considerable pleasure to realize that many jazz artists were teenagers themselves when they embarked on musical careers. For instance, Ella Fitzgerald, one of jazz's most esteemed and prolific recording vocalist, had won numerable singing contests as a teen at Harlem's legendary Apollo theater. Her first recording with the renowned Chick Webb Band was at age 17. By the time she was 20, Fitzgerald and Webb had achieved considerable fame with their recording of "A-Tisket, A-Tasket" (Nicholson, 1994). As an adolescent I saw—and this continues to be my view—the jazz musician as the supreme personification of talent, giftedness, artistic discipline, and brilliant creativity. Vaughan, the inimitable jazz singer, was known as "Sassy." When I was a child, "sassy" was a term elders often used rather jokingly to describe "fast" and "womanish" behavior of young females. Later as a young teen growing up in a segregated society, the meaning of "sassy" became magnified when I learned it was an affectionate name for Vaughan. Vaughan's consummate musical gifts and stage charm captivated her listeners. She also demonstrated perfect control of her voice. She was a woman in control; in sociological jargon, she possessed self-efficacy. Like many black songsters, Vaughan's talent was nurtured and developed in the black church.

The term "sassy" has unparalleled and magnified meaning when equated with Vaughan. I was a teenager just discovering the beauty, the passion, and the intelligence of jazz music. At the time, not knowing the source of this sobriquet, it seemed natural to associate "sassy" with the images that her voice aroused—the smoothness and sophistication of velvet; heartfelt emotions of love gained, of love loss; the passionate, cheeky, and ebullient joy in the jazz scat. "Sassy" became associated with a black woman who commanded above all intelligence and competency. Despite the hardships of a segregated society and the sufferings of subjugation, the black jazz artist represented the paradox of American racial life. Here were persons esteemed for their artistry, who possessed an independence of spirit, yet were subject to the Jim Crow laws of a segregated society. The conditions of legal-social apartheid did not deter them from their ambitious calling—they were impassioned men and women dedicated to the pursuit of the music.

After Vaughan's death on April 4, 1990, I learned that she enjoyed the ribald companionship of the male musicians with whom she worked: "Like her male colleagues she could drink hard, work hard, and swear like there was no tomorrow" ("Sarah Vaughn, the divine one," 1991). A woman of considerable complexity, she guarded the privacy of her home to protect herself and her family. She was known to be both a good mother and a good daughter. Her sassiness was attributed to her courage, her confidence in her enormous talent, and her astute business sense in managing her career. Unsuccessful in love, Vaughan poured her soul into her music. She knew both the happiness and pain of love, which found its expression in her interpretation of a song.

Many people were supportive as I undertook the writing of this book. Melvin Delgado was the first person to encourage me to write this text. He believed that writing a book was a project that I could successfully accomplish. I am especially grateful to the faculty at the Boston University School of Social Work who read a first draft. Special thanks to Gail Steketee, Robert Hudson, Scott Geron, Maryann Amodeo, and Judith Gonyea for their encouraging and positive responses to the first draft. Darren Bennett was especially helpful in lending his expertise to help me develop the illustrations used in the text. Special thanks to Dean Wilma Peebles-Wilkins, who was especially supportive on those days when I thought that I could not possibly write another sentence. Last, thanks go to my two wonderful adult daughters, also my friends, Melinda and Janet, who believed that their mother could "do anything she sets out do and certainly write a book since she is a lover of books."

A Book about the Strengths of Inner-City Black Girls

Real wonder, however, lay in the amazing shapes and substances God's grace took: gospel in times of persecution; the exquisite wins of people forbidden to compete; the upright righteousness of those who let no boot hold them down—people who made Job's patience look like restlessness. Elegance when all around was shabby.

(Morrison, 1998, p. 62)

To be sure, the cataclysmic social-cultural changes of the future will be forged by contemporary youth. Ideally, public policies should be designed with foreknowledge to address both current and future societal needs. Current public discourse about the failure of public education, rising college costs, the collapse of manufacturing industries, employment downsizing, and the ruin of blue-collar employment mirrors the grave social conditions that will seriously influence the developmental course of contemporary youth. Moreover, as seismic shifts in racial/ethnic demography occur, social and economic investment in the development of youth of color seems all the more urgent. Yet public educational institutions, where the majority of youth of color are educated, seem ill prepared to meet the challenges of a technological informational age that point to a digital divide for inner-city youth. Certainly, impoverished social-economic conditions warrant an empathic, intelligent, and committed response from educators, policy makers, and human service professionals if positive and lasting changes are to take place in the lives of youth of color. Hopefully, this text will contribute to the knowledge building of future social workers who will join the ranks of those social service helpers who are unswerving in their dedication to helping poor and underserved minority youth lead productive, caring, and successful lives.

At present a significant proportion of black and Latino youth are disengaged from basic social institutions that instill values for responsible adult living. Premature parenthood, school dropout, substance abuse, and incarceration are disproportionately high among youth of color. Moreover, when economic opportunities are scarce, adolescents typically engage in illegitimate activities that lead to poor social outcomes (McLaughlin, 1993; Wilson, 1996). African American poor male adolescents, for instance, are motivated to achieve material success, but some have suspended ethical or lawful standards of behavior to attain success. Thus marketing illicit drugs can constitute a profitable enterprise for urban males of color. More importantly, many inner-city youth are alienated from cultural communal values of educational achievement, care, and nurturance, consequently putting them more in danger of involvement in antisocial behaviors.

Of course, not all poor urban youth engage in antisocial behaviors: Some embark on legitimate career paths that upgrade socioeconomic status (Jarrett, 1995; Stevens, 1993). These youths demonstrate resourceful ways in which personal and social identities are constructed for successful social investment. I postulate that many inner-city adolescents and their families have much to teach policy makers and helping professionals about successful living in adverse circumstances. Numerous economically disadvantaged families have been successful despite scarce social mobility opportunities. An examination of such families can provide information about the competence and social assets that affect healthy development and positive social adjustment.

In this text, I propose a person-process-context formulation within an epidemiological public health model to examine poor adolescents and their families in at-risk environments. While I make use of the terms "at-risk" or "high-risk," the intent here is not to use these terms as deficit labels but to view them as conceptual categories within a larger theoretical paradigm of health—the person-process-context model. I have argued elsewhere that competent practice must be related to a health paradigm that considers strengths and assets of individuals, families, and communities. A health paradigm is essential if social workers are to develop a knowledge base that will enhance understanding of the person-in-situation configuration in all its complexities. At the same time, however, I have indicated a caveat regarding the limitations of a strengths-based model in its omission of social redress (Stevens, 1995–96, 1997b). Currently, the National Association of Social Work (NASW) espouses an approach of adolescent health as opposed to at-risk or high-risk labels and individual intervention. NASW asserts that this new focus means

> moving social work in a direction that fosters preventive health strategies for adolescents through education and family and community collaboration by acknowledging the positive traits of the youth population, rather than singling out the individual problems. (Beaucar, 1999, p. 11)

While I support the NASW approach, I reason, nonetheless, that health and risk models are not in opposition, but are in juxtaposition *within* a comprehensive theoretical formulation of human development.

The person-process-context formulation outlines mediating processes involved in the interactive relationship between person and social context. I have adopted this formulation from Spencer (1995) and have borrowed her conceptualization to inform my own theoretical constructions. Spencer theorizes that a phenomenological approach applied to Bronfenbrenner's (1979) ecological systems model is a way to conceptualize the person-process-context. A phenomenological approach, according to Spencer, focuses on "meaning-making processes and the power those processes has in the interaction between African-American youth and their context" (p. 39). To this end, she contends that an at-risk model should be expanded to include the capacity for self-relatedness or intersubjectivity. Self-relatedness captures adolescents' ability to understand mutually shareable experiences within a given culture. Moreover, I have borrowed fundamental principles of knowledge from the disciplines of theology, philosophy, sociology, human development, and psychodynamic theory to theorize, understand, and interpret how and why black female adolescents create meaningful identities. It is my conviction that while this text makes use of black female narratives to theorize about identity development, the theoretical constructs used to do so are not class, race, or ethnicity specific, but can be applied across such categorical boundaries. Ethnic distinctiveness is derived from cultural expressions that occur within ecological domains, such as family, school, and neighborhood.

Although scholars have placed considerable emphasis on social assets or social capital as protective factors in mediating risk, less attention has been given to the interactive connection between individual attributes and social assets in negotiating life circumstances. Certain identifiable attributes have been associated with disadvantaged children, such as positive social skills, a sense of empowerment, and problem-solving abilities (Garmezy, 1991). The person-process-context model would suggest that despite chronic adversity, meaning-making processes and personal attributes could be used to mediate at-risk environments. I theorize that black female adolescents develop intersubjective attributes of assertion, recognition, and self-efficacy to mediate exposure to risk elements. I also postulate that such attributes are intrinsically connected to specific developmental domains (see Figure 3.1). Further, social assets or social capital reinforces personal attributions in the mediation of risk.

The theoretical/empirical database for the text is drawn from various knowledge areas. Consequently, the knowledge base of the text is diverse, including pertinent literature, my previously published work, and study findings from research I conducted with inner-city black adolescent girls. Based on these three knowledge areas, the adolescent developmental domains, augmented by biographical stories, are delineated to frame the book's substantive content. The domains are racial, ethnic, and gender role resolution; role model formulation; decision making; dating and mating expectations; care protective sensibility; opportunity mobility; and adulthood preparation (Stevens, 1993). The domains are context dependent and provide a framework for understanding how black female adolescents make meaning of their social environments. Consequently, resilience, social assets, and risk are identified within the domains.

The biographical narratives describe the developmental themes within the person-process-context model. While the narratives are largely drawn from my empirical studies of the lives of inner-city black adolescent girls, other literature sources are also used. The narratives portray how black girls cope with at-risk environments and manage negative racial/gender appraisals. Anecdotal material from the lives of celebrated black women is also cited to illustrate strengths analogous to those of the adolescent females depicted in the text. Personal strengths are conceptualized from a person-process-context model. Clinical approaches that bolster resilient capacities and develop social assets in adolescent girls are delineated. Clinical interventions are based on a strengths perspective that suggests that persons can identify and access their own inner resources to realize growth potential (Saleebey, 1992).

Traditionally, the study of poor minority adolescents has been severely limited in adolescent research and scholarship. Jessor (1993) has argued that the present state of knowledge about adolescent development is largely based on studies of middle-class white male youth. Consequently, there is a gap in the knowledge base of adolescent developmental theory. A few notable texts address the concerns of black economically disadvantaged adolescent girls. Specifically, Ladner's (1972) now classic ethnographic study, *Tomorrow's Tomorrow*, outlines the developmental course of poor black girls, many of whom became pregnant during adolescence. Three recent books—*Between Voice and Silence* (Taylor, Gilligan, & Sullivan, 1995), *Reviving Ophelia* (Pipher, 1994), and *Altered Loves* (Apter, 1991)—deal with gender-specific developmental issues among adolescent females of various ethnic and racial groups. The Taylor, Gilligan, and Sullivan work, based on empirical research, distinctively addresses the developmental trajectory of at-risk inner-city females. Still, there is a scarcity of literature about disadvantaged black adolescent females who do not engage in at-risk behaviors (Way, 1995).

This book tries to show that adolescence is a developmental period characterized by healthy psychosocial behaviors. This view finds support among other scholars who no longer view adolescence as an inevitable tumultuous developmental phase for subsequent normal personality integration. Rather, theoretical conceptualizations of this period are formulated from empirically based descriptions of adolescent adaptation and growth. What makes this new research especially compelling is the insight that the adaptations youth undergo during this period are socially structured (Offer, Ostrov, Howard & Atkinson, 1988; Powers, Stuart, & Klinder, 1989; Schulenberg, Maggs, & Hurrelmann, 1997). From its conception by G. Stanley Hall in 1904, adolescence was hypothesized as a stage of turbulence caused by the upsurge of hormonal development and earlier psychosocial experiences. Hall's thesis set the stage for the development of the more sophisticated psychodynamic recapitulation theory of storm and stress. Later, the psychodynamic interpretation of adolescence well formulated by Anna Freud (1958) became culturally embedded. Despite evidence that contradicts the recapitulation storm and stress thesis, this interpretation continues to hold sway. My hope is to present a more balanced depiction of adolescent well-being. To this end, this text describes and analyzes the successful management of adolescence in at-risk environments. The objective of this analysis is to generate knowledge about positive effects that promote mental health. Practice wisdom suggests that individuals and families cope successfully in adverse environments, evincing healthy life practices that transcend particular circumstances. As I have mentioned, black girls develop attributes of assertion, recognition, and self-efficacy to mediate exposure to risk. To support this hypothesis, I argue that black girls learn to construct healthy meaningful lives, despite poverty, blocked opportunities, and racial stigma. Central to this argument are three assumptions, all of which undergird the text:

- The first is the commonsense idea that human beings evolve certain strategies (strengths) to manage adversity in their lives. Over time individuals become proficient and disciplined in coping with life's misfortunes. Ralph Ellison pointedly captured the substance of this supposition: "American Negro life is, for the Negro who must live it, not only a burden but also a discipline—just as any human life which has endured so long is a discipline teaching its own insights into the human condition, its own strategies of survival" (quoted in Washington, 1994, p. xivi). Moreover, survival and adaptation infer that human behavior is goal directed, purposive, and intentional. The intentionality of human actions transpires within a relational world, thereby making psychological growth possible vis-à-vis mutually shared meanings and connected knowing.

- The second assumption, based on the findings of new mind research, is that mental activity is always oriented toward the meaningful actions of others. As such, the intentional state of another is easily grasped, bringing about a meeting of the minds—a mutual tuning in or empathic intentionality. Conceivably, because of the necessity of learning to negotiate racially hostile environments, empathic intentionality is more intensified in ethnic minorities. Psychological life is considered relational and contextually embedded. More importantly, empathic intentionality enables the individual to sort out the legitimacy and illegitimacy of another's belief system. What is remarkably different in this reconceptualization of mind is that it is context dependent, not the isolated entity that scholars heretofore posited (Bruner, 1997; Crossley, 1996; Orange, Atwood, & Stolorow, 1997). Essentially, humans are story/myth-making animals and thus have a need to attach meaning to experience. Human beings bear the burden or freedom of memory that must be storied with coherence and continuity. Further, all cultures create meaning systems to explain the reality unperceived by the senses. As such, cultural meaning systems embodied in myth, narratives, metaphor, and ritual are anchored in the dimension of the spiritual and thus give definition to quotidian encounters.

- Last, the third assumption relates to the spiritual domain of African American life. Cultural spiritual narratives are sustained through time by belief and faith (Becker, 1964; Worgul, 1980). Recognizably, spirituality has distinctive significance in the lives of African Americans. The supposition is that to be human is to be spiritual in nature. Human beings covet a personal relationship with the transcendent God(s). For black folk, spirituality has been a consummate source of support and resilience. Cone (1972) convincingly argues that Christian spirituality has its genesis, for black Americans, in the slave experience. African slaves, according to Cone, recontexualized the slaveowners' Christianity to reflect God's involvement in their bondage and liberation. Further, slaves ritualized meanings of persecution, bondage, liberation, resistance, and suffering in music—slave songs, spirituals, and blues. Songs became oral histories recounting the triumphant liberation of the spirit. By placing God in the midst of communal suffering, slaves interpreted their lives as both tragic and heroic. Fueled by an African analogical vision of life as sacred and imbued with ritual, the slaves' capacity to see their lives as a seamless tapestry of courageous suffering and joy gave life mythic moral meaning and thus framed an American ethnic culture.[1] Integral to the African's sense of being in the world, in relation to self, nature, and others, the slave's analogous imagination was animated by the Hebrew-Christian biblical text. The Negro spirituals, according to Cone, pointedly illustrate that: "The slaves felt assured that they would make it through, and neither death, Satan, nor white people could prevent God from effecting the liberation of black people from bondage" (p. 73).

In a similar vein, philosopher Martin Buber (1970) illuminates the meaning of self-relatedness to a personal God. He affirms:

> The designation of God as a person is indispensable for all, who, like myself . . . mean by "God" him that, whatever else he may be in addition, enters into a direct relationship to us human beings through creative, revelatory, and redemptive acts, and thus makes it possible for us to enter into a direct relationship to him. (p. 181)

The essence of Buber's faith argument is that a genuinely human person realizes that cognition is really never adequate; thus knowledge propels itself beyond to the realm of the spiritual, which ultimately leads to the power of faith. Hence faith and intellect are inextricably joined. In human suffering and adversity is the recognition of one's limitation and vulnerabilities. Personal weaknesses are the very conditions necessary for the expression of faith (Sawicki, 1997). Buber's comment well defines the personal God of faith professed by African Americans. Thus, it seems that one can assume that many African Americans hold profound religious beliefs.

In the intersection of mind and social space, where the encounter between subject and subject takes place, a spiritual vitality occurs that infuses self-relatedness and hence adaptation. A belief in the spiritual essence of life transforms the self in such a way that living is more than survival; life becomes valued, principled, joyful, and hopeful. What is needed to fully understand this life-generating dynamic are new explanatory models. For instance, medical researchers currently investigate the domain of spirituality to better understand its effects in the healing process.

In this text, I examine the assets of neighborhoods, families, and their daughters in meeting life's challenges. Further, the book's perspective of strength is a framework to affirm the assets of those who are often viewed as being without human or social capital. While adolescent negative and destructive behaviors are certainly addressed in the text, developmental pathology is not a central focus. This text emphasizes meaning, context, and narrative in the lives of black girls. Especially important in this focus is how black girls enhance self-agency through the creation of personal and communal meaning.

The book contains eight chapters divided into three parts. The first part presents a theoretical overview for the text, the second part introduces the discussion of the developmental domains of adolescence, and the third part includes the final chapter of the book, which considers clinical implications in addressing the needs of at-risk, economically disadvantaged black girls. The book has a concluding commentary, or Epilogue, which provides closure for the text.

Chapters 1, 2, 3 in Part 1 deal with the theoretical framework for the text. In Chapter 1, a definition of resilience and risks within a social context is presented. An overview of the three risk models—additive, cumulative, and interactive—is outlined. Chapter 2 critiques both traditional and new emergent theories that explicate adolescent developmental tasks. Chapter 3 explicates the person-process-context interactive model, including a description of the seven developmental domains.

In Part 2, Chapters 4, 5, 6, and 7 address the developmental domains and explicate, based on self-reports, accounts of the girls' daily experiences. The racial, ethnic, and gender role commitment domain is explained in Chapter 4. The chapter explores how black female adolescents create meaningful identities derived from varied experiences based on race, ethnicity, and gender and explicates identity development within the context of a hostile environment where race and gender are devalued. Protective care sensibility and role model formulation domains are discussed in Chapter 5. In Chapter 5, a care protective sensibility is explored to reflect black female adolescents' sense of care and protection in relation to self and others. Behaviors that demonstrate care, loyalty, and kindness in relation to others are examined as they relate to the formulation of role models in one's environment. The chapter also explores how prosocial behaviors become part of an evolving self. The role model formulation investigates how black adolescent females develop judgments about valued and nonvalued behavior as personified by persons within jeopardy environments. The chapter examines the process of formulating appropriate social conduct from esteemed persons found in the adolescent females' immediate family or community. The effects of social class on role model formulation are also explored. The domains of decision making, dating, and mate selection are addressed in Chapter 6. This chapter explores the development of problem-solving skills within the contexts of family and peers and undertakes an analysis of how coping skills are refined for effective decision making in meeting the challenges of environmental jeopardy, including drug trafficking, gang related behavior, and sexual harassment. The chapter also discusses the issue of what black girls expect of black boys. Dating and mating expectations are explored in relation to black girls' developing behavioral expectations and criteria used to select dating partners. A discussion of developmental struggles related to parental discipline and romantic attachments is also provided in the chapter. Opportunity mobility and adulthood preparation domains are explicated in Chapter 7. The chapter examines adolescents' self-perceptions of behavior and affective responses felt necessary for a well-functioning adult. Conceptualizations of strengths necessary for a productive life, as evident in case examples, are also presented in this chapter. The chapter discusses the impact of restricted opportunities on the developmental course of adolescence, particularly the structural strain of racism and its effects. The chapter provides substantive content on opportunity venues. Coupled with the adulthood preparation theme, the chapter provides a pointed analysis of the future direction of clinical practice with at-risk black girls and their families.

Chapter 8 in Part 3 discusses various clinical approaches, including assessment and intervention. Specific practice principles are identified and explicated. Strengths derived from the developmental domains are reviewed, and a family-collaborative clinical prevention program is introduced to aid adolescent girls and their families. The Epilogue briefly summarizes lessons learned from clinical practice and the results of empirical investigation about the resiliency of black girls. The commentary ends on a hopeful note, suggesting that practitioners are more effective when those they serve are seen from a model of health and strength. The Glossary provides a quick reference for key terms and concepts used in the text.

Why scholars in the past saw little benefit in investigating the strengths of undervalued populations is unclear. Perhaps because of overriding concerns about the ill effects of poverty, the assets of impoverished communities and the personal strengths of their inhabitants were overlooked. In the interest of concerns about the paucity of scholarship in this area, this text seeks to advance knowledge about the personal and social resources of the black adolescent female. It is hoped that in so doing, a more complete and realistic portrayal of her life will be seen in the fullness of a light that reveals her strengths.

Methodology and Theory

While I have dealt with the assumptions that undergird this book, equally important are its scientific underpinnings. I have noted previously that a person-process-context model is introduced as a theoretical framework for the text. It is worthwhile to reiterate the major thesis of the model for the purposes of highlighting its significance in understanding the contextual lives of individuals. The model specifically borrows from Margaret Beale Spencer's (1995) seminal elaboration of an interactive at-risk person-context model and includes meaning-making intersubjective processes and their relationship to developmental imperatives within an ecological perspective. Spencer has raised concerns about the limitations of existent theoretical models to examine the lives of black youth. She argues correctly that new models must be formulated that are more inclusive—that encompass the social context of black life. Spencer's model addresses the relationship between environment and developmental outcomes. To this end, she describes her model as a "phenomenological variant of Bronfenbrenner's ecological systems theory" (p. 39). I have taken up Spencer's challenge to consider new theorizing about black youth. As a scholar and theoretician, I stand on her shoulders and am indebted to her work. Linguistically, I have changed the terminology of Spencer's model to person-process-context (see Figure 2.1). In so doing, I have introduced meaning-making processes as a point of nexus between persons and their contexts. Thus, I locate intersubjectivity at the center of the model's formulation (see Figure 3.1). In Chapter 3, the concept of intersubjectivity is discussed from three perspectives: psychological, social, and the epistemology of empathy. I use Bronfenbrenner's theory of "nested contexts" (see Figure 3.2) to consider the social structural effects of a racialist society as well as to provide an ecological theoretical perspective for the model itself. I borrow from multiple and diverse disciplines for the elaboration of black youth experiences.

I have been influenced in my thinking of culture by the writings of anthropologist Edward T. Hall (1969, 1977), especially his works *The Hidden Dimension* and *Beyond Culture*. Hall uses the term "context" both as a noun and a verb. As a noun, he infers, I believe, the common understanding of cultural situations where transactional processes of behavior and cognition take place. Hall's use of the term "contexting" suggests internalized mental actions—that represents the analytical or recursive processing of information in a given cultural or environmental situation. According to Hall, "contexting" is our capacity to think about things conditioned by varied social perspectives. This capacity, Hall argues, is deeply embedded in our evolutionary biological system. Contexting enables individuals to build and develop complexity in their patterned thoughts and behavior. Hall's contexting fits perfectly the recursive thinking that commonly occurs during puberty. The recursive thinking in which adolescents engage represents the need to infuse the world with contextual meaning. Adolescents want to develop a worldview from their particular social perspective. The generational divide between youth and adults occurs because both cohorts see their worlds from different social contextual perspectives. For example, adolescents perceive their social world as pliant and stimulating and that of the adult world as dull and fixed. The need to contextualize the worlds in which we play and work is always characterized by both harmony and dissonance. My reflections about contexting have led me to consider the art form of jazz as a metaphor for thinking about the way life is created and lived. I view jazz as an improvisational conversation that is characterized by the responses of empathy, assertion, and recognition among its musicians. I extend the use of this metaphor in my explication of the person-process-context model explained in Chapter 3. The improvisational nature of jazz is the bringing together of all the contexting experiences of individual players to create a harmonious collective whole. In my view, the need to create a well-balanced coherent whole from disparate experiences is what occurs when individuals try to create meaning in their lives. Additionally, developmental theory, psychoanalysis, cultural anthropology, literature, music, and theology are some of the disciplines that I draw upon to advance theorizing about black female youth and the contexting of their experiences.

Importantly, key interpretative analyses and theories employed in the text are based on empirical research data from two principal investigative studies that I conducted at different time intervals from 1992 through 1997. Although both studies were carried out to learn more about black adolescent females and their social environments, the second study was specifically designed to effect change in the psychosocial adjustment of early aged adolescent females. Specifically undertaken to explore issues of adolescent pregnancy and adolescent perceptions of adult role functioning, the first study (N = 36) was exploratory and designed to generate hypotheses about adolescent pregnancy and early coital behavior among black urban female adolescents. Sample subjects were randomly selected from the prenatal and family planning clinics in a large teaching hospital in a metropolitan midwestern city. The hospital served inner-city communities that experienced many social problems, such as poverty, school dropout, unemployment, and teen births. The sample consisted of 20 pregnant and 16 nonpregnant African American female adolescents. The initial design called for equal numbers of subjects (N = 40), but some of the nonpregnant girls selected proved difficult to reach. Some of them were either away at college or working full-time. The pregnant sample did not include any females in the first trimester to ensure that subjects had made a decision to carry their pregnancy to term. Respondents who had experienced abortions were not eliminated from the study since this was viewed as an exercise of choice and a form of birth control. The adolescence pregnancy research, known as Pregnancy Adulthood Negotiation of Status Inventory (PANSI);[2] was designed to contrast and compare sexually active pregnant and nonpregnant low-income urban late-aged black female adolescents, age 17–19, with respect to their perceptions about an adult lifestyle (Stevens, 1993, 1994, 1995–1996). A significant characteristic of the study was the descriptive analysis of intergroup comparisons while controlling for race, age, and class. Another notable feature was the analysis of data utilizing both qualitative and quantitative procedures.

The research design posed limitations in validity; however, it was believed that the strength of the design was in the collection of narrative experiences of the research subjects themselves. Thus, it was considered that the investigation would open up new lines of inquiry into the subject of adolescent pregnancy. The overall objective of the research was the identification and description of study subjects' perceptions and understandings relative to (1) parenthood as a rite of passage and (2) the negotiated achievement of adulthood status. The study described variant patterns of intergroup social actions while analyzing intergroup attitudinal perceptions about the meaning of becoming a grown-up. The research was guided by three fundamental hypotheses about the significance of adult identity:

1. Black female adolescents view pregnancy and motherhood as a means through which to attain adulthood status.
2. Pregnancy and motherhood, as a primary means for attaining adulthood status, are more common themes among female adolescents who are pregnant than among their peers who seek to postpone pregnancy.
3. There is a significant difference between the pregnant and nonpregnant adolescents in that the pregnant adolescents are more likely to establish linkages beyond the immediacy of the family and peer group. These linkages are reflected in their engagement in church, community, work, and educational environments.

For the statistical analysis of quantitative data, t-tests, chi-squares, and the Mann-Whitney U test were used. A qualitative data analysis computer program (Ethnograph) was used for the text-based data, which were subsequently reviewed and refined resulting in seven thematic categories. Altogether, research findings tended to provide support for the three hypotheses posited for the study. The two sample cohorts were compared by the thematic codes. Importantly, the two groups differed at a <.05 level of significance on certain variables: psychological (a sense of care and protection in relation to self and others, self-expectancies for social mobility, and dating and mate selection patterns); situational (church affiliation); and behavioral (college attendance, registered voter status, and abortion history). Pertinent study results are introduced in the respective developmental domain chapters of the text. The developmental domains represent thematic categories derived from the qualitative data. I reasoned that the domains are conceptual and grounded in the research data and are representatives of adolescent maturational issues and thus have abstract and universal characteristics.

The second empirical investigation, Growing Up: Learning to Make Choices, (GULTMC), was a 3-year longitudinal study developed as an intervention model for pregnancy prevention (Stevens, 1997b, 1998a, 1999). The research was conducted in a naturalistic setting, a middle school in an inner-city community in a metropolitan northeastern city. A random sample of 38 black girls was selected from a roster of students with school adjustment problems evidenced by referrals to the principal's office or temporary suspensions. Due to attrition, the final sample of girls was 36. Two girls dropped out of the study because they were no longer in attendance at the school because of a change in residence. The GULTMC research built on the PANSI study of pregnant and nonpregnant adolescents. The GULTMC study was specifically designed to measure the effectiveness of a culturally sensitive 10-week curriculum of self-esteem, school adjustment, racial identity development, and academic performance among at-risk black female adolescents ages 11–14. The research sample self-identified as black but represented various ethnic groups—African American, Dominican, and Haitian.[3] Thirty-three of the sample girls were African American. The study curricula, tested in a simple experimental design, included skill acquisition, goal attainment, and role model access elements in two process components, the Self-Image Life Skills and the Role Model Mentor segments. The Self-Image Life Skills component used therapeutic games to develop skills for effective social skill acquisition and goal attainment. The Role Model Mentor component provided cultural-recreational field excursions with a college student mentor. The study incorporated both quantitative and qualitative measures. The Rosenberg Self-Esteem Scale, the Hare Self-Esteem Scale, and the Helms Racial Identity Attitude Scale (RIAS) were used at pretest, posttest, and 3-year follow-up time intervals to measure the effectiveness of the curriculum. Qualitative data included audiotape transcriptions of both the curriculum group sessions and the mentor planning/reporting meetings as well as field notes. A second intervention took place when 18 months after posttest the experimental group participated in 10 focus group sessions to explore concerns regarding community role models and drug use. The experimental females were paid $10 per group session, including both curriculum and focus group sessions. Refreshments were served at all sessions. The study hypothesized that the experimental females (who received the curriculum intervention) would show higher self-esteem, improved school adjustment (less misconduct, tardiness, absence reports), better academic grades, and the internalization of a positive racial identity when compared with the control females (who did not receive the intervention). Data were collected on sexual activity, drug use, self-esteem, racial identity, academic performance, and school adjustment. Study findings were the result of statistical analysis (t-tests, chi-squares) and a qualitative data analysis (QDA) computer management program (Hyper-Research). The Hyper-Research computer program yielded thematic categories from the qualitative raw data.

Overall, quantitative findings showed that there were very few differences between the females in the experimental group (who received the intervention) and those in the control group (who did not receive the intervention). There are several possible explanations for these findings. First, the small sample sizes could serve to mask the effects of the intervention. Second, the primary intention of the intervention (i.e., pregnancy prevention) was met, but the indirect effects hoped for may not have been realized. It is worth noting that none of the girls who completed the follow-up survey (in either the experimental or control group) became pregnant between the end of the curriculum training and the administration of the follow-up survey. Third, the effects of the intervention may not have been apparent at follow-up (or may have only been detected during a shorter or longer period of time following the intervention). Last, the intervention could have had no impact. Because of the small size of the sample, this may be the most plausible explanation, and the other possible explanations may only be verified if the study is replicated with a larger sample size. However, findings did indicate notable trends that suggested that there were fewer incidents of misconduct for the experimental group than the control group at posttest trials. Additionally, results suggested that the longer the girls remained in school, self-esteem within the context of the school environment lessened. These results find support in other empirical findings that indicate that black adolescents receive high levels of personal regard within the social contexts of family and community, whereas low levels of esteem are experienced in the school setting (Spencer, 1982). While the research had significant limitations, mostly related to sample size and attrition, qualitative findings were richly textured and yielded data accessible to the interpretative analysis and conjectural presentations found in this text.

Last, I try to ground my theories not only in the research raw data, but also in more than 30 years of practice experience in both the public and private sectors in urban areas. The case material is offered to advance student learning in the application of interventions as well as learning to master the concepts and ideas that are use to theorize about the lives of black inner-city girls. For three decades, I have practiced social work in poor and working-class inner-city communities in school, child welfare, mental health, hospital, and private practice settings. The case illustrations throughout the text are constructed from actual practices with real adolescents and their families and are presented in a block format throughout the text. The case material is not necessarily designed to provide ideal intervention solutions but to help students reflect on intervention practices and the contextual meaning of adolescent girls' lives. The adolescent girls presented in the case material are resilient girls who experience real problematic situations and developmental dilemmas. Certainly, in my early career, I had not fully conceptualized the model of practice and the theoretical underpinnings set forth in this text. However, it is clear that my social work interventions were sincere attempts to be empathetically related to those whom I served. Clients have taught me that *perfect* interventions do not exist, but useful empathic interventions can be accomplished. In one case illustration, I include information from an adolescent's girl's life as it has unfolded some years after the clinical work was completed. On occasion girls with whom I have worked have contacted me years later to let me know the outcome of their lives. This view of seeing how individual girls' lives unfold over a period of time has been instructive. Many seasoned practitioners, I am certain, have had this experience, as will most students when they eventually become experienced professionals. The years of work in a hospital setting offered an opportunity to observe intergenerational changes in the lives of families. From those experiences, I learned that while clinical services end, the relationships we develop with clients do not. Another exemplary illustration is concerned, in particular, with racial and ethnic identity. An adolescent's severe response to a social context where she is the lone person of color may appear to the social work student to be extreme in its intensity. The case is included in this text because it demonstrates the intense need for adolescents to reconcile identity issues related to race and ethnicity. As practitioners we help clients change their lives, but we too are changed by our involvement in their lives. The experiences that we have with those with whom we work become a part of who we are as persons. I recognize that students *do* want to help those they serve, but all too often in their eagerness and wish to be good social workers, perfect solutions are sought to very complex issues and problems. At best, what social workers really do is to help people change their lives so that life will be lived more fully with dignity, integrity, respect, and mastery.

I imagine that the case material and raw data presented in the text will be the first time that some students will learn about the lives of inner-city black girls who are economically indigent. However, I trust that students will come to recognize what is universal about the adolescent experience in the lives of the girls presented in this text. Paradoxically, this means that students must understand those social categories—race, ethnicity, and class—that contextualize experiences as well as become aware of what is developmentally universal in these experiences. This kind of sophisticated awareness, I am certain, demands that students learn to confront their own biases about who inner-city economically disadvantaged black girls *really* are. An additional responsibility is placed on students to learn highly conceptual material. However, I do believe that learning concepts and theories will provide students with the intellectual tools to deliberate not only about black girls, but also about all adolescents in general. Too frequently, minority adolescents are seen as "other," as outside the domain of what is considered normal. I hope that students will make use of the case illustrations for reflective theorizing, a practice commonly engaged in by social workers. Case illustrations range in length from very brief to comprehensive and lengthy. The extended narratives are used in multiple instances to explain perspectives about theory and practice. Essentially, the case illustrations are designed to unpack particular theories and concepts. At the same time, however, a case may also be used to explicate concepts not specifically selected for a case example. A particular case illustration may represent multiple subtexts that address various concepts and theories. It is likely that a particular developmental domain is always an inferred subtext in a case illustration.

At the end of each case illustration, I delineate study questions and issues to assist students in their reflections. Students are advised to think seriously and empathetically about the practice issues involved in the case vignettes. In so doing, students should consider the intervention principles presented in the social work practice model in Chapter 8. While I do not address specific social policy issues in the study questions, I believe it is important that students reflect on substantive policy implications that may be inferred from the case illustrations. Clinical practices and the daily praxis of people's lives are always carried out within the social milieu determined by policy initiatives. I believe that this text has something unique to offer students in that the case illustrations are derived from both empirical study and practice wisdom. Moreover, the case material introduces the student to authentic data from the field in the learning context of the classroom. I also encourage students to make use of the figures as tools to aid in their conceptualization of the strengths, developmental issues, psychosocial experiences, and social ecologies that characterize the adolescent journey.

Notes

1. To the enslaved African American, the biblical text of the enslaved Jew in the land of Egypt represented the revelation of a complete identity in the fullness of a divine Being. Thus, life became sacred. The refrain from a popular spiritual song, "Go down Moses, way down to Egypt land, Tell old Pharaoh to let my people go," embodies this sacred revelation. In such instances, the enslaved African American made use of an *analogical imag-*

ination. See also Lourdeaux (1990) and Gordon (2000) for the use of this concept regarding the spirituality of the one person reflected in the communal persona of many.

2. PANSI was the titled name for the interview instrument that I constructed. I select to use this title to identify the study itself.

3. Girls who identified themselves as African American represented girls who were descendants of "American African Slaves" (the slave as a nonvoluntary immigrant, who has a caste status to use John Ogbu's (1978) terminology). There were no descendants of first- or second-generation African immigrants.

SMART and *Sassy*

THEORY OVERVIEW

1   Risk and Resiliency in Social Contexts

*Black [resistance] in America did not begin with the Civil Rights movement
and Martin Luther King, or with Black Power and Stokely Carmichael or the
Black Panther Party. Black resistance has roots stretching back to slave ships,
the auction blocks, and the plantation regime. It began when the first black
person decided that death was preferable to slavery.*

(Cone, 1991, p. 24)

*They had learned to withstand and endure rather than to conquer and destroy.
Their precarious position had taught them to weigh and to deliberate, and the
sorrows of their enslavement had filled them with mercy instead of vengeance.
Theirs was more often a wisdom of the spirit than of books, and their natural
instinct was to share rather than withhold.*

(Murray, 1978, p. 145)

Resilience in Historical Context

The Early Period

The resilient survival of human beings exists a priori. Conventional wisdom suggests that moral strength exists in the lives of the impoverished (Coles, 1986). This moral stamina provides the impetus to confront life's hardships. I define "resilient" to mean moral steadfast perseverance, demonstrated by hardiness and courage in the face of dangerous and hazardous conditions. Certainly, in civilized societies, moral tenacity is necessary for exercising protest and resistance to overcome or survive oppressed conditions. Cultural and political resistance includes a range of expressions from the most subtle (i.e., unproductive work habits) to the most violent (i.e., armed insurrection). While not central to this text, it seems necessary to recount black resistance in some measure to corroborate historical continuity and to fortify cultural memory. Black women survived the holocaust of the middle passage and its aftermath of chattel enslavement with hope and fortitude, qualities necessary to cope with inhuman living conditions (Hine & Thompson, 1998). Contemporary black female adolescents, like their ancestral sisters, display strengths of boldness, courage, fortitude, and assertiveness in confronting mundane social life. Paradoxically, the history of black women chronicles a cultural legacy of both resistive protest and caretaking. From the proverbial "ain't I a woman" voiced by Sojourner Truth to Rosa Parks's symbolic gesture "I will not move," the resistant activities of these two historical luminaries symbolizes communal qualities of care, resistance, and strength. The simple courageous qualities of ordinary folk, as represented by these notable resisters, were needed to survive the hostile oppressed environment of a racialized society.

In particular, Harriet Tubman, a prudent and adept resister, transported slaves to the free North by way of the Underground Railroad. Further, the social activism and charitable works of Negro[1] women at the end of Reconstruction in 1877 and through the Progressive Era was considerable (Hine & Thompson, 1998). The gender-based charitable work of Negro women was initiated to care for aged freed men and women who were alone and without the care of relatives. Paradoxically, the altruistic work of middle-class Negro women paralleled that of upper-class white Anglo-Saxon Protestant women who helped European immigrants assimilate to American culture. Mutual aid and benevolent societies were the means by which Negro women organized and provided services to the needy (Peebles-Wilkins, 1992). Like their upper class white cohorts, Negro middle-class women saw a moral calling in charitable works. Charitable caregiving was regarded as a means of racial uplift, and Negro women saw themselves foremost as race women.[2]

Devalued as biologically inferior and morally depraved, black women were then, as now, uniquely positioned to comprehend the interlocking oppression of race and gender. It is not surprising, then, that they identified themselves as consummate race women. Extreme poverty, violent lynchings, racial bigotry, and their consequences were sufficient cause to become, as they were called, "bothersome busybodies" or "meddlers" (Pollard, 1997). Indeed, "meddling" women were active resisters, reformers, and protesters against racial injustices. They also advocated for women's suffrage. Prominent women of the ilk of Ida B. Wells and Mary Church Terrell were passionately persistent in championing the cause of racial and social injustices. The irascible and radical Wells, probing journalist and newspaper owner, campaigned unceasingly for antilynching laws, albeit unsuccessfully. Terrell organized the first sit-in, a resistance strategy that would decades later be put to effective use in the civil rights movement. As a prolific writer, organizer of voluntary associations, and social reform spokesperson, Terrell campaigned for service provisions in a number of areas—juvenile delinquency, child welfare, and parent education—all activities to strengthen Negro families (Giddings, 1984; Peebles-Wilkins & Koerin, 1992). Both Wells and Terrell were peers of Jane Addams—the settlement house pioneer. Similarly, all three campaigned for the fair and just treatment of the downtrodden, including involvement in suffragist activities. Historical accounts suggest that the three women were friends (Giddings, 1984). Unfortunately, the realities of race in American society ensured that the reform efforts of Negro and white women would diverge. Both Wells and Terrell, for instance, seriously contested Addams's philosophy of expediency, which was often at odds with the cause of justice and equality for the Negro (Giddings, 1984).

The Contemporary Period

In subsequent decades, the celebrated resistance of Rosa Parks, a domestic worker and seamstress, and of Fannie Lou Hamer, a Mississippi sharecropper and plantation timekeeper, is legendary. Parks's refusal, on Friday, December 1, 1955, to move to the back of a segregated Montgomery, Alabama, bus ignited the civil rights movement. Hamer, a convert to the civil rights movement by way of voter registration ac-

HISTORICAL LEGACIES AND SELF-NARRATIVES: "I LIKE THESE WOMEN 'CAUSE I CAN SEE ME"

In the GULTMC social skills curriculum a session was devoted to developing a name and motto for the group. The girls were asked to think of stories about black women who demonstrated courage and strength in their lives. The girls were to try to think of stories that they had heard in their own families. Family stories could be about relatives or non-relatives. The social worker emphasized that it was important to identify stories that showed that women had guts, intelligence, and power. The girls were also introduced to 10 historical narratives (usually a paragraph in length) of famous African American women who had these identifiable qualities. The girls were then asked to select one or two of the famous women's stories and one or two of their own oral stories and to choose a partner. Once the girls were paired, they were to discuss their stories with their partners. In the discussions, the girls were first to reflect on why they had selected a particular story and the meaning of the story to them. Second, the girls were asked to identify what it was that they both liked and disliked about the women in their stories (e.g., the way she wore clothes, the way she stood up to people, etc.). Third, the girls were to take everything that they liked about the women in their stories to see if it matched any of the things they saw in themselves or their partners. Upon completion of the exercise, the girls were surprised to learn that some of the qualities they identified in the women that they held in esteem were qualities they possessed themselves. The girls began to see themselves differently once they identified their own strengths as grounded in ethnic pride. Terisa, a 14-year-old, summarized perspicaciously the experience of participants: "I like these women 'cause I can see me." *Study Questions and Issues:* (1) Discuss why you think this exercise could enhance agency. (2) Is this an exercise that you think could be adopted in individual work with an adolescent girl? Explain. (3) Identify and discuss resilient historical narratives, from your own life experience, that enhance agency and self-efficacy. (4) The therapeutic exercise presented focuses on assets rather than deficits. Discuss how you think such a focus might be more beneficial than stressing behavior patterns that reflect negative or deficit narratives. *See also:* Figures 3.1, 3.2, and 3.3; the Collaborative Intervention Context Model's (*CICM*) Third principle, which involves the practitioner's efforts to maximize personal agency and self-efficacy by consistent analysis of social, contextual, or relational inequities that intersect the participant's life.

tivities for the Student Non-Violent Coordinating Committee, was catapulted to national fame as a spokesperson for the Mississippi Freedom Democratic Party at the 1964 Democratic National Convention. Institutional bondage and social and legal Jim Crow apartheid attest that black women have been forced to cope in extreme toxic and hazardous environments. Throughout history, resistance for liberation and caretaking actions has been the typical response of black women in oppressive environments. Certainly, perseverance in such environments has not been without personal and communal cost. Nonetheless, black women have been amazingly resilient—courageous, bold, and brave.

Rutter (1987) asserts that as early as 1957 three key findings in human development research and scholarship created interest in resilience. First was the consistency in quantitative research findings that documented that notable variations occurred in individual psychosocial outcomes even in the most onerous social circumstances, such as the children of mentally ill parents. Second, the findings from temperament studies indicated that those children's "disposition" affected interpersonal interactions. This was an important insight regarding the intersubjectivity of relationships indicating that children themselves influenced their environments in significant ways. Third, person-environment scholarship highlighted the individual's capacity for coping and mastery during life's critical turning points. Explorations in this substantive area drew attention to the fact that individuals were, in fact, active self-determining agents interacting within their environments.

A significant consideration is that the social science literature conspicuously omits historical reference of the resilient youth of the 1960s civil rights movement. As freedom riders, marchers, and voter registrants, black youth challenged the white power structures of the South, demanding just and equal treatment. Escorted by federal law enforcers, black children, for instance, entered schools surrounded by enraged, threatening, malevolent white protesters. These children (alongside their families) demonstrated extraordinary courage in life-threatening environments. Perhaps Coles's (1967) classic study, *Children of Crisis*, which examined the integration of white southern elementary schools by black children (and their families), represents embryonic scholarship on resilience. This monumental but rudimentary work did not use the resiliency construct as an explanatory descriptor.

Indeed, in retrospect, the children and youth of the civil rights era were resilient. Irrespective of Coles's study, the investigation of the strengths of black children did not gain currency. However, given new theoretical insights on resilience, a retrospective examination of the children and youth of the civil rights era is needed. Despite the lack of documentation from the social science disciplines, Halberstam (1998), a journalist, chronicles the civil rights protest era as a campaign initiated and sustained by youth. He suggests that, through civil disobedience, youth were the infantry in a campaign for democratic ideals. In the postcivil rights period, however, cultural protest has taken different forms. Many contemporary youth believe that the civil rights legislation of the 1960s has had little if any intergenerational impact on their lives and the lives of their peers. As a form of social protest, the social decay of inner-city life is exploited in the ethnic music of "gansta rap" bards. These urban troubadours engage in recitative protest poetics about the moral and economic impoverishment of inner-city life. Hip hop and gansta rap music has resonated with disillusioned youth worldwide (Sunday, "Japan's Youth," 1998). Additionally, the music has been appropriated by youth of diverse cultures to express their disaffection in society. Unfortunately, as gansta rap is increasingly exploited for consumer consumption, much of the music ceases to be cultural protest, but increasingly dramatizes a romanticized social world of drugs and violence.

As significant benefits were gained from affirmative action policies in the post–civil rights era, a greater proportion of blacks acquired middle-class rank. Still others remained trapped in impoverished racialist environments separated from mainstream America (Hacker, 1992). Countless poor black families have loss hope in the American dream of future possibilities (West, 1993a, 1993b; Wilson, 1996). Research findings document the fact that chronic poverty produces cumulative adversities that may account for negative consequences, such as criminality or psychiatric disorders among children (Garmezy, 1993). But this is a skewed perspective, as most children of mentally ill parents or of all parents do not necessarily have these problems themselves (Long & Vailant, 1989). I argue, nonetheless, that many economically disadvantaged families cope in ways that transcend the limitations of hazardous restrictive racialist impoverished environments. Since such families have been understudied, little is known about what it actually takes to counteract multiple stresses for healthy psychosocial outcomes. Fortunately, scholars have begun researching this area to explore how poor families cope as a kin network to promote the resilience and social mobility of their offspring (Jarrett, 1995).

Definition of Resilience

Fittingly, resilience is a standpoint from which to explicate risk and protective factors. Although resilience is commonly understood in the literature in terms of correlation between attributed causes of outcomes and the outcome itself, the concept, according to Kaplan (1996), is ambiguous. Not surprisingly, the resilient models researchers use are quite variable. Notwithstanding, constructs common to all models are outcomes, risk, and protective factors. Kaplan, in particular, has noted that the concept of resilience as outcome, as cause, or as influence is a quandary for researchers. According to Kaplan, definitions vary in light of which questions the researcher is attempting to address:

> Is resilience defined based on the nature of outcomes in response to stress or regarding the factors that interact with stress to produce the outcomes? Is resilience the variation in good outcomes among individuals who are at-risk for bad outcomes, or is resilience the qualities possessed by individuals that enable them to have good outcomes? Is resilience a phenomenon that would moderate the influence of risk factors on more or less benign outcomes? Or is resilience the fact of having achieved benign outcomes in the face of adversity? (p. 4)

I support the view that resilience is achieving a good outcome from misfortune as well as the successful management of risk factors to avoid misfortune. To support the thesis of this text, resilience is understood to mean factors that interact with stress to moderate risk factors that ordinarily would produce negative outcomes. In the use of this definition, I infer that resilience is evolutionary, evolving over time, and a characteristic that can be promoted by stress. Thus stress encompasses "constructive confrontations" of life crises that can promote growth and development. Life crises are opportunities for the reorganization of psychosocial resources to promote and enhance psychosocial functioning (Schaefer & Moos, 1992). Similarly, Werner and Smith (1982) tersely define resilience as "the self-righting tendencies within the human organism" (p. 152) In such an evolutionary perspective of resilience, Bronfenbrenner's ecological paradigm indicates the role of resilience within the transactional encounter of person and the environment (see Figure 3.2). Kaplan (1996) has argued that resilience is a muddied construct for researchers and should be discarded, as it no longer has empirical usefulness. The perspective and the goal of this text are to provide a description of African American adolescent females that focus on their strengths. Widely used in the social work literature, the concepts of strengths and social supports are interchangeable substitutes for resilient and protective factors, respectively. The strengths perspective, a therapeutic service model, suggests that human beings, through lived experiences, are endowed with positive attributes, abilities, talents, and resources. A person's endowed proficiency enhances self-empowerment tendencies and advances the therapeutic helping process (Saleebey, 1992). Succinctly, social supports are social resources or assets that promote social structural opportunities (Stevens, 1997).

Models of Risk

Conventionally, risk is seen as exposure to anyone or anything that represents danger or injury. During the past decade, researchers from several disciplines, including psychology, psychiatry, sociology, and social work, have conducted studies that examine individual adaptability in the face of serious environmental risks (Dryfoos, 1990; Dubow & Luster, 1990; Grossman et al., 1992; Haggerty et al., 1994; Kolvin, Miller, Fleeting, and Kolvin, 1988; Jessor, 1993; Kagan, 1992; Rutter, 1998). Nonetheless, risks and protection, constructs borrowed from epidemiology, are relatively new to social science research. Unlike the actualized "risk" of epidemiology, which figures in the manifestation of disease processes, social science researchers currently investigate the relationship between high-stress situations and adaptive functioning. Economic impoverishment, poor housing, marital discord, divorce, parental mental illness, maternal psychiatric disorder, child foster home placement, and racial hate crimes are all regarded as risk circumstances that threaten psychosocial development. Research findings conclude that healthy adaptive psychosocial functioning can occur despite exposure to threatening circumstances. Equally important are findings that suggest that individuals present distinct and varied responses to physical-social environments, the least of which may be pathological (Demos, 1989; Garmezy, 1993; Kolvin et al., 1988; Rutter, 1987; Sameroff & Seifer, 1990; Stevens, 1997b; Werner & Smith, 1982).

Risk models are either cumulative, additive, or interactive. While the terms additive and cumulative are sometimes used interchangeably, both infer that stresses are summative, that they pile up over either short-term or long-term periods or occur in parallel circumstances. In particular, cumulative risk is the term more commonly used and specifically indicates continuous exposure to jeopardy over time. Individuals or families are at greater risk for adverse effects when stress events occur in equivalent situations in a given period. Generally, such stresses in environmental situations persist over generations. Research findings indicate that cumulative exposures to risk elements are significantly associated with the likelihood of psychiatric disorders in offspring (Garmezy, 1993). In this regard, it is reasoned, for instance, that chronic poverty generates other risk circumstances, thereby compromising adaptive intergenerational functioning. Adolescent pregnant females, for example, are likely to be economically impoverished before childbearing. Or children who experience chronic poverty, for example, are likely to be malnourished and subject to the many health problems caused by poor nutrition. Cumulative risks can be triggered by the occurrence of a single stress event that generates multiple sequential risks. One family may experience an array of stresses, such as severe mental illness, parental loss of employment, severe physical illness, and marital discord. Researchers find it difficult to disaggregate elements of risk.

The interactive risk model undergirds the person-process-context configuration used to explain human adaptation (see Chapter 3). The interactive model facilitates the appropriation of a resiliency construct. Strength and hardiness, features of resilience, can be observed in transactions that occur in certain ecological domains, such as family, peers, and school. Granted that social contexts can comprise risk, the interactive model has special significance for adolescents of color precisely because the model incorporates the person-in-situation transactional construct and an ecological perspective. Consequently, it is best suited to clarify how social stigma is negotiated in a hostile environment whether in a healthy or maladaptive way (see Figure 3.1). For example, in the application of the interactive model, the societal attribution of racial stigma need not be internalized as self-hate. Individuals may confront the inevitability of hostile social circumstances or micro-aggressive actions without attributing self-blame. A strength perspective suggests that resilient life practices can evolve from malevolent social circumstances. An individual can develop a critical or discriminating conscience in negotiating one's social world. Thus, a sense of self-efficacy is attained. While the three conceptual risk models may well overlap, I proposed that the person-process-context paradigm is one that directly deals with the transactional nature of the person and environment and is itself a type of interactive model.

Seemingly, in the interactive model, protective factors can be more transparent. By and large this is due to the intersubjective process elements involved in the transaction of person and environment context. Relatedly, a more recent development in risk research is the study of protective factors that are considered to counteract or buffer extreme risk effects (Garmezy, 1993). Interestingly, such studies were undertaken because it was found that psychosocial outcomes of children who suffered cumulative risk conditions were not always severely compromised. While this knowledge certainly pointed to the resilience of such children, it made researchers aware of the fact that not enough was known about this topic. Notwithstanding, to date, empirical findings reveal a number of protective factors that are likely to contribute to beneficial social outcomes. A few notable protective factors are active church membership, employment, and proximal role models (Stevens, 1997).

Social Stigma, a Risk Factor

The consideration of stress is also experienced from the allocation of particular social categories, such as race, age, and sexual orientation, which constitute social stigma (Goffman, 1963). Accordingly, social stigma engenders unkind, harmful, or even lethal social responses. Social responses of this kind are not only stress inducers, but may also represent a risk syndrome. I suggest that a risk syndrome represents a set of co-occurring factors that characterizes a special pattern of risk. Simply put, poor adolescents of color may experience social stigma in three categories: socioeconomic status, age, and race/ethnicity. Ordinarily, personal manifestations of impoverishment provoke uneasiness, shame, or embarrassment in those who are privileged. Undoubtedly, the poor are aware of the sentiments their condition evokes. Certainly, in

SOCIAL STIGMA IN A SCHOOL SETTING: "I DON'T WANT THE STUDENTS TO KNOW I'M FROM THE PROJECTS"

Fourteen-year-old Avon was referred to the social worker by the parish priest. Avon is having considerable difficulty adjusting to a predominately white school environment. The school is located far from Avon's inner-city neighborhood. Avon has won a competitive four-year scholarship to attend the school. The school, considered to be one of the best high schools in the city, is located near a Catholic university and selects the best and brightest students from both suburban and urban areas. The school is noted for its high scholarship, and most of the student population comes from families of middle- and upper-class backgrounds. Avon is one of five students of color enrolled in the school. Avon is quiet in class and has difficulty speaking when called upon by her teachers. She has no friends at the school. After attending school for 6 months, Avon thinks that she may want to attend a high school in her own neighborhood. At the same time Avon would like to take advantage of the opportunity to remain at the school but is uncertain about what to do. She wants advice about what to do from the social worker. Avon resides in public housing with her mother and two older brothers, ages 16 and 18. Avon has lived in public housing all of her life. Avon's elder brother works and attends junior college. Avon's father deserted the family when she was 2 years old, and his whereabouts are unknown. Avon and her family are considered good practicing Catholics and are active in parish activities. Avon's parish is one of the few in the city that has a black priest. Avon and her siblings were educated in the parish's primary school and her brothers in parochial high schools in black neighborhoods in the city. Currently Avon's mother is employed part-time as a hotel housekeeper. She has a hard time making ends meet. Once fully employed, her work is now irregular as she has rheumatoid arthritis. Avon is exceptionally bright, well mannered, and attractive. She was the valedictorian in her eighth grade class. In the initial contacts with the social worker, Avon complained bitterly about the high school environment. She feels the students look down on her because she is black and poor. She says, "Sometimes being poor may be worst than being black." She relates that the one other black girl in the school, an eleventh-grader named Becky, is "uppity," comes from a better background than she does, and is popular with her white classmates. Avon says that she would like to get to know Becky, but she is really unfriendly toward the students of color. Avon complains that the school's Big Sister Program that assigns upper-class students to help incoming freshman become acquainted with a new school environment has not worked for her. She does not feel comfortable with her Big Sister, Penny, and rarely meets with her. Avon is mortified that Penny will discover that she lives in the projects. Avon is aware that many of the white students commonly use derogatory racial epithets, tell off-color racial/ethnic jokes, and believe that the students of color are the "dumb kids." She claims that white students or either condescending or dismissive toward her. *Study Questions and Issues:* (1) Discuss the salient developmental issues reflected in Avon's adjustment to the school environment. Consider all the developmental domains. Give special consideration to the racial, ethnic, and gender role commitment domain (see Figure 3.4). (2) Discuss the difficulties you think might be experienced by the practitioner in engaging Avon for therapeutic work considering that the practitioner may be of a different racial/ethnic and/or class background. (3) Discuss practical interventions that you would use to communicate sincerity, authenticity, and acceptance of Avon's dilemma. (4) Discuss whether you would support Avon in remaining in her current school environment or transferring to a neighborhood school. (5) Discuss ways you would recognize Avon's strengths. (6) Do you think social stigma is an issue in this particular case? Explain your point of view. *See also:* Chapters 4–6 and Figures 3.1 and 3.4.

American society, race is a contaminated social category. Historically, race has been used to depict a hierarchy of power. The American Negro has represented the most inferior or tainted biological human condition—often depicted as sinister—and thus has a stigma.

I infer that age is a source of social stigma because of conflicting cultural responses about youth in American society. In American society, "being young" is exaggeratedly esteemed, especially in the marketplace of consumerism. The underside of such excessive veneration is that adults are fearful of youth's brashness and unpredictability. Adults are also anxious about their own aging and loss of vigor. Given the demonization of race, the societal view of black youth, especially black males, is that they are dangerous, impetuous, and menacing. Here let us note the important consideration of social categories as risk factors themselves. On this account it seems that while both cumulative and additive risk models have merit, the interactive model captures the reciprocal exchanges between subject and subject or subject and social context. Within this conceptual framework both social categories and social circumstances constitute risk factors. In this regard, it is posited that the successful management of adolescent development in at-risk environments can provide knowledge about positive effects that promote mental health. Moreover, the hypothesis that individuals develop the attributes of assertion, self-efficacy, and recognition, which mediate risk elements despite chronic adversity, finds support in an interactive model. These issues will be taken up more thoroughly in Chapter 3 within the person-process-context model.

Notes

1. To account for the occurrence of historical differences in the usage of diverse racial/ethnic identity vocabularies, I use Negro, black, and African American interchangeably. The decision to adopt these respective terminologies was to depict historical accuracy rather than a personal commitment to any particular nomenclature.

2. During the early 1900s black Americans who became social activists in the cause of promoting racial equality were identified as "race men or race women" to distinguish their activities as guided by an obligation to the social and economic advancement of American blacks. Such women were committed to the social and moral uplift of the Negro race.

2 Adolescent Developmental Theories

I am as dark—but lovely,
Oh daughters of Jerusalem
As the tents of Kedar,
As the curtains of Salma.
Do not stare at me because I am swarthy,
Because the sun has burned me

(Song of Songs)

Betsey could hardly believe it was she when she looked in the mirror. What a woman she was going to be! Betsey felt beautiful. She felt brave. She knew it now. There was a difference between being a little girl and being a woman. She knew now. She'd never see Regina again, but they'd never be separate either. Women who can see over the other side are never far from each other.

(Shange, 1985, p. 139)

Introduction

Black females find their voice in the chorus of other black female voices. It could be argued that the coming of age of the black female is in the personal and communal connection created in friendships, in mother/daughter relationships, and in community institutions. Historically, black women's relational connections served as safe sanctuaries from the trauma of racism and oppression (Cannon, 1996). Until quite recently, black female self-empowerment narratives were documented in literary creations rather than in social science scholarship. The denouement in Ntozake Shange's coming of age novel, *Betsey Brown*, for example, is Betsey's self-discovery of the pleasures of sisterhood and the revelation of her own lovableness and beauty. In a first-time visit to a beauty parlor, a farewell gift from her summer caretaker, Regina, Betsey is attended to as if she were royalty. She is given a stylish new hairdo, manicure, and pedicure. More importantly, the storytelling and behavior of the older women customers captivate her. The beauty shop is magically figured in the novel. For Betsey, the beauty shop is an enchanted place where women rule—where women's ways of knowing and meaning making are mutually shared. Equally important, she is schooled in folk practices for dealing with racial inequities. From this experience, Betsey realizes a prudent life lesson—that confidence, courage, beauty, and sisterhood is the bequest of women who see the future (hope) in the present. Shange has encapsulated a rather commonplace experience to depict a young girl's self-awakening and maturation. Yet what developmental theory can clarify a black girl's self-awareness of strength and beauty poignantly symbolized by the character of Betsey Brown? Betsey Brown's character unfolds within the social context of her daily experiences in the same ways that I try to portray the real lives of inner-city black girls' lives in this text.

Developmental Theories and Praxis

Currently, researchers consider that the complexity of adolescent development warrants consideration of the sociocultural contexts of ethnicity, gender, and culture. Relatedly, because of the multiple contextual factors that influence development, it is argued, no one single developmental model fits all adolescents (Santrock, 1999). Historically, adolescent developmental theories have not genuinely addressed the authentic realities of the praxis of black lives. Unquestionably, Betsey Brown, a fully artistically conceived character, has experiences that altogether reverberate as authentic. In *Betsey Brown*, Shange repudiates three fundamental racial banalities: One is that black girls are culturally deprived and economically disadvantaged. Another is that beauty is not found in the person of the female Negro, but that black signifies negativity or ugliness. And finally is the cliché of strained and discordant black male-female relations. What is explicitly illustrated in *Betsey Brown* is a tapestry of ethnic richness, complexity, and diversity reflected in the distinctive resilience of its characters. Betsey, much like the author, is a middle-class girl growing up in St. Louis at the dawn of the civil rights movement. Despite the loving care of family, Betsey needs to be resilient to deal with the social devaluation of being Black and female. Betsey's parents, both professionals, have a stable, loving marriage. The father is a physician, the mother a psychiatric social worker. Middle-class black girls and their families are rarely depicted in American literature. Class is used descriptively in *Betsey Brown* to distinguish economic dissimilarity between Regina, the children's summer caretaker, and Betsey. Class is also used to differentiate the quality of the two girls' lives. Yet Shange pointedly clarifies that there is an emotional connection between Betsey and Regina, despite the fact of significant class differences. Although Regina's specific age is unknown, she is a recent high school graduate and expectant mother, estranged from her boyfriend, the expectant father. Betsey's relational connection with the women in the beauty salon transcends age and class.

Betsey learns an important lesson from the beauty shop women when she discovers that comeliness is not merely in the dressing of hair, but in communal belonging and relational connection. The beauty salon is employed metaphorically by Shange to portray the meaning of being grown up. Or, rather what Alice Walker (1983) has referred to as being *Womanish*—audacious, courageous, and willful—the serious and unaffected behavior of black women. Herein Shange reveals the continuity of personhood in the communal context—the gathering of sisters. Shange makes symbolic use of the beauty salon to reveal the ordinary practices and conduct of black women's lives. Actualized here are the daily pulsating jazzlike rhythms of communal life.

Scholars have noted the significance of pubertal development in the life cycle. It is considered one of the most significant developments in the life cycle and second only to infancy in the marked rate of physical and hormonal growth (Dubas & Petersen, 1993). A theory is needed that places Betsey's important developmental marker within an ecological life span framework, as Smith (1997) has argued. In such a framework, praxis is temporal, complex, and richly multifaceted. Certainly Shange illustrates this in *Betsey Brown*. While Betsey is a fictionalized character, the portrayal of her self-awakening is no less real. Fiction writers have profound insight into human nature and social experiences. A developmental theory of adolescence is needed that helps illuminate girls' lives as actually portrayed in the real-life situations illustrated throughout the text. The lives of the girls exemplified in the case illustrations in this text are punctuated by the pulsating jazz rhythms of life no less than that of the character of Betsey Brown.

Psychoanalytic Theory and Adolescent Development

More than a decade ago empirical studies discredited the commonly held notion of the inevitable occurrence of adolescent angst (Offer et al., 1988). Study results documented that adolescents were not rebellious or conflicted, but mediated developmental trajectories by engaging in rather quotidian behaviors. American educator and psychologist G. Stanley Hall (1904) has been credited as chiefly responsible for the adoption of Freudian theories to explain adolescent psychological development (Coleman, 1974). Traditional psychoanalytic metatheory hypothesized that the mind, engineered by biological instinctual sexual drives, was an independent and objective entity that metabolized developmental processes. At critical age-graded developmental periods, the mind was believed to function as a dynamic and unconscious processor and organizer of emotional experiences. The mental intrapsychic structuring and synthesis of psychosocial experiences could either advance or retard emotional growth. In the case of adolescence, it was theorized that during this period earlier intrapsychic developmental conflicts reemerged once again for resolution. For Erikson, adolescence was a time of moratorium—a time of respite in which one's social world could be explored and intrapsychic conflicts worked through. Psychoanalytic theorist Anna Freud (1958) hypothesized that adolescence was a period of intense angst. The resurgence of earlier conflicts stimulated such intrapsychic turbulence and confusion that the adolescent's emotional state was akin to psychosis. If such conflicts were unsettled at the end of the adolescent period, the individual was likely to be emotionally disordered in later life.

Despite the fact that scholars currently consider these earlier formulations no longer tenable, the psychoanalytic view has had profound influence in shaping and delineating the empirical agenda in adolescent development (Steinberg, 1990). Grounded in the metatheory of psychoanalysis, Blos (1962, 1976) and Erikson (1964, 1968, 1969) are largely responsible for the present theoretical interpretation of adolescence, so much so that constructs from their psychoanalytical framework have been extracted for independent empirical use. Blos and Erikson have explicated constructs such as identity, moratorium, separation, detachment, autonomy, individuation, and differentiation that are now considered integral to adolescent developmental theory and empirical investigation. For the most part, untangling constructs from the metatheory of psychoanalysis has been problematic for researchers. This is because psychoanalytic constructs are dealt with both as scientific practices and as neurotic symptoms that require therapeutic interventions. Psychoanalytic theory's crucible is its essentialist assumptions that makes it nearly impossible to distinguish between cause and motivation (Sawicki, 1997). Simply put, the unconscious is not subject to measurable validation. Moreover, when compared to the empirical social accountability methods of most researchers, psychodynamic principles exist in a social context devoid of the social group and social accounting approaches of empirical science (Williams, 1995). The psychoanalytic conceptualization of normal development derived from clinical cases of psychopathology—and in turn, clinical postulations became the theoretical foundation for the treatment. Thus, a recursive feedback loop of theorizing developed that is both teleological (the theory conceived instinctual drives as fundamentally causative) and tautological (redundant explanations of the unconscious as the motivation for behaviors).

Perhaps influenced, in part, by feminist theory and findings from developmental research, the psychoanalytic view of adolescence is undergoing fundamental revisions. The specific proposition that adolescence is a recapitulation of earlier developmental (oedipal) conflicts that stimulate chaotic reactions has been reconceptualized. One could speculate that adolescents who undergo experiences of intense angst are themselves troubled youth. No longer is it regarded reasonable to view adolescence as normatively characterized by hostility, rebellion, detachment, and relational conflict (e.g., with parents). The new theoretical reconstruction depicts puberty within a sociopolitical context. Adolescence is considered a period of meaning making and the family as the locus of harmony, attachment, and relational connection (Mirkin, 1994; Palombo, 1985, 1990; Steinberg, 1990). Increasingly, empirical studies show that most adolescents have warm, harmonious, and open relations with their parents. Additionally, substantial empirical evidence suggests that families simultaneously undergo maturational alterations as their offspring experience developmental changes (Steinberg, 1990). These findings, all on white youth, find support in the idea of transactional processes occurring in families. Still to be considered, however, is how these new conceptualizations and results figure in the lives of economically disadvantaged teens of color.

Critics contend that new theorizations of adolescent development are based on empirical investigations of white middle-class youth and thus have limited generalizability (Jessor, 1993). The question arises as to why this has occurred. Conjecturally, white adolescent populations have been easily accessible to researchers. Or, as some scholars have argued, white social scientists have had little or no interest in African American adolescents (Gibbs, 1990). Moreover, during the 1960s black communities were closed to researchers. The inaccessibility of the black community to researchers can be explained, in part, by a generalized fear of being harmed by the experiments of white researchers and by the rejection of the deficit explanatory models researchers have used to investigate black communities (Myers, 1989). Nevertheless, the demographic characteristics of white youth are in stark contrast to those of poor inner-city adolescents of color. Research findings document that even when African Americans and whites share similar socioeconomic status, they reside in substantially different neighborhoods. Whites are more likely to reside in neighborhoods representing varied social classes, while blacks generally reside in segregated poverty localities. Consequently, whites are more likely than blacks to live in higher-quality neighborhoods

(Henley, 1995). Generally, scientific investigations of white youth are those of middle-class status, in two-parent households, and in suburban communities. Research scholars correctly question whether investigative findings of white youth can be generalized to other adolescent populations. What is needed is research about familial processes in economically disadvantaged single-headed households among adolescents of color (Steinberg, 1990). Notwithstanding that many poor black neighborhoods may reside in communities that represent social risks, empirical data about how those resilient families interact in such environments to enhance their adaptive capacities are also worthy of investigation.

Feminism and Adolescent Development

As mentioned earlier, the oedipal situation embodied the nucleus of the psychoanalytic developmental hypothesis. The core intrapsychic oedipal conflict of competitive striving occurred in childhood and reoccurred in adolescence. Emotional maturation was achieved, the theory posited, with its resolution. The oedipal resolution necessitated that the male relinquish the maternal figure as love object, forego fears of castration, and identify with the autonomy and independence of the father. Developmentally male-centered, psychoanalytic theory, feminists asserted, was theoretically flawed in its postulation of the severance of parental ties to achieve independence and autonomy during adolescence (Chodorow, 1989; Gilligan, Ward, & Taylor, 1988). Despite the fact that Freud tried to explain girls' development, the oedipal thesis, feminists claimed, omitted the true characteristic of female development—penis envy was hardly a concern of girls.

Feminist theoreticians argued that, unlike males, the socialization of females is based on mutuality, care, and connection rather than competition and separation. Females are socialized to value relational attachment, mutuality, and care. Females differed from males in that they sustained identification with the same-sex parental figure or love object throughout the life span. Hence females undergo a uniquely different set of psychosocial experiences within the nuclear family (Belenky et al., 1986; Gilligan, Ward, & Taylor, 1988). Further, it was theorized that females have a separate developmental trajectory, one where relational connection is nurtured and sustained throughout the life cycle. From a feminist standpoint, the maturational anxiety girls experience at puberty onset is due to conflicting demands encountered in the social expectation for increasing autonomy and the emotional need for relational attachment.

While significant paradigmatic shifts exist in adolescent development theory, additional empirical research is required in the new and developing relational theory posited by both feminist and neopsychoanalytic scholars. Implicit in the female relational attachment argument is the fact that males and females experience dissimilar socialization processes within the culture based on gender. But the fact remains that male and females, aware of such gender socialization differences, sustain and maintain them by active participation in the culture. Thus, the feminist argument may relate more to cultural considerations than psychodynamic theory does. Consequently, the issue of a separate developmental line thesis may be more appropriately addressed within a sociopolitical framework. The question feminists must address is how males are relationally connected within the context of family—or what intersubjective attributes males develop to negotiate the context of familial life. *Once gender is recognized as situated in the context of culture, a separate gender line of development is not necessary.*

From another view, albeit simplistically conceptualized, the angst of adolescence appears to be no more than a developmental dilemma sparked by a felt intensity of longing to fulfill simultaneously both dependent and independent emotional needs. I do not postulate that from a life cycle and ecological perspective, the modulation of independent and dependent longings is not determined by gender nor is it peculiar to adolescence. Rather, I theorize that such longings represent a normative maturational occurrence throughout the life cycle. Simply put, independent and dependent desires embody a basic existential predicament—the paradoxical need for both aloneness and togetherness, or the need to experience the self as distinctly unique and at the same time as like or akin to those with whom communal membership is shared. What occurs that makes this dilemma peculiar during adolescence is the transition to adulthood with its concomitant developmental challenges of learning how to manage reproductive maturity, how to handle intense affect, and how to foster and sustain empathic relational connections. Further, the developmental demands of adolescence are exacerbated when meeting ethnic identity challenges in a hostile environments (see the case illustration *"Social Stigma in a School Setting"* concerning 14-year-old Avon).

Unquestionably, feminists' postulate of relational attachment in the development of adolescence girls exposed the limitations of psychoanalytic formulations of adolescent development in general. Accordingly, feminists significantly challenged the psychoanalytic interpretation of familial realignment within a milieu of emotional detachment, conflict, and disharmony during adolescence. Postmodern ideas positing the improbability of objectivity or that reality is never independent of subjective perception have, undoubtedly, contributed to a reconceptualization of human development as uniquely context dependent. But here too additional empirical data are needed to strengthen or confirm this thesis.

Contextualized Development, Identity Complexity, and Meaning

The hypothesis that development is context dependent—a reciprocal and transactional process of engagement within multifarious domains, such as family, neighborhood, peer group, school, and church—is a relatively novel notion. It is an idea well suited to the ecological life span developmental model since it suggests that decisive developmental challenges be calibrated by transactional relationships occurring at pivotal periods and in critical domains throughout the life course. This viewpoint also suggests a preventive perspective that indicates that social work intervention should occur at decisive times throughout the life course. Relational connection, mutuality, and caring are psychosocial qualities of significant import, and they must be seen as contingent on context. Such is the case that even when the relational qualities are personally avowed they function as part of the social expression of the communal values and customs of a given society, an organization or an institution, or a specific ethnic cultural group. In the case illustration "Nested Contexts," 14-year-old Ramara adopts caring and empathic values that are deeply rooted in the family's religious beliefs. Thus, one could say that Ramara is maturing in the developmental domain of care and protective sensibility. Certainly, empathic relational qualities contribute to the maturational process since they constitute adaptive intersubjective responses (see Figure 3.1).

The idea that I advance here is that the authentic mark of maturity in American culture is self-efficacy, which is thus a maturational goal of puberty. I consider this developmental marker culturally based in that it is derived from a cultural ethos of individualism. The attribution of self-efficacy among African American adolescents is both complex and problematic. Attributed self-efficacy presents a social dilemma for black adolescents, as they must deal with the effects of racism in a hostile environment. (A more detailed discussion of this issue is presented in Chapter 4.) Essentially, self-efficacy is the ability to exercise mastery and competence in one's social environment or to feel that one has control over one's environment because of proficient abilities. Self-efficacy is a developmental marker that can be accomplished by a variety of means. Self-efficacy can be achieved in the competition of athletic games learned in the school setting, in the autonomy and independence of decision making learned by taking part in family and community processes, and in the mutuality and caring of friendships developed in the peer group and neighborhood. Apparently, it is in the larger social contextual domains of school and work that African American adolescents experience difficulties. These examples of self-efficacy presume that skills of mastery and competence are exercised not only in morally legitimate contextual domains but also with a personally avowed code of principled ethics. Moreover, the development of a moral sensibility is set forth as integral to healthy maturation in adolescents. While the genesis of moral development is laid down early in life, it remains an ongoing process consistently tested by life's praxis (Coles, 1986). Obviously, in real-life circumstances, self-efficacy skills can lack propriety. The drug dealer or Mafia hit man, for instance, functions with adept skill, but in a exploitative amoral context or a context that is idiosyncratic and peculiar to the criminal world.

The Family Constellation and Individuality

I theorize that the family in the life course-ecological framework is considered expansive—a kinship network that extends beyond the nuclear family constellation. Moreover, the kinship network represents an ethnic/racial collective that embodies its peculiar values and customs necessary to ensure intergenerational continuity. Within this framework, the adolescent does not sever parental bonds but self-differentiates within the familial context to achieve a unique personhood that accommodates membership in the makeup of both the family and the social community. The adolescent must learn to manage the needs for self-assertion, self-efficacy, and recognition within the "nested contexts" of family and neighborhood. Maturational development that occurs within relational connection and interdependence is understood contextually. Paradoxically, in a mature adult, familial connection is defined no less by the uniqueness of self-differentiation within the family as it is by a common resemblance to the familial character. The makeup of identity is defined by one's distinctiveness within the family group as well as the identity of the family as a group entity. During adolescence, the familial character may be experienced as both liberating and restrictive. The family exercises control over expressions of individuality. In most families, extreme eccentricities are generally not tolerated. They often are the cause of familial conflict and can alienate the individual from the kinship body. For instance, families often tolerate commonplace idiosyncrasies and use them to define the character peculiarities of different family members, for example, "Aunt Ruby gossips too much" or "Uncle Earl is always late for family functions." Additionally, the family distinctiveness as an entity is defined in expressions such as, "All of us Mitchells have been earnest hard workers and don't complain about the hard knocks of life." Familial relations can be problematic during the adolescent period, precisely because it is the time adolescents may experiment and discover who they are by adopting new behaviors and new interests and outlandish or faddish behaviors and dress. Identity complexity is a construct in which to interpret the intricate processes that occur in identity exploration and formation during the adolescent period.

The Significance of Gender and Race

In the previous section it was noted that gender socialization had particular import in identity development. Gender, however, is only one variable among several that uniquely impact the adolescent trajectory. Indeed, in the explication of contextualized development is the consideration of race/ethnicity as significant variables consequential to the development of identity. In the case of adolescents of color, race/ethnicity alongside gender are equally pivotal in identity formation. Notwithstanding the significant influence of these variables in the developmental process, the chief unit of socialization is undeniably the family unit, in which gender, race/ethnicity, and class assume meaning within context. Family epitomizes attachment to one's cultural reference group, an attachment central to racial/ethnic identity formation.

Race/ethnicity is fundamental to identity development in adolescents of color (Biggs, 1998; Boykin & Ellison, 1995; Collins, 1990). Collins, in particular, advances the ideas that gender, race, and class uniquely converge in the self-experiences of African American females to form personhood. The intersection of these three variables, she argues, are always operative in the context in which African American females model their existence, even though the experiences of black females are richly culturally diverse, insofar as they are bicultural. Moreover, their lived experiences, according to Collins (1990), are structured by the interlocking variables of gender, race, and class. Black females, Collins argues, function not only on the basis of knowledge received from the dominant culture but also on knowledge that is constructed for change and resistance and situated in the context of their lived experiences, but suppressed from the dominant cultural context—subjugated knowledge. As an oppressed minority, subjugated knowledge provides the means by which black females resist negative definitions of self rendered by the dominant group. Subjugated knowledge as concrete and personal provides only a glimpse into the human condition; it is a

SELF-ASSERTION, SELF-EFFICACY, AND RECOGNITION: "THOSE BAD GIRLS"

Sixteen-year-old Anna Mae Anderson and her 48-year-old mother were seen in an inner-city hospital's family planning clinic. Mrs. Anderson brought Anna Mae to the clinic because she wanted her to have birth control pills. Mrs. Anderson believed her daughter to be sexually active, although Anna Mae had told her mother that she was not having sex. Mrs. Anderson was also requesting counseling services for Anna Mae. According to Mrs. Anderson, "Anna Mae is getting out of control and always with those bad girls." Mrs. Anderson wanted to know whether the clinic visit was confidential, as she did not want her husband to know that she had brought Anna Mae to the clinic. Mrs. Anderson was advised that clinic records were confidential and that Anna Mae could request contraceptives without parental consent and that it was Anna Mae's decision as to whether she shared this information with her parents. Mrs. Anderson said that she brought Anna Mae to the clinic because she did not think that she would have come on her own. The family lives in a large high-rise public housing complex. Anna Mae is the youngest of three daughters. The older daughters Batheada and Clarissa are ages 28 and 26, respectively. Both daughters are college graduates and have jobs in bordering states. Both are unmarried. Batheada and Clarissa generally visit the family during Thanksgiving and Christmas holidays. Fifty-five-year old Mr. Anderson is a janitor at the housing complex where the family resides. He has maintained his job for 30 years. Mrs. Anderson is a homemaker. The Anderson family is a member of a large extended group of kin. Both Mr. and Mrs. Anderson come from large families. Mr. and Mrs. Anderson are well respected in the community, active in community affairs, and regular churchgoers. However, Mrs. Anderson complains that things have gotten worse in the housing development and it is harder to raise children. She is especially concerned about the selling of drugs in the community. She says, "There are too many young girls having babies who don't know the first thing about being parents. A lot of those bad girls who are friends with Anna Mae have mothers who are much younger than I am and they don't know nothing about raising children either." Mrs. Anderson related that she was really worried that something bad would happen to Anna Mae. When the counselor wanted to know what Mrs. Anderson meant by "Anna Mae getting out control," Mrs. Anderson had a difficult time identifying specific behaviors. Mrs. Anderson said that she didn't know if she could name anything specific, but that she knew "those bad girls that are friends with Anna Mae have a lot of problems." According to Mrs. Anderson, Anna Mae's friends "are sexually active, smoke marijuana, play hookey from school, and talk back to grown-ups." When the counselor saw Anna Mae alone, she shared that she thought her mother was just too nervous about everything and is always listening to gossip. Her mother doesn't give her much credit for being able to make good decisions. She related that she didn't have bad girl friends. Some of her friends had family problems, but they themselves were not bad. She thought her friends looked up to her and mostly wanted her advice about things. They used to visit her a lot, but her mother acts funny when they're around so they don't come around much anymore. She misses them. She talks to her older sisters a lot and will be glad when she graduates from high school. She wants to be like her sisters and go away to college. She goes to a high school outside her neighborhood that she likes all right, but she doesn't forget where she comes from. Some of her friends are girls she grew up with. She believes her family has a reputation, in the community, for being uppity, but it's her mother who people mostly have in mind. Her friends don't do the things her mother says they do. Some of the girls in the neighborhood do the crazy things her mother talked about. She doesn't date, but there is a boy at her church that she likes. She has not told her mother about him because it would make her too upset, but her sisters know. She's also told her Aunt Mae, her mother's sister, whom she talks to a lot. The two of them get along well together. When she started her menstrual period it was Aunt Mae that she first told. They do lots of things together; they go shopping and to the movies a lot. The two of them are thinking about having a family book club. It was Aunt Mae who told her mother to let her wear lipstick. Aunt Mae is a few years younger than her mother, with no children, and divorced. She said that she is still a virgin. She is looking forward to the summer because she will visit Clarissa, who is getting her a summer job. Sometimes she thinks it's easier to talk with her dad than it is with her mother. When she turned 12 her mother began to act differently toward her—too worried about everything, always thinking about the worse possible things that could happen to her. She thought her mother had done a pretty good job of raising her, but when she got in her teens everything changed. In the last segment of the interview session, the counselor saw Anna Mae and her mother together and advised, with Anna Mae's permission, that Anna Mae had decided that she did not want birth control pills, as she was not sexually active. Anna Mae wanted a counselor to talk to about things. She thought that if she had someone to talked to it might help her to get along better with her mother. Her sisters were far away and phone calls were too expensive. Mrs. Anderson said that if Anna Mae wanted a counselor to talk to it was OK. She never wanted anything but the best for her children. The counselor referred Anna Mae and Mrs. Anderson to a family service agency. *Study Questions and Issues:* (1) Discuss the ways you think Anna Mae might be protected against the obvious social risks in her community. (2) Discuss the ways you believe Anna Mae's family context or familial relations counterbalances the mother's overprotective attitude. Or do you think Mrs. Anderson's concerns about her daughter's safety in the neighborhood is warranted? Explain. (3) Do you think Anna Mae is at risk for engaging in antisocial behaviors? Explain. (4) Write a brief assessment and discuss in a small group of three or four students what you believe the clinical issues to be if you were the family service practitioner that would see Anna Mae. Explain how you would engage her for services when using the Collaborative Intervention Context Model (CICM) (see Chapters 1, 3, and 8). (5) What do you think are the key developmental issues for Anna Mae? Explain how she manages issues of assertion, self-efficacy, and recognition within her family and neighborhood. Discuss how other girls in Anna Mae's neighborhood may manage these same issues in maladaptive ways. *See also:* Figure 3.1.

partisan angle—and not intended as a claim of universal truths for all oppressed persons/groups. In the case of African American females, subjugated knowledge is likely to make up the basic socialization experiences of their cultural reference group. Yet such experiences must be synthesized to accommodate equally meaningful socialization experiences from other contextual domains.

In an effort to address the complexity of identity formation in adolescence, I theorized that a normative core adolescent developmental task is synthesizing coherent meaning systems from varied experiences of socialization. In the case of African American females, I have postulated that synthesizing coherent meaning systems from three experiences of socialization must take place. One socialization experience is that of the dominant society (Euro-American worldview); second, a devalued societal status (affected by the status convergence of race and gender); and third, a cultural reference or ethnic group (Afro-American worldview) (Stevens, 1997a).

Identity and the Creation of Meaning

Similarly, from an essentialist psychological view, Palombo (1985, 1988, 1990) has addressed meaning construction in adolescence. Using the self-psychology model of psychoanalyst Heinz Kohut, Palombo contends that a major developmental task of adolescence is the "crystallization of a meaning system" directed at an inner program that affirms a sense of self. Palombo seems unclear about the exact meaning of an inner program—in the tradition of psychoanalytic speculation one surmises that he uses the expression to refer to intrapsychic processes. Palombo's expression *inner program of personal needs* seems imprecise and esoteric. Importantly, the phrase is used to suggest three concrete elements: (1) the need to be mirrored for competence, value, and worth; (2) the need to idealize personal-societal goals and values; and (3) the need to participate in a community of others. The precise significance of Palombo's conceptualization is its inferred attribution of intersubjectivity—self-meanings are constructed in relation to the other. More importantly, perhaps, the three elements have particular significance for practice theory, especially if clinical work is viewed as the construction of meanings. The practitioner, in working with adolescent clients, must be able to integrate all three elements in the clinical work. For instance, the practitioner will want to mirror the self-worth of the adolescent to assist the adolescent in adopting positive societal goals and values and to support the adolescent in developing prosocial behaviors among a peer group. Moreover, insofar as socialization experiences in American culture are and will continue to be culturally diverse, adolescents of color must develop the capacity to articulate and integrate a multitextured self that comprises multiple and diverse meaning systems. This supposes that adolescents have a well-developed capacity, augmented by cognitive development, for meaning coherence and synthesis (Palombo, 1988; Spencer, 1995).

Identity complexity and social identity are postulated as heuristic constructs in explicating the adolescent developmental trajectory. Saari (1991) refers to identity complexity as the conscious experience of self as coherent, versatile, creative, and differentiated, noting in particular that conflict may exist in coherence. Identity complexity, as so defined, may well be placed within a phenomenological paradigm, and not exclusively in a psychodynamic one, as Saari asserts (Atwood & Stolorow, 1984). Identity is an evolving differentiation in relation to self, others, and the surrounding world, while sustaining connection to significant others. It is the intersubjective connection to significant others that makes coherence within differentiation possible (Stevens, 1997a) (see Figure 2.1). I postulate that intersubjectivity is the intervening variable between person and context. Without taking an essentialist viewpoint, I propose that meaning is created between subject(s) and subject(s) and decidedly influenced by the context or ecological domains within which the co-creation occurs. Sawicki (1997) has noted that psychoanalytic theory has inadequately dealt with its essentialist assumptions of causality and, therefore, requires phenomenological critique. Spencer (1995) contends that this particular formulation of person-process-context constitutes a "phenomenological approach to and application of ecological systems theory" (p. 49) which typifies the interactive synthesis of person and context. I have suggested elsewhere (1994) that the idea of the complexities inherent in identity development may well be placed in a phenomenological paradigm. Orange, At-

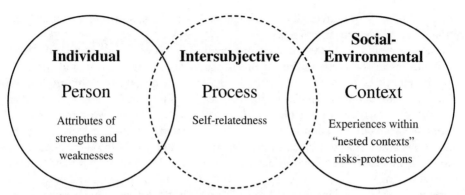

Figure 2.1. Person-process-context model of intersubjectivity processes (an open and changing interactive process of empathy, recognition, and assertion.

wood, and Stolorow (1997), scholars within the psychoanalytic perspective, have asserted that the contextualist view is neither theory nor practice, but an attitude and sensibility toward both. Others argue that context is more than outlook and awareness, that it represents a theoretical framework in which to view development. Lerner, Ostrom, and Freel (1997) conceptualize developmental contextualism as an integrative theory of development that bridges the gap between existent developmental theories and the actual lives of at-risk poor adolescents. The authors argue persuasively that developmental contextualism affords a multi-integrative view of adolescent psychosocial problems. Thus, such a view permits multiple interventions (see the case illustration "Nested Concepts") in addressing problems since adolescent problem behaviors are interrelated or can co-occur (Stevens, 1998b).

A mature individual reflects a coherent differentiated self that mirrors experiences of complexity, choice, fluidity, creativity, and articulation. Such self-experiences are organized by meanings created from social-cultural life and embodied in a social identity. Adolescents are just beginning to evolve this coherent differentiated self. Social identity here is conceptualized as the cultural anchorage of the self. A social identity differs from the concept of social role in that social identity has to do with the meanings embedded in social roles, not just the role itself. A social identity develops by engaging in social and personal meaning-making actions that are legitimated by the praxis of daily life. On the surface, social identities may seem commensurate with the various social roles assumed by an individual. While the inference here is that an individual may have multiple social identities, the two constructs differ in the psychological mechanisms of choice and self-assertion. For example, the role of teacher, student, senator, mother, wife, or sorority sister are all positions that are defined by culturally constructed meanings. When social roles constitute social identities, however, the individual chooses to personally own the cultural meanings inherent in the roles assumed. To make such a claim of ownership, cultural role meanings become an integral and a coherent part of one's unique self-system. Moreover, in the ownership process, the individual can reorder, rearrange, or reinvent conventionally constructed role meanings and in so doing they become actual social identities that bear the indelible mark of individual distinctiveness. In the self-assertion for mutual recognition, a social identity is created.

Developmentally, adolescents are just beginning to create and own particular social identities in the construction of the narrative self. The creation and ownership of social identities can be problematic for adolescents despite the exciting activities that come with identity development. In the case illustration "Social Stigma in a School Setting" Avon, a poor black girl, is trying to figure out what the social role of student means in a predominately white school environment. Perhaps for the first time, she is aware that the social categories of black and poor can be grounds for derision and belittlement, which affect her personally. Within Avon's neighborhood community, the social role she assumed as student meant intelligence and ethnic pride. In the white school environment Avon wishes to portray these positive characteristics, but her self-assertion, she feels, is compromised by social rejection. The social identity of an adolescent can be reinforced negatively or positively in the ecological domains of the school and peer group. Unquestionably, the family and community represent central nested contextual influences in the adolescent's psychosocial development. Nonetheless, the school and peer groups also have profound influences and may undermine the positive effects of family and community. The constructs of identity complexity and social identity will be used in subsequent chapters in a discussion of the seven developmental domains (see Figure 3.4).

Age-Related Developmental Markers

For the purposes of this text, a rudimentary definition of adolescence is *a transitional developmental period between childhood and adulthood marked by vital biological, cognitive, and socioemotional changes.* Developmental researchers distinguish the adolescent period by two decisive age-related transitions, reproductive and social (adulthood status) maturity. And while the two are not coterminous in American culture, they represent vital benchmark transformations. Reproductive maturity, a developmental transition of profound consequences, is, perhaps, one of the most difficult challenges adolescents face. Commonly, we think of adolescence as comprising one period of development. And while this is generally the case, it is important to recognize that the adolescent period in American society is protracted, one that extends from approximately age 10 through age 23. This prolonged temporality is determined by critical social factors, such as compulsory education and the timing of entry into the labor market. Pubertal maturation is differentiated by age-related subphases with accompanying evolutionary tasks. Developmental theorists vary, however, in how the subphases of adolescence are classified. For some, the adolescence life stage cycle is comprised of comprehensive substages: early adolescence and late adolescence. Accordingly, the early period (age 10–17) includes the middle school and high school years, and the late period (age 17–22 years) involves the completion of high school or college. Differentiated by specific developmental markers, the early period incorporates most pubertal changes, including physical maturation, formal operational thought, emotional development, membership in peer groups, and heterosexual relationships. Clearly, the changes in cognition and reproduction clearly distinguish adolescence from childhood. The late period, characterized by career interests, dating/mating, and identity exploration, encompasses some autonomy from parents, sex role identity, internalized morality, and career and vocational choices (Newman & Newman, 1987; Santrock, 1998).

Similarly, Elliott and Feldman (1990) identify vital adolescent maturational tasks, but rather divide the period into three pivotal subphases: early adolescence, middle adolescence, and late adolescence. Accordingly, early adolescence, age 10–14, typifies the profound biological and social changes that decide racial/ethnic and gender resolution and culminate in identification with a sexual orientation. Middle adolescence, age 15–17, is characterized by increasing autonomy and individuation, and for a significant proportion (generally those with limited socioeconomic advantage) signals the conclusion of the adolescent period. Late adolescence, age 18 to the mid-20s, typifies the adolescent experiences of those who because of protracted schooling for career development postpone entering adulthood. The adolescent years are prolonged for adolescents who attend college for adulthood preparation and who are not likely to enter the labor force until about age 22–25. Admittedly, substantive developmental tasks occur regardless, but the differentiated time frames allow for a more discrete analysis of maturational milestones.

The ages of adolescent study participants involved in the two research projects outlined in the Prologue were from 11 to 19, thereby encompassing all the developmental subphases outlined here. Notwithstanding the normative age-related milestones, I postulate that adolescents of color engage in identity exploration earlier than white (majority) teens and are more profoundly affected by their experiences of personal discovery. Among black adolescents, early identity exploration is necessitated by the need to enhance self-efficacy capacities in the face of socially denigrating experiences. Concomitantly the adolescent must integrate as an evolving self-narrative the subjugated knowledge about the ethnic group to which she belongs. Thus, black adolescents must deal with identity issues early in order to deal with the stigma of a socially devalued minority status (see the case illustration "Social Stigma in a School Setting"). I term the affirmed knowledge about minority ethnic cultures "subjugated knowledge." I use subjugated knowledge to suggest the ways minority populations develop not only ideas and ways of knowing, but also fact-based information about who they are and how they fit in the society at large. This type of knowledge may well exist outside majority epistemologies, discourse, or erudition. For example, the accumulated historical data about black people often celebrated annually in such events as Black History Month are a concrete example of subjugated knowledge. Black History Month, albeit now legitimately recognized in the post–civil rights era, was initially developed independently of mainstream culture and celebrated as a form of cultural resistance. The celebration, when initially introduced by black educators in segregated (black) educational institutions, was not, as now, a monthlong celebration, but an ethnic commemoration of only one week. Subjugated knowledge (a minority standpoint) generally exists in opposition to the prevailing dominant knowledge (a majority standpoint) about the minority group's placement in and contribution to society's cultural life. The standpoint of subjugated knowledge is one of historical truthfulness and inclusiveness. Its aim is to provide fact-based stories that contest the harmful and prejudicial typecasting of a particular racial/ethnic group (see the case illustration "Historical Legacies and Self-Narratives). Essentially, subjugated knowledge works as a form of cultural resistance. Moreover, cultural resistance can sanction self-defining experiences in alternative social locations, such as music and literature, and in daily idiomatic expressions in behavior and language (Collins, 1990; Stevens, 1997a). Rap music, including the more strident gansta rap, is an example of this observation. What implications does this examination have for clinical practice? Foremost, the normative adolescent identity exploration experience for African American youth is problematized. For black adolescents, the journey of self-discovery involves constructing an identity as a member of a socially devalued racial/ethnic group. Most importantly, if not properly channeled, cultural resistance for black youth can go awry and be maladaptive. Further, the adolescent period for poor black teens is likely to be completed at age 17 or 18 for those who are not college bound, thus shortening the period of identity exploration and self-differentiation. On a practice level, this suggests that practitioners should be attuned to how black youth manage identity issues. Additionally, practitioners must become knowledgeable about the history of the various ethnic minorities with whom they work, especially with at-risk adolescents. Many poor inner-city black adolescents are ignorant of their very rich ethnic heritage. A positive cultural heritage once owned by adolescents can be integrated into the self-narrative that they construct. Social workers will want to develop interventions that enable youth of color to learn about ethnic personages of historical and contemporary importance who symbolize competence, value, and worth and have made significant contributions to society. Practice wisdom suggests that the idea of the professional helper as culturally competent is exceedingly presumptuous. Practitioners are most helpful to the people they serve when they recognize their personal prejudices and biases, become knowledgeable about varied cultures, and openly recognize and disclose their cultural ignorance with clients.

Key Adolescent Developmental Constructs

Apparently, some psychoanalytic constructs are sound given their use in scientific studies. Reasonably, it seems necessary to elucidate key constructs that originated in psychoanalytic thought since they are now central to the lexicon of the adolescent developmental process. For even where research has been conducted among poor adolescents of color, these constructs have empirical use. Key adolescent developmental constructs are discussed in this section and will be referred to in subsequent chapters.

Used extensively in explications of developmental theory, the concept of *identity* tellingly has become synonymous with the adolescence process itself. Identity, for instance, is central to Erikson's theory of adolescent psychosocial development. Erikson explains identity as an inner sense of coherence and meaning that gives the adolescent a sense of well-being and harmony in relation to others. Moreover, Erikson posited that adolescence was a moratorium from the responsibilities of adulthood, thus allowing time to achieve identity formation. The developmental identity process, according to Erikson, resulted in either a healthy state of identity consolidation or the less healthy condition of identity foreclosure. Identity foreclosure was likely to occur when adult experiences or responsibilities were assumed too early. The temporal factor was a critical factor in the identity process.

In later years Erikson (1968) modified his identity construct to incorporate culturally attitudinal shifts about sex. With the sexual revolution of the 1960s, premarital sex became more widely socially sanctioned (Alan Guttmacher Institute, 1994). Subsequently, Erikson postulated that sexual abstinence and virginity were no longer a condition for marriage or considered necessary during adolescence—especially during the later teen years. He conjectured three new sexual patterns condoned by society: (1) celibacy for a special period, (2) promiscuity without personal commitment, and (3) masturbation. A serious omission in this listing, however, is sexual activity with personal commitment. Despite the fact that Erikson accommodated these social observations into his basic theoretical framework, the essence of his conceptualization regarding identity development remained unchanged. The emphasis on self-development by way of communal validation is perhaps Erikson's most significant contribution to the understanding of identity.

Clearly, Erikson compels us to acknowledge the significance of social referents of behavior and affect, yet his identity construct is problematic. For one thing, he theorized identity as unitary, formed in late adolescence with an outcome of consolidation or foreclosure. More importantly, Erikson's theoretical formulations of race and gender in identity formation were seriously weakened by historical biases related to the social status of females and Negroes in American society. For instance, Erikson reasoned that female identity was realized through spousal attachment and that African American identity was decidedly compromised. Because of racism and oppression, Negroes, Erikson argued, tended to form negative identities.

Unlike Erikson, Blos focused less on the social aspects of adolescent development. He considered the adolescent developmental process as limited to the context of the nuclear family. In Blos's theory communal experiences were inconsequential to pubertal development. For Blos the centrality of the maturational process was the adolescent's separation and individuation from nuclear parental figures. Borrowing the separation-individuation thesis from the empirical research on early childhood development of Margaret Mahler, the British psychoanalyst, Blos reasoned that the adolescent underwent a second phase of separation-individuation. Separation and individuation from parental figures was necessary, according to Blos, if the adolescent was to achieve emotional autonomy. During puberty, the adolescent undergoes a second phase of individuation, the initial phase having taken place during the childhood toddler years.

In some respects, Blos's theory is akin to the traditional recapitulation thesis—that is, the reconstitution of earlier conflicted developmental phases for intrapsychic solution. Certainly the family is considered the primary context for the socialization of its offspring. But notable intersubjective experiences do occur outside the familial context. Contrarily, a contexualized or ecological view suggests that varied temporal relational contexts can be intense and coherent—occurring independently of the familial context. Such encounters contribute to solid configurations of self-experiences that are necessary for identity organization (Orange, Atwood, & Stolorow, 1997). The strength, the consistency, and the coherence of contextual intersubjective experiences characterize development. The aim herewith is not to entirely dispense of the key adolescent constructs derived from psychoanalytic theory but to modify and integrate them into a person-process-context paradigm.

In particular, I have identified seven developmental domains that characterize the adolescent trajectory. Through self-assertion, agency, and relational connection to her social world, the adolescent girl engages the maturational tasks of each growth area.

Developmental Domains and their Definitions

Racial, Ethnic, and Sex Gender Role Commitment refers to valuative judgments about a standard of behavior for males and females that embodies a commitment to taking on a gender role firmly situated in a racial/ethnic social identity. Judgments may reflect issues of sexuality that relate to understandings about body image, menses, sexual activity, and reproduction. Judgments also portray racial/ethnic identification. The adolescent commits to a racial, ethnic, and gender social identity with minimal ambivalence and anxiety for a cohesive and coherent self-presentation.

Care Protective Sensibility speaks to a sense of care and protection in relation to self and others. It also refers to the perception of the importance of affective and behavioral expressions of care, loyalty, and nurturance in relation to others as an evolving self-defining personal view. The adolescent develops the capacity to recognize self-relatedness in others and to be empathic. The adolescent's developed sense of empathic perspective taking enhances her capacity to respect and care for others.

Role Model Formulation refers to valuative judgments about valued and nonvalued behaviors as personified by persons within both proximal and distal "nested contexts." From admired and esteemed individuals, the adolescent begins to construct meaningful behaviors and values. The adolescent revises the idealized images of parents and other role models constructed during earlier developmental periods.

Decision Making refers to the development of problem-solving strategies that are practiced and carried out in the proximal ecological spheres of family, peers, and school. This domain is especially focused on the formation of coping skills that involve coping with immediate problems in living as well as the anticipation of future goals that involve the preparation and the planning of activities that make possible the realization of those goals. The adolescent makes effective use of new capacities in cognition for self-efficacy and self-assertion. The adolescent realizes a sense of self-empowerment through effective decision making.

Dating/Mate Selection refers to valuative judgments about the behavior of male peers or males in general based on observations or experience. Judgments are made about the behavior of males with whom girls are involved in a committed supportive partner relationship—a boyfriend or an expectant father. Additionally, appraisals are made about noncommittal partner relationships. The adolescent develops new understanding and acceptance of self as a sexual being who has the capacity for reproduction. The adolescent's capacity for emotional and sexual intimacy is enhanced while maintaining a core sense of self-differentiation and coherence.

Opportunity Mobility refers to self-expectancies for social mobility as well as engaged activities of social mobility where there is awareness that such activities are designed "to improve one's lot in life." The self-actualization of social mobility goals includes socially sanctioned activities that open pathways to enhance upward mobility, such as jobs, school, and social development clubs. The adolescent recognizes and seeks available opportunities for social investment in society through educational and vocational channels. The adolescent's self-perception includes the social investment in society as a full citizen who can realize future goals.

Adulthood Preparation refers to awareness for the self-expectancies of character development traits within the social environment of family, school, and peers. Such character attributes are perceived as effective for coping and necessary in becoming a functioning adult. These traits include, but are not limited to (1) gaining independence socially and financially to become a grown-up in one's right, (2) a beginning awareness of self-responsibility for reproductive choices, (3) assuming responsibility for one's actions, and (4) developing a sense of respect for self and others. The adolescent develops an awareness of the attributions of adulthood, such as duty, responsibility, and care for and protection of others. This self-awareness leads her to engage in prosocial activities where adulthood attributions can be learned and acquired.

3 Person-Process-Context: An Ecological Transactional Model

*Had she paints, or clay, or knew the discipline of the dance, or strings;
had she anything to engage her tremendous curiosity and her gift for
metaphor, she might have exchanged the restlessness and preoccupation
with whim for an activity that provided her with all she yearned for.
And like any artist with no art form, she became dangerous.*

(Morrison, 1973, p. 121)

*Nor are defiance and contestation less fundamental to human well-being than are
worship and propitiation. Indeed they seem to be precisely what such indispensably
human attributes as courage, dignity, honor, nobility, and heroism are all about.*

(Murray, 1978, p. 38)

*As the pieces of Bessie's character and career were amassed, it became clear that
Bessie could not be another book for the jazz enthusiast alone; the extraordinary lifestyle and personality of this woman contributed as much to her renown as her voice
did. Bessie had to be more than the story of the world's most famous blues singer;
it had to be the story of a woman who was black, sassy, beautiful, and proud
long before that became the acceptable thing to be.*

(Albertson, 1972, p. 12).

Introduction

The psychological and social insights embodied in the opening quotes represent the two-sided thesis of this text and are especially germane to the focal point of this chapter: *How do socially stigmatized individuals reconcile basic humanness in daily praxis?* The person-process-context paradigm (Figure 2.1), an interaction-transactional-ecological explanatory model, is presented as the principal paradigm of this text that tries to answer this question. I regard a jazz/blues idiom as a metaphor[1] for the person-process-context model. The jazz musician must be able to act spontaneously to create the personalized aria that contributes to the ensemble's musical expressions. At the same time, the jazz musician is always a member of the group. Her or his responses are in almost perfect attunement (mental and emotional) to those with whom she or he is playing. In the spontaneous improvisational form of jazz, new rhythms are created and integrated into traditional rhythmic patterns. The process of the creation of free and spontaneous musical harmonies represents intersubjective processes formed by persons within the context of the jazz ensemble. Without question, camaraderie of assertion, mutual recognition, and empathy are created between jazz performers, the very process of intersubjectivity.

The improvisational structure of blues/jazz music typifies the lives of people everywhere that live inventively in the present. When social contextual spaces are inhabited to mete out creative and spontaneous processes of existence, it can be said that persons live imaginatively. More often than not, a readiness for living creatively in the present seems somehow characteristic of people with minimal economic means or those who live with incomparable existential suffering. Frequently, people in such circumstances have a hopeful spontaneous quality about their lives, which embodies a quality of spiritual essence. In jazz, improvisation means that "musicians are in a state of constant creative alert, of habitual readiness to invent" (Dyer, 1996, p. 198). Dyer's observation takes on added significance when one recognizes that a certain tranquillity is required about the natural order of things to be in a state of open responsiveness to life's fluctuations. Creative alertness to mundane realities indicates certain self-possession in the face of life's demands. For African Americans, this sense of agency has anthropological roots in an existential religious tradition that considers the upheavals, calamities, and storms of life as adversities that must be transcended, not avoided (Brown, 1998). African Americans' expressive cultural traditions allowed that life's adversities are confronted with irony and humor—as manifested in the blues, in comedy, in oral literary texts, and, above all, in black language. In the arresting mode of humor, the absurdities, the anomalies, and the contradictions of life could be observed. Metaphor and hyperbole, in both sacred and secular mediums, embellished folk songs and folk tales to mask their subversive subtext. All in all, these various modes of relational connection gave existential sublimity to the biracial and bicultural life that continues to exist for most African Americans to this day (Lowe, 1994).

The person-process-context model, similar in its function to a jazz ensemble, allows for the improvisational nature of daily life, as it involves what I call the *intersubjective praxis* found in the mundane lives of African Americans. This intersubjective praxis comprises daily actions of assertion, mutual recognition, and empathic caring (Figure 3.1). Simply put, I use improvisation in the person-process-context model to mean that feature of existence where persons are constantly making up self-defining practices to meet the demands of daily living. I recognize that my claims of black agential self-possession are contrary to many eminent scholars who view the oppression of subordinate groups as mostly lacking personal agency and self-definition. The case illustration *"Nested Concepts"* is a narrative of a young 14-year-old girl whose teen brother died in a violent gang fight. The case exemplifies how the social worker enhanced existing strengths of personal agency and self-definition to help a young girl work through issues of mourning and loss. Despite the oppressive and often fatal conditions of poor communities, resilient families manage to live their lives with dignity and hope. Moreover, the practitioner in the case illustration does not have a preconceived clinical agenda, but merely tries to figure how services will be delivered and in what context. The focus and content of the clinical sessions, like the improvisation of jazz music, are dependent on how the practitioner and client/participant listen to or construe one another's meanings about who they are and how that identity is given recognition. I postulate that it is nearly impossible for any group, subordinate or otherwise, to be entirely without a sense of agency. Moreover, the self-reports of the girls from both the PANSI and the GULTMC studies

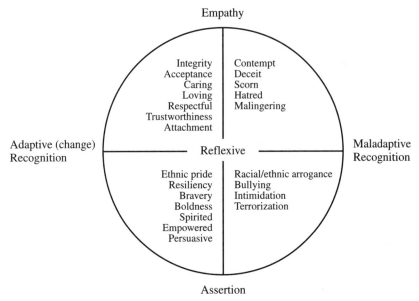

Figure 3.1. Varieties of intersubjective responses.

document, I believe, agential functioning in their daily lives. I address the expressive particularities of this type of functioning in subsequent chapters that discuss the developmental domains of the adolescent period.

I began this chapter with three quotes selected because of their pertinence to the thematic issue of the vitality and resilience of African Americans' cultural heritage. Thematically, all three quotes are inextricably related despite the fact that they reflect the insights of authors writing from the perspective of different standpoints and representing different racial/ethnic backgrounds. Both Murray and Morrison are African Americans, whereas Albertson is a European born and reared in Iceland and Denmark. Murray is an essayist and social critic, Morrison represents the eye of the novelist, and Albertson reflects the view of the biographer. Both Morrison and Murray have demonstrated, in their writings, a pragmatic perspicacity in portraying an African American sensibility. In Morrison's citation, we discern the alienation and hopelessness of her novel's title character Sula. Anomie befalls Sula when her passionate inquisitiveness, intelligence, and talent lack contextual legitimacy. On the other hand, the Murray quotation from *Stompin the Blues* (1978) articulates the artistic impulse that creates beauty and order from chaos. Recognizing the jazz/blues idiom as anchored in a legitimate social context of resistance, Murray clarifies the presence of the artistic tendency in the everyday life of black folk. Tellingly, Murray's insights instruct us that an artistic disposition is not an elitist phenomenon, but an element of the mundane. Morrison, however, accentuates the sorrow, suffering, and pain of profound loss and extinction that underscore African American life. For Morrison, loss and extinction are integral to American Negro life, whether in the legacy of slavery, in the social death of a segregated community, or, in the person of Sula in the death of the female self (Grewal, 1998). These quotes depict the realities of the lives of African Americans: hopelessness and alienation and struggle and resilience.

The third quote is from the biography of Bessie Smith, who lived during one of the most racist periods of American history.[2] Albertson's *Bessie* (1972) captures the legendary artist's persona of cultural pride and assertiveness. Interestingly, Bessie's personality characteristics, recognized by Albertson as positive self-regard, self-efficacy, and assertiveness, are those considered by present-day scholar/researchers as resilient attributes worthy of empirical investigation. As in Chapter 1, here I recognize Bessie Smith not only to restore cultural memory to honor the strengths of black female luminaries, but also to highlight common assumptions about *who* has positive self-regard in *what* conditions. Ordinarily it is assumed that the influences of poverty and racism cause a negative self-identity (Erikson, 1969). Without question, impoverished circumstances and insidious racism can contribute to a negative social context. Most importantly, we need to know more about those phenomena that take place between the psychic-physical space of self-regard and that of social context. Inspired by Murray's observation of the mundane quality of African American creativity, it seems not too far-fetched to consider black creativity as a form of strength and resilience as well as an appropriate idiom for processes that occur in that transitional space of person and context. Black creativity is considered interactive, stylistic, and rhythmic and includes Hall's "contexting" process, which underscores not only the unique expressive culture of African Americans, but also American popular culture in general. Thus, in the public space, black expressive culture is used to sell consumer products—from soap to automobiles (Chapelle, 1998; Hall, 1977; White & White, 1998).

In this chapter, I explicate the principal elements in the person-process-context model, including concepts of interactionism, social capital, structural strain, and intersubjectivity. In the chapter's final segment the developmental domains are briefly introduced to indicate their relationship to the model. The person-process-context explanatory model is used to clarify how black female adolescents utilize attributes of assertion, recognition, and self-efficacy to make meaning of risk circumstances and to mediate exposure to risk elements (see the case illustration "Self-Assertion, Self-Efficacy, and Recognition"). Equally important in this analysis is how social assets, social supports, social resources, or social capital reinforce personal attributions in the mediation of risk as elucidated by the model. The developmental domains are critical areas in which to examine these personal attributes.

An Interactive-Transactional Model

Kilty and Meenaghan (1995) argue that an at-risk model highlights the fact that psychosocial processes are connected to social structures. Notwithstanding the explanatory cogency of their argument, the at-risk model constitutes a serious weakness. The model lacks clarity regarding *how* psychosocial processes connect to social structures. Consequently, explanations about relational properties and interactive effects are needed to correct this conceptual flaw. Spencer (1995), a social psychologist, remedies this shortcoming by broadening the person-context model to include mediating

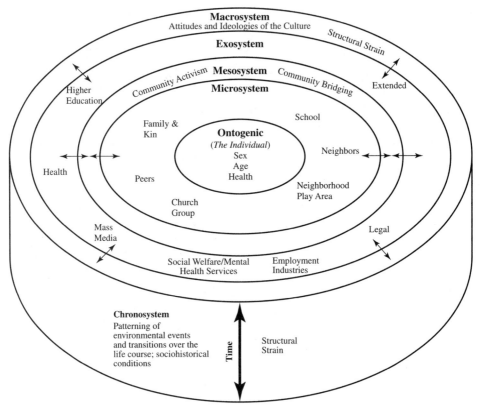

Figure 3.2. Social ecologies. Adapted from Santrock (1998).

coping processes that capture self-relatedness or intersubjectivity. Thus, a more exact formulation, she argues, is represented by the inclusion of intersubjective processes. According to Spencer, a person-process-context model, while still conceptualized as an interactive risk model, postulates intersubjective processes as a necessary and integral ingredient. Certainly, environmental jeopardy demands a new look at how adolescents manage developmental tasks. The reciprocal relationship between the person and the environment and how this relationship mediates larger societal influences, that is, structural inequalities, can be explicated by Bronfenbrenner's (1979) hypothesis of "nested contexts" (Figure 3.2). If an at-risk model is to have sufficient explanatory power, it must lend itself to the examination of the constructs of resilience, social assets, protective factors, and self-relatedness. Bronfenbrenner's ecological model offers a framework to augment epidemiological theorization about the person-in-environment, resilience, risk, and protective factors. Bronfenbrenner's theory of "nested contexts" suggests successive bidirectional domains of biopsychosocial-historical-contextual influences that affect individual development during the life span. Nested contexts are the underpinning substructure of Bronfenbrenner's ecological model (Figure 3.2). The construct clarifies the paradoxical transactions of individuals and environments in two areas: (1) transactions that involve individuals as co-

NESTED CONTEXTS: "A GIFT FOR ROBERT"

The initial phase of clinical work requires that complete strangers come to know one another in a rather unique context, that of the therapeutic encounter. The client/participant's most intimate life issues are encountered in the relationship with the practitioner. The practitioner and the client/participant build a relationship of trust, acceptance, empathy, and hope. The practitioner and the client/participant learn about each other as they engage in therapeutic interventions that are directed toward change in the person, the situation, or the context. The successful engagement of the client/participant occurs in the beginning phase of work (the first one to three sessions). The practitioner may involve the engagement of other "nested contexts" that will support and promote ongoing clinical work [see the collaborative intervention context model (CICM) in Chapter 8]. Such was the case of Ramara Collins, a 14-year-old eighth-grader who was referred for services by the school nurse to a family service agency. The nurse was concerned about Ramara's mental health status and school adjustment. One month prior to the opening of school, Ramara's 16-year-old brother, Robert, was killed in a gang war shoot-out. The city's many schools were serviced by a few social workers. Thus, students were often referred to various community agencies located throughout the city for social services. The family service practitioner immediately arranged for a conference with key school personnel (nurse and teachers) to assess psychosocial issues and to formulate a service delivery plan. Observations of Ramara's responses in the school environment were identified as socially withdrawn, failure to complete class and homework assignments, frequent visits to the school nurse with complaints of abdominal pains and headaches, and recurring requests to leave school early because of illness. According to the nurse, Ramara's physical symptoms had no medical basis. It was believed that Ramara was feigning illness or that her complaints were mainly psychosomatic. The nurse reported that Ramara's mother, Mrs. Collins, had been unresponsive to repeated requests to complete a health history record needed for Ramara's graduation and transfer to high school. Mrs. Collins's unresponsiveness was atypical. In past years, Mrs. Collins had been an active participant in the school's several parent activities. A year ago Mrs. Collins was laid off from a shoe manufacturing company where she had worked for 15 years. Mrs. Collins had been unable to obtain new employment. The teachers were especially worried that Ramara would not have the required academic credits needed to graduate, since she was failing her classes and 2 months of the first semester had already transpired. Summarized findings of the case conference were: (1) Ramara's behavior was symptomatic of the grieving process, as she was mourning the loss of her deceased brother. (2) Ramara had considerable strengths. Her GPA the previous school year was at the "B" level. She was perceived, under normal circumstances, as a good student, affable, eager, and ambitious. (3) Although Ramara's parents were separated, the family was known to be a close-knit extended kinship group. Ramara had good relationships with both her paternal and maternal grandmothers. Prior to the death of her son, Mrs. Collins had been responsive to the school's solicitations for parental involvement. It was believed that Ramara and her mother had a good relationship. (4) The social worker was to arrange weekly counseling sessions at the school site until the end of the school year. No plans were made regarding the therapeutic focus of the counseling sessions. (5) The school principal was to authorize alternate releases from gym and study periods so that Ramara could attend counseling sessions. The social worker met with Ramara to share conference findings and to contract for services. Ramara agreed to participate in the counseling sessions. Mrs. Collins was also contacted to obtain parental consent. In a home visit, Mrs. Collins expressed outrage about what she believed to be the school's lack of sensitivity about her son's death. "How could Ramara be doing well in school, after her brother had died? The school shouldn't expect so much. Ramara's school performance is the least of my worries right now." The social worker thought in the long run it would mean a great deal to Ramara to graduate on time with her classmates. She related that she realized that it was a painful and difficult time for the family right now, but she believed that she could be of help to both Ramara and Mrs. Collins. The social worker thought it might help if Ramara had someone to talk to about how she was feeling about things. She thought having Ramara to talk to someone might take some of the pressure off of Mrs. Collins. The social worker suggested that Mrs. Collins could also participate in some of the counseling sessions. Mrs. Collins admitted that she and Ramara were usually close, but of late they had little to say to one another. She said that she was really worried about how Ramara was taking in everything about Robert's death. Mrs. Collins said that her son was not really a gang member, but on occasion would be with a neighbor who was in a gang. Mrs. Collins believed that her son was in the wrong place at the wrong time. She said that the gang was really after the neighborhood boy. Mrs. Collins consented to having Ramara participate in the counseling sessions. Mrs. Collins thought that periodic phone contacts would be a good way to stay in contact with the social worker. Ramara was always on time for appointments and presented as warm and friendly, but talked little. The counseling sessions were initiated with games, such as cards, checkers, and the like. The social worker did not pressure Ramara to share information but would usually ask how things had gone during the week. In the third session the social worker disclosed that she had lost a nephew some years ago in a similar situation as Ramara's brother, Robert. The social worker said that she knew how painful and hurtful it was to lose a loved one so young. After the social worker's self-disclosure there was a marked shift in the therapeutic relationship. Ramara opened up more and talked about her feelings about her brother, her anger with her mother, and nightly visits to her brother's room. The game-playing format remained the same. Subsequent sessions remained productive. The social worker enhanced Ramara's capacity for self-awareness, enabling her to examine her feelings, wishes, intentions, and interactive patterns. Tutoring services were arranged with a community after-school program. The social worker supported Ramara's involvement with a community group of Family Survivors, a group devoted to families who had lost teens through violent deaths. Ramara's maternal grandmother had been attending the group meetings shortly after Robert's death, but Ramara initially had been reluctant to attend. Ramara and her mother began to talk more and share positive memories about Robert. Ramara began once again attending church services with her maternal grandmother. The social worker and Ramara took a couple of "Big Sister" field trips together to the local museums. The worker attended a special prayer service with the family for community youth that had lost their lives violently in the streets. All the work accomplished by Ramara and the social worker was successful. Ramara worked through her grief. She came to believe that improving her grades and graduating from the eighth grade was a gift to her brother. She believed that Robert would have wanted her to graduate and move on with her life. *Study Questions and Issues:* (1) Discuss the issue of self-disclosure in clinical practice. Do you think that the social worker was appropriate or inappropriate in sharing personal information? Explain. (2) Identify and discuss how you think various "nested contexts" supported and promoted the therapeutic process. (3) Why do you think the work with Ramara and her family was successful?

creators of their immediate social context and (2) social structural elements that limit the co-creation of contextual transactions. The Bronfenbrenner model allows a consideration of opportunity pathways in social contexts in the depiction of social structural strain elements.

The interactive-transactive explanatory model takes into account the fact that some youth are in jeopardy for poor life outcomes due to the interaction of individual attributes and environmental factors (see Figure 3.1). Although I consider risk as an element in the person-process-context model; I do not place the word "risk" in my lexical equation. For example, the model is not equated as person, risk, and context. I have done this so as not to restrict the application of the model to only circumstances of jeopardy. Burt (1998), in an explication of the meaning of risk, has suggested that current explanations of risk relate to sensation seeking, hazardous environments, antecedents and markers, and risk as certainty. Risk as certainty, according to Burt, proposes that once particular problem behaviors occur the adolescent can be identified as at risk. Recall that the GULTMC girls were selected to participate in the curricula intervention based on demonstrated negative behaviors such as school suspensions, poor academic performance, repeated absences, and the like. On this account, Burt argues that while this approach is not primary prevention, it is attractive because the interventionist can document actual problem behaviors of specific youth rather than environmental jeopardy or familial and personal characteristics indicative of risk. Moreover, if I am consistent with an intellectual commitment to a model of health, to indicate risk in the model's nomenclature would, in effect, disclaim an emphasis of well-being. Nonetheless, the person-process-context model indicates that despite environmental risk, some youth are resilient and protected by social assets such as friendships and membership in formal/informal organizations, parental supervision, and monitoring. Recent evidence supports the view that resilient capacities are multidimensional and elastic. Resilient individuals display sturdiness, a focused commitment to follow events through, and a strong sense of self-efficacy. Additionally, social resources that serve as shock absorbers for life's adversities protect resilient individuals. Increasingly, scholars look to risk-protective approaches to study adolescent problem behaviors, such as drug use, childbearing, and early coital behavior (Grossman et al., 1992; Page et al., 1993; Rhodes, Gingiss, & Smith, 1994; Smith, 1997). As well, protective prosocial approaches are viewed as well-suited frameworks for the development of adolescent early intervention-prevention programs (Stevens, 1999).

Scientists claim that interactionism is central to understanding the individual and his or her environment. Social science disciplines have traditionally emphasized the dynamic interplay between environmental circumstances and personal attributes. In particular, social work has established a person-in-situation construct to indicate a systemic process involving the interaction of person and environment. The construct infers that the whole is greater than the sum of its parts. The construct advances theorization about the impact of the environment on personal adaptation. Ordinarily, the person-in-situation describes three interdependent dynamic processes: internal mechanisms, external conditions, and interactive operations. Internal processes are both biological and psychological in influencing the individual's preferences, needs, and his or her perception of the situation. As well, internal processes influence the degree of access to emotional-cognitive inner capacities and resources required for coping with the situation. Interactive operations are regarded as coping strategies. Certainly the person-in-situation construct recognizes the interdependence of person and environment. Thus, the nexus for the identified three processes is that of internal mechanisms, thereby rendering psychological change as the ultimate goal of treatment.

In social work's conceptualization of the person and environment within an ecological framework (Germain & Gitterman, 1980), the environment, for the most part, is considered as independent and interdependent. In this framework, the relationship between person and environment is posited as transactional. The person-in-situation construct presumes that the social reality beyond the self necessitates collaboration with the environment in a way that results in a healthy adaptive psychosocial outcome. Theories must correlate with daily life practices even in applied disciplines such as social work. In this regard, Saari (1991), theorizing from a psychoanalytic essentialist framework, has proposed that a person's relationship to the environment necessitates understanding the personal meaning system through which the environment is comprehended. Accordingly, she posits that a meaning system is the intervening variable between the person and environment, a "required element in any theory regarding human behavior" (p. 46). Both personal and cultural meaning systems are described as dynamic and complex. However, this theory, while valuable, seems not to go far enough in explaining how it is that meaning systems are related to contexualized experiences and how the self (as subject) experiences the subjectivity of other. More recent concepts, namely context and intersubjectivity, are omitted altogether in Sari's explication of meaning systems.

Current thought among social scientists is that the transmission and acquisition of societal values, norms, and expectations take place in multilevel contextual domains, such as peer groups, family, neighborhood, and social institutions. The conceptual shift from environment to context suggests that the individual participates in a reciprocal, subject(s)-to-subject(s) interactive-transactive relationship within multiple and discrete social domains of influence that constitute particular meanings and values. The conceptual shift embraces *subjectivity*. Simply put, as the individual is changed by the context in which she is temporally situated, she in turn changes the makeup of that context. This shift in thinking, I believe, has enormous implications when practice interventions are seen as occurring within varied contexts. It suggests that clinical work intersects with client's lives in ways that are strength-enhancing and authentic. In contextual or social-ecological spheres the person functions as an assertive agent seeking and negotiating recognition and self-efficacy through intersubjective engagement. Rather than adaptation to environment, negotiation or mediation within context is considered essential to healthy psychosocial functioning and to the model posited in this text. Assertion, recognition, and self-efficacy are intersubjective attributes, all of which are central to the development of self-relatedness, the faculty that makes negotiation and mediation possible.

Henceforth, "ecology" and "context," when appropriate, will be used interchangeably. These two concepts supplant the term "environment." Social workers have given a static inference to the term "environment" in the use of the phrase "environmental manipulation." Context and ecology indicate dynamic, interactive, reciprocal, and transactional processes taking place between individuals and their surroundings. "Interaction" and "transaction" are terms used to capture the dynamic intersubjective processes that occur in the person-process-context model. As such, dynamic mediating processes are situated in the individual's intersubjectively configured experiences. Additionally, attributed characteristics of assertion, recognition, and self-efficacy are instrumental in confronting structural strain dilemmas. Moreover, social capital and protective factors buttress individual efforts of negotiation of structural strain dilemmas. Ecologically, social structural strain represents contextual spheres of racial tension or pressure that constricts opportunities of social mobility. In the present model, structural strain exemplifies systemic racism and the barriers to social mobility. The explication of social structural strain, social capital, intersubjectivity, and developmental domains discussed in the following sections provides a general framework for the reader. This framework will aid the reader in the examination of the developmental domains and their relationship to intersubjective processes that are discussed in subsequent chapters.

Structural Strain and Social Capital

Protective factors can be seen as social supports, social assets, or social capital. Investigated at the level of at-risk environments, researchers seemingly incorporate all three constructs under the rubric of protective factors. I employ the term "social capital" to reflect an ethnic attribute of organized cooperation for the perceived communal good. I argue that structural strain influences the ways in which ethnic groups develop social capital. The extent of structural strain that an ethnic group experiences will influence how that group utilizes protective factors.

Despite the element of dynamic change within the person-process-context model, the limitations of change processes is found in the ecological sphere of structural strain. Unfortunately, structural strain has endured and, therefore, occurs regularly within specific ecological domains (see Figure 3.2). As previously noted, deficits in an ethnic group's social assets or social capital can delimit social opportunities. Nonetheless, opportunity mobility limitations are also created by conditions of social structural strain. Structural strain represents social structural barriers that prevent access to opportunity, privilege, and power. Historically, structural strain, in the case of American blacks, included institutionalized racism that led to legally discriminatory practices designed to restrict access to social and economic opportunities. While in the past such practices were sanctioned legal laws, albeit hidden from public view, many covert discriminatory racist practices persist in the post–civil rights era. Government policies to eradicate discrimination and provide access to social, educational, and economic opportunities have wavered in the last decades. Empirical evidence suggests that black youth are increasingly pessimistic about the future of fair and just racial practices (Feagin & Sikes, 1994).

Merton (1957), particularly skilled in analyzing social structural effects on individual adaptation, hypothesized that social structural factors significantly influence social opportunities. Based on an elaboration of Durkheim's theory of anomie, Merton hypothesized that, when legitimate access to social status is denied or blocked, deviant routes to achieve social success are sought—and thus social deviance occurs. Accordingly, Merton asserted that lower classes are deprived of social status by virtue of their location in the social hierarchy. Scholars use a structural strain thesis to understand social problems experienced by black urban adolescent populations, such as premature pregnancy and drug use (Brunswick, 1999; Stevens, 1994, 1995–6). For instance, I use a social structural framework to explain early coitus and nonmarital pregnancy among African American inner-city females (Stevens, 1993, 1994, 1995–96). Findings documented that 17- to 19-year-old urban lower-class black females perceive adolescent parenthood as a pathway to adulthood when opportunities for social mobility are blocked. In the examination of adolescent pregnancy, I argued that social status is immediate and contextual, based on proximal experiences negotiated, designated, and conferred within the immediate context of community. A major difficulty with Merton's thesis is that status deprivation as a cause of social deviancy is questionable.

Contrary to Merton's theory, Rubington and Weinberg (1989) argue that social status deprivation, while an important consideration, is not the cause of deviancy or unconventional behavior. Moreover, such reasoning, the authors contend, is contrary to empirical evidence. Unconventional behavior need not be deviant, as the legitimacy of middle-class values is not unrecognized by those who are deprived of higher status. More likely, social status is not necessarily distant and abstract, but proximal and contextual. Those who are in proximity to one another, that is, in neighborhoods, communities, and groups where face-to-face relationships are primary ways of relating, often confer status. Consider the case illustration *"Nested Contexts."* Ramara's maternal grandmother in her church congregation had the status of Elder and Mother. This particular status infers that older women of the church have acquired gifts of wisdom and knowledge. The women are seated in a special place in the church known as the "Mother's Bench." Ramara's grandmother took great pride in her achieved status and willingly shared her gifts with younger members of the church congregation. The use of this kind of status appropriation is an established tradition among African Americans.

During slavery, black Americans appropriated biblical scripture to create meaningful identities. Group designated names were often based on function—Harriet Tubman became known as "Moses" as she led runaway slaves to the North to freedom. The designation of the biblical name Moses signified a transformation from that of property to liberator. Further, the African American indigenous church offered social status unattainable in a discriminating and hostile society. Indeed, church members assumed influential status roles, such as minister, deacon, deaconess, and trustee. Church members negotiated meanings for the creation of norms, status, and values within the context of their environments. Although aware of traditional external norms, ethnic groups develop and exercise behavioral repertoires grounded in the norms they themselves create and negotiate within the proximal domains of family, peer, and community institutions (Stevens, 1996). Norms are not necessarily internalized as universal standards for all time, but are contextual and can change over time (Cancian, 1975). Conjecturally, proximal norms may diverge from conventional distal norms because of their expressed ethnic specificity and because of the reality assumptions upon which they are based. Proximal norms seen from this viewpoint embody recognized social status created within immediate environments. In this regard, social status may constitute either aberrant or exemplary behavior. I suggest that proximal norms figure prominently in the development of social capital among ethnic Americans.

Economists have conceptualized the term "social capital" to depict social progress and social development among American ethnic groups (Coleman, 1988a,b; Loury et al., 1972). Fukuyama (1995), a policy analyst, has defined social capital simply as "the existence of a certain set of informal values or norms shared among members of a group that permit co-operation among them" (p. 4). However, Fukuyama cautions that the cooperative sharing of group norms and values does not in itself create social capital—since values and norms must have the moral, legal, and social sanction of a just and civil society. The argument Fukuyama sets forth is troublesome in that social capital, for some American ethnic groups, has not always been based on legal or moral sanctions. For instance, the Italian American Mafia uses illegal resources to purchase legitimate capital ventures. Mafia criminal operations may have over time (through several generations) generated capital for legitimate ownership of business enterprises. Simply put, the illegal activities of some American ethnic groups (Italians, Irish, and Jewish) may have been used historically to gain a foothold in American institutions—such as unions and corporations (Fox, 1989; Gage, 1971). Social capital comprises an ingredient of chronological temporality that is contextual. Fukuyama limits the context of social capital if his meaning relates only to legally sanctioned activities. Concern for moral codes, lawful practices, and legal customs, for instance, is given full attention in a court of law where contextual meaning carries little weight, but in daily praxis, context *is* meaning (Hall, 1977). Proximal norms are generally grounded in daily praxis—people make them up as the situation demands. The moral integrity of subjects' actions is based on the self-respect and recognition sought in the intersubjective encounter in praxis. More importantly, proximal values change over time (Cancian, 1975). Apparently, the intra-ethnic collaboration that achieves social and economic gains may produce social capital, but it is affected by a historical temporality. Moreover, the term seems directly related to the subject of proximal social norms.

The supposition that proximal social norms are group-created should not diminish the significance of distal social structures that oppress or restrict opportunities for social mobility for American ethnic minorities who are without social status. Unquestionably, distal social norms influence proximal group norms. Conjecturally, the social capital of varied American ethnic groups is due, in large part, to a racial/ethnic group's investment in certain proximal social norms that promote social and economic empowerment. Correspondingly, the *natural helping networks* construct, as used in social work (Lewis & Suarez, 1995) encompasses both proximal and distal societal norms in its correspondence to social scientists' operational definition of social capital. Natural helping networks are alliances of like-minded persons loosely or formally organized to focus on group needs in which trust develops and the group's communal knowledge is used for its empowerment. The fluidity of the boundary maintenance of such networks is influenced by historical-social conditions at a given time. For instance, one could postulate that Irish immigrants brought the hierarchical religious structures indigenous to Catholic parishes to bear on American political and educational institutions. Certainly, the social capital of an urban political patronage system advanced Irish immigrants' social, political, and economic assimilation. Equally important was the attribution of social status based on color or race. Despite the fact that Irish immigrants experienced ethnic discrimination, the assimilation was aided significantly by their location in the social hierarchy by the designation of whiteness, thus distinguishing themselves from the pariah status of America's black minority—blacks (Ignatiev, 1995). Seemingly, the two terms "social capital" and "natural helping networks" differ in significant ways. Social capital refers to the cumulative natural resources of a single entity, such as an ethnic community or ethnic group, where boundary maintenance is fixed, determined singularly by ethnicity, race, or culture. On the other hand, natural helping networks imply flexible boundary maintenance, with the needs of the group distinguishing its parameters.

The significance of racial stigma and institutionalized racism in preventing the maximal benefit of social capital investments of American blacks must not be minimized. Unable to assimilate into American society because of the externalized stigma of color, the social capital of the American Negro was lodged mainly in racially segregated institutions, such as churches, newspapers, fraternities and sororities, mutual aid societies, social clubs, and historical black institutions of higher learning. Subsequent to the emancipation of the Negro slave, the social capital of black institutions was used to resist oppressive racial practices and to advance racial progress. Certainly, from an ecological perspective, one of the primary benefits of ethnic institutions was the transactional process that led to the achievement of middle-class status. Certainly social capital made for significant changes in the social mobility of some blacks. Still, social progress was incremental or nonexistent for the Negro masses. Apparently, social status advancement created largely through successful intergenerational educational attainment was responsible for the development of an upper-class Negro elite, a significant number of whom achieved social status as teachers, lawyers, and physicians. Historically, the rise of a Negro elite, although numerically negligible, did indeed provide role models who could articulate the needs of the masses, champion the advancement of civil rights, and advocate social and economic parity.

Despite the impediments of structural strain, the social mobility of a small, but significant black middle-class intelligentsia positively affected the Negro masses by strengthening group identity and legitimating exemplary group racial consciousness. Unquestionably, the social capital of middle-class attainment by the Negro intelligentsia made it possible to engage in legitimate enlightened protest that was endorsed by an ethnic press and adopted by established civil rights organizations. Paradoxically, such cooperative efforts of social capital were supported and sustained by the structural strain of racism. Despite traditional efforts of social protest, Negro social capital did not bring about assimilation, nor did it dismantle America's legal racial apartheid (Cruse, 1967). It was not until the 1960s civil rights movement that the cooperative organizational efforts of ethnic-based institutions brought about consequential social structural modifications. Assuredly, the civil rights movement of the 1960s, characterized by both civil disobedience and judicial litigation, contributed significantly to the transformation of America's social order for the postmodern era. The consideration of an ecological perspective indicates that within the chronological nested context, the patterning of sociohistorical social protest conditions over time may have converged to produce a unique set of circumstances that brought about the distinctive civil disobedience that fostered the civil rights movement of the 1960s.

While I have set forth an argument that black cultural creativity represents social capital, a social structural critique of the commercialization of black creativity seems important, insofar as black teens are inundated by popular entertainment culture in the form of movies, television, radio, and recordings. The current exploitation and appropriation of black creativity in the marketplace seems unprecedented. From an ecological perspective, the elevation of the marketability of black cultural artifacts may be due, in large measure, to historical shifts and trends in the sophisticated development of media technology in the selling of consumer products. Evidently, there is some evidence to suggest that African Americans are more media conscious with respect to persons of color in ads, brand names, and labels than most other groups (Chapelle, 1998). Thus, media technology is yet another social context that may significantly influence adolescent developmental maturation. Television and movies, both noninteractive media forms, transmit the cultural ethos of individualism, materialism, and violence. Notwithstanding, black cultural artifacts, a form of social capital, have fueled and undergirded America's entertainment, fashion, and advertising industries—integral ingredients of mass culture. Moreover, black artists have made innovative use of technology to produce novel rhythmic sounds in popular music. Unquestionably, black artists have used production technology expertly ("Partners in the Engine Room of Rap," 1999).

The limited benefits African Americans historically have accrued from these industries are due, in part, to a lack of economic control of the cultural products themselves. Corporate America's interest in African American hip hop music and fashion is attributed to the almost $447 billion buying power of blacks as well as its spin-off or residual markets among white adolescents. White youth enthusiastically embrace the hip hop culture of baggy clothing and its angry stylistic urban lyrics (Chapelle, 1998). Recent trends in the entertainment industry have created a few young female rap and rhythm and blues stars of the likes of Missy Elliott and Lauryn Hill, who are redefining the parameters of the music but more importantly are bright and discerning businesswomen creating their own music labels. Like Bessie Smith of an earlier period, Missy Elliott represents the New Negro as designated by a white-controlled media:

> The New Negro is an inventive amalgamation of past and future trends that are indigenous to black American style. Generally, the New Negro—who is "new" every decade or so—is female, a woman who considers her marginal status a form of freedom and a challenge: she takes the little she has been given and transforms it into something complex, outrageous, and ultimately, fashionable. She is outrageous because no one cares what she does—until, that is, she begins to make money. (Als, 1997, p 144–169)

Entertainment aside, it is questionable whether this new trend of artist empowerment will benefit black female teens overall. The entertainment industry represents the most exaggerated form of materialism and individualism. Its caricature of social values cannot provide for positive role model formulation, but it can constitute fodder for the fierce cycle of narcissistic celebrity culture that is supported by the insatiability of consumers.

The ecological perspective suggests that individual development is fused and integrated within multilevel contextual domains, including the sphere of historical temporality (Lerner, Ostrom, & Freel, 1997). Although scholars have documented the significance of social assets or social capital as protective factors in mediating risk, was previously mentioned, less attention has been given to the interactive-transactive connection between individual attributes and social assets in negotiating life circumstances. Certain identifiable attributes have been associated with disadvantaged children, such as positive social skills, a sense of empowerment, and problem-solving abilities (Garmezy, 1991). It can be argued that the resilient attributes of recognized difference in mutuality, self-efficacy, and assertiveness comprise intersubjective processes that form the nexus in the person-process-context construct. Simply put, I propose that the *process* element in the ecological construct of person-process-context infers intersubjective operations. It was suggested earlier, in the Prologue, that the intersubjective processes of recognition, self-efficacy, and assertion be used to mediate exposure to risk elements as well as promote prosocial behaviors that are intrinsically connected to specific developmental domains. Given this hypothesis, it now seems appropriate to examine the concept of intersubjectivity and its related themes of contextualism.

Intersubjectivity

The exegesis of intersubjectivity is grounded in the phenomenology movement of the nineteenth-century German hermeneutic tradition. Its preeminent scholar, German philosopher Edmund Husserl, literally defined the canon of phenomenology (Sawicki, 1997). The epistemology of phenomenology attempts to answer the question of the existence of other consciousnesses and the individual's relationship to them—this is the heart of the Husserlian idea of intersubjectivity (Crossley, 1996). Or, in light of its contemporary and elementary use, "*Intersubjectivity* means that humans can perceive reality through their senses and communicate that experience to others" (Williams, 1995, p. 880). There are varied theoretical perspectives from which the concept is defined by seemingly disparate disciplines: philosophy, theology, political science, sociology, psychology, and psychoanalysis. Intersubjectivity, Crossley (1996) suggests, is interdisciplinary in its application. Indeed, intersubjectivity is a complex concept. Accordingly, it would be impossible to fully examine the concept in all its dimensions and applications. Thus, the examination of the intersubjectivity presented herein is selective. Expectedly, the term is examined regarding its relevance to the topical subjects of the text, namely the psychological and social-structural issues of black adolescent girls as related to environmental risk, strengths, and resilient adaptation within an ecological context. I view the term from four viewpoints: from the perspective of psychological/ecological consciousness/unconsciousness (Benjamin, 1995; Orange, Atwood, & Stolorow, 1997; Stern, 1985), from the position of social-structural elements (Crossley, 1996), from the epistemology of empathy (Sawicki, 1997; Stein, 1964), and from the reflexive mode of symbolic interactionism (Becker, 1963; Berger & Luckman, 1967; Cancian, 1975; Goffman, 1973, 1976; Meade, 1934). (See Figures 3.1 and 3.3.)

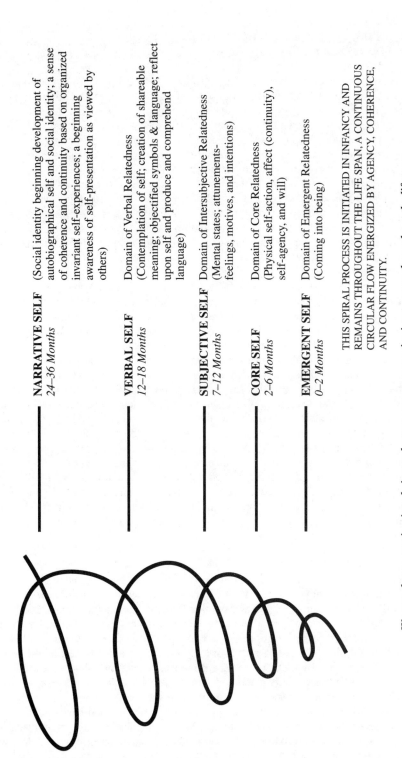

NARRATIVE SELF
24–36 Months
(Social identity beginning development of autobiographical self and social identity; a sense of coherence and continuity based on organized invariant self-experiences; a beginning awareness of self-presentation as viewed by others)

VERBAL SELF
12–18 Months
Domain of Verbal Relatedness
(Contemplation of self; creation of shareable meaning; objectified symbols & language; reflect upon self and produce and comprehend language)

SUBJECTIVE SELF
7–12 Months
Domain of Intersubjective Relatedness
(Mental states; attunements-feelings, motives, and intentions)

CORE SELF
2–6 Months
Domain of Core Relatedness
(Physical self-action, affect (continuity), self-agency, and will)

EMERGENT SELF
0–2 Months
Domain of Emergent Relatedness
(Coming into being)

THIS SPIRAL PROCESS IS INITIATED IN INFANCY AND REMAINS THROUGHOUT THE LIFE SPAN, A CONTINUOUS CIRCULAR FLOW ENERGIZED BY AGENCY, COHERENCE, AND CONTINUITY.

We are always coming into being as human persons, continuing to grow throughout the life span.

Figure 3.3. Formation and reformation of domains of experience throughout the life span. Based on Stern (1985).

"Varieties of Intersubjective Responses: "My Mother Always Drinks"

Seventeen-year-old Maxine Givens gave birth to a premature 3-pound newborn boy. She was discharged after a 3-day hospital stay. The infant, Matthew, remained in the hospital's special care nursery in order to gain the appropriate discharge weight. It was the nursery policy to encourage parents (especially mothers) to visit regularly to enhance infant bonding. A week had transpired and Maxine had not seen her son. The case was referred to social services. The Givenses had no telephone, so the social worker made a home visit. The social worker arrived at the Givens' home at 11:00 A.M. A woman, who, after the social worker explained the nature of her visit, said that she was Maxine's mother, Mrs. Givens, greeted the social worker and invited her into the apartment. Mrs. Givens related that Maxine was at school and not expected home until later that afternoon. The family occupied a small second floor two-bedroom apartment in a three-storey apartment building in an economically impoverished neighborhood. The building's hallways were dirty with litter and the windows and stairways were in need of obvious repairs. The Givens' apartment was tidy but sparsely furnished. Mrs. Givens appeared disheveled and slightly inebriated. She said that she had a lot of health problems and that she was very upset with Maxine getting herself pregnant. She related that she was only 36 years old and thought that she was still young enough to have a good time in life. She didn't believe that she was ready to be a grandmother. Mrs. Givens related that she was a diabetic and not well. Her doctor had told her that she might lose her sight. Although she can see now, she is up all hours of the night worried sick that she might end up going blind. She said that she isn't in any kind of position right now to take care of a baby, especially a "sickly" one. The social worker explained that Matthew's prognosis was excellent and that he was not really a "sick" infant. He had only to gain the proper weight and could then be discharged from the hospital. Mrs. Givens related that Maxine was an only child and that having Maxine had been a mistake. She said that she'd had to do everything herself and that "raising a child is no picnic." She laughed quietly and said that she never tells Maxine that giving birth to her was a mistake though. She said that she tries hard to be a good mother and that she didn't want the social worker to think that she didn't do right by Maxine. Maxine calls the hospital every day to see how the baby is doing. She said that she would have her call the social worker to arrange an appointment. Mrs. Givens said that her neighbor across the hall let Maxine use her phone to make emergency telephone calls. The following day, Maxine visited Matthew and also saw the social worker. Maxine related that as soon as she got home from school, her mother had told her that the hospital social worker had visited. Maxine explained that she wanted to see Matthew, but she had already missed a lot of school days and she didn't want to miss too many and get too far behind in her assignments. She said she calls the nursery every day to see how Matthew is doing. She has been really scared and worried that Matthew might not live. She's spoken with the doctors and knows now that he will be all right. She is working hard to try to graduate with her class in the spring. She has made plans to have Matthew's father's mother, Mrs. Murphy, help her take care of Matthew. "My mother always drinks. It was never my plan to have my mother help take care of my baby," Maxine said. She claimed that she was mostly raised by her grandmother, who died a couple of years ago. Mrs. Murphy is a real nice person and wants to help, although she and Matthew's father, 18-year-old Ray, no longer go together. Mrs. Murphy will visit Matthew when she is able to. She did not believe that Ray would visit Matthew. "Ray is acting really crazy, just hanging out in the streets, drinking, smoking pot with his friends, and not looking for work." Weeping softly, she related, "Ray doesn't care about Matthew. He wanted me to get an abortion. I could have had an abortion but I don't believe in it. It would have been wrong to kill my baby." The social worker said that it must be hard for her to take on so much responsibility, trying to plan and care for Matthew and still go to school. She said that she thought Maxine showed a lot of courage wanting to take care of Matthew and complete school. Maxine said that she had plans to go to school after graduation to become a court stenographer. She was sorry that she had gotten involved with Ray. She had not wanted to get pregnant, but just one time she had not taken the proper precaution. She said that she was really disappointed in Ray and sometimes in herself too. What's really been bothering her lately is her friend Norman. "It's blowing my mind, I can't figure it out." She's known Ray since they were in grammar school and they've always been just good friends. Norman graduated from high school last year and is working and going to college part-time. She said that she believes Norman wants to be her boyfriend even after all that's happened to her. "It's blowing my mind. I never thought of him as a boyfriend just a friend, but he's always been there for me." At the close of the session Maxine said that she didn't realize that she had so much to talk about. She thought that maybe she's been holding everything inside too long: "Everything is all penned up." She wanted to know if she could see the social worker each time she visited Matthew: "It feels good talking to you." She said that she misses her grandmother; she used to talk to her a lot. Regular counseling sessions were maintained with Maxine until she graduated from high school and entered a postgraduate program to become a court stenographer/reporter. The clinical work was supportive structured intervention that focused on Maxine's (1) role as mother, (2) goals to complete high school and enter a postgraduate study program, (3) relationships with Ray and Norman, and (4) relationship with Mrs. Murphy, paternal grandmother to Matthew. The social worker was unable to engage Mrs. Givens for collaborative work. Mrs. Givens did think that it was a good idea for Maxine to see the social worker on a regular basis. Mrs. Murphy provided childcare once Matthew was discharged. Matthew was followed at the hospital for pediatric care. Ray was killed in a street fight several months after Matthew's hospital discharge. Mrs. Givens refused to seek help for her drinking problems and remained emotionally uninvolved with both Maxine and Matthew. Maxine continued to live at home. The social worker attended Maxine's graduation along with Norman. The social worker bought Maxine a graduation gift of jewelry, a charm bracelet. Norman brought a camera to take pictures. Mrs. Givens did not attend Maxine's graduation. Eighteen years later, Maxine contacted the social worker by telephone at a different place of employment. She said that she had gone to the hospital and was given the phone number of the social worker's new job. Maxine said that she still has the graduation picture of her and the social worker placed on her living room end table. She thinks of the social work often. She related that she had married Norman and everything had worked out. "Norman encouraged me to try to locate you." Maxine has two young boys, ages 12 and 14. Matthew recently joined the Marines. Maxine is a court reporter and pretty much contented with the way her life has turned out. Her mother finally went to AA. *Study Questions and Issues:* (1) What specific developmental challenges do you think the practitioner and Maxine encountered in the clinical work? Discuss how you think Maxine's developmental challenges might relate to issues of intersubjectivity. (2) Discuss whether Maxine is an at-risk adolescent. Identify what you consider risk and protective factors in her contextual situations. Evaluate Maxine's connection to kinship networks or social institutions. Consider factors of intersubjectivity in your evaluation. (3) Discuss Maxine's strengths and how they might be related to intersubjective factors. (4) Discuss how you think Maxine constructs a social identity and autobiographical self. (5) Discuss gift-giving to clients. Do you think it was appropriate or inappropriate for the social worker to give Maxine a graduation gift? Explain. *See also:* Chapters 5–8; Figures 2.1, 3.1, and 3.2.

The reference perspectives that I have adopted allow for a more complex use of the *psychosocial* nomenclature commonly used in social work to describe both psychological and social-structural phenomena. Orange, Atwood, and Stolorow, eminent neo-psychoanalytic theorists, approach intersubjective theory from the focus of the clinical dyadic relationship as contextual, in that the therapist and patient bring what Hall would call "contexting" experiences. These authors' position has some merit. Obviously, a dyadic relational field is of paramount significance to the clinical therapeutic course. The therapeutic journey is not just a matter of two minds meeting. Still, the intersubjective view adopted here is one that is irrevocably inclusive of an external perspective and is not wholly dependent on the contextual experiences of the therapist and client. From a context perspective, in this text I am concerned about *who* is doing *what* to *whom, under what social circumstances,* and *what one gives attention to* within the intersubjective fields that exist outside the therapeutic relationship. What exists outside the therapeutic relationship is of paramount significance to the client and essentially becomes the therapeutic work. The practitioner engages the client in a way that will encourage the client to share his or her social contextual experiences so that they can be scrutinized and examined in the therapeutic encounter. Such therapeutic examination and scrutiny reflect, overall, an emphasis of personal (client) agency that is critical for any therapeutic encounter, but especially salient when considering adolescent development.

In the case illustration *"Varieties of Intersubjective Responses,"* Maxine Givens resides in a family context of restricted emotional and social resources. Nonetheless, it cannot be said that Maxine's familial resources are completely depleted, as she apparently had a nurturing relationship with her maternal grandmother. However, Maxine's sense of personal agency is not weakened by her familial situation. Maxine selectively chooses other adults (the paternal grandmother of her baby and the social worker) in her social milieu from which she can acquire personal validation. Maxine's capacity to select caring adults from her environment to whom she can become respectfully and lovingly attached is an indication of her resilience. Contextual stimuli are selectively adopted; they are never ratified totally. Thus, Maxine has a realistic recognition and acceptance of her mother's limitations without her sense of personal agency being compromised.

As in the case of Maxine, the resilient individual will engage in situational contexting to the extent that adaptation is productive. The resilient individual tries to bring disparate components into some kind of harmonious whole in order that self-experiences are coherent, interconnected, and meaningful. Moreover, in adolescence, while significant maturational milestones have already taken place, adolescents are still developmentally amenable to cognitive restructuring and the reorganization of emotional experiences. This cognitive and emotional reshuffling constitutes the *meaning-making processes* in which the adolescent is engaged and that become evidenced in social behaviors for which validation is sought. Maxine seeks validation from those adults who she holds in esteem. Most important is the adolescent's attempts at unraveling the subtext of daily transactions to hone a sense of coherency in their lives—this perspective allows for a more contextual and nuanced understanding of culture and social structures (Hall, 1977). Maxine seeks social coherency in her contacts with esteemed, trustworthy, and sincere adults within her varied so-

cial contexts. For instance, adolescents are particularly adept in ferreting out the social hypocrisies in the social world of adults. As was previously noted, Orange, Atwood, and Stolorow adopt a phenomenology perspective in their recognition that intersubjectivity theory transcends the monadic Freudian view of human beings. The
authors' define intersubjectivity as the subjective organization of experience into patterns of meaning to the subject, including both unconscious and unconscious experiences.

Other psychoanalytically trained scholars have made important contributions to
the theory of intersubjectivity. The contribution that psychoanalytic thought makes
to both phenomenological and symbolic interactional perspectives is an elaboration
of the internal dynamics of the egological processes of the problematic relationship
between the "I" and the looking-glass "Me" (Pile, 1996). Stern (1977, 1985) and Benjamin (1988, 1995) have been influential in the elaboration of the construct of mutual recognition as a component of intersubjectivity. Benjamin, in particular, has integrated symbolic interactionist thinking in her psychoanalytic theorization of
intersubjectivity. She persuasively argues that the need for recognition is the unify-
ing concept in intersubjective theories. She clarifies:

> Recognition is the essential response to the constant companion of assertion. The subject
> declares, "I am, I do" and then waits for a response "you have done." Recognition is thus
> reflexive; it includes not only the others confirming response but also how we find our-
> selves in that response. (1988, p. 21)

The development of the self in interactionist terms is a set of identities that require the response of others and the acceptance of the response designation by the
actor herself (McCall, 1966). The two principal symbolic interactionist terms that I
employ to capture meaning-making actions are "negotiation" and "norms." In interactionist terms, negotiation means the navigation of a particular course of action in
the ecological space in which the actor finds herself situated or located. The term implies that interaction is dialectical and that meanings are socially constructed and created. Similarly, social norms embody the idea of socially constructed meanings. Social norms represent situated social actions that cause others to validate identity
(Cancian, 1975). Social norms conceptualized in this way are emic in that they evolve
from near or immediate experiences that consist of life's daily operations. Accordingly, social norms are "is" statements (as opposed to "should" statements). An example of an "is" statement is: A young child is dependent on her parents. An example of a "should" statement is: A young child should obey her parents.

Personal "is" statements define the social world in ways that inform an individual about what identities exist and what actions and attributes validate such identities, whether those identities are positive or negative. Resilient adolescents construct
"is" statements that define the realities of their lives that must be confronted daily.
Moreover, the comment "my mother always drinks" is itself an "is" statement that
gives meaning to Maxine's life. Maxine's "is" statement allows her to respond to a
situation that although painful is not maladaptive. Maxine's response to her mother's
drinking problem disallows denial about how her mother functions. This theorization is yet another window in which to view the person-process-context model, as it
can illuminate those intersubjective responses that become most important in con-

fronting daily hassles. Maxine learns to recognize her mother's limited abilities without being unempathic. The lesson learned here is that one's failures and limitations can generate empathy or sympathy. One could speculate that "should" statements (e.g., Mothers should be emotionally responsive to their children) can represent declarations as counterpoints to "is" statements for empathic understandings.

The postulation that mutual recognition incorporates empathy—the capacity to share emotional and cognitive states with another person—is the substance of relatedness between two subjects (see Figures 3.1 and 3.3). While empathy is fundamental to intersubjectivity, it is, perhaps, the more complex and difficult concept to integrate in a meaningful way in the person-process-context explanatory model. Primarily drawn from secondary sources, the understanding of empathy presented for this discussion is based on the theories of Edith Stein. Stein's hermeneutics of empathy meant that individuals have direct access to the experience of other individuals—a doubled *i* experience, or a dual side of intramonadic reproduction. Stein's meaning differs from Husserl in that empathy, for Stein, represented a *recognition of difference in sameness*, whereas for Husserl empathic subjects coincided or were perfectly congruent and constituted the "pure i." Stein and Husserl were both concerned with the *content* of empathy, but they differed in concerns about *whose* experience of "the who" of empathic experiences—Stein thought to take into account the *characteristics* and *culture* of the monadic *i*, which in itself indicates the *particularistic constitution in context*. Accordingly, Stein's hermeneutic, Sawicki (1997) argues, was considerably more comprehensive than Husserl's. Stein considered science as limited in its understanding of phenomena. Science alone, she argued, could not shape the totality of meaning or understanding. To simplify Stein's thesis, I suggest that empathy must be differentiated by cultural context since the individual or person is molded by meanings shared within a given culture.

I have tried to incorporate Stein's idea of empathy in the person-process-context model. Stein contended that on three fronts every kind of understanding forms individual activities: "empathizing an alien *i*, contracting a relationship of responsible following with that *i*, and constituting objects affirmable by that *i*" (quoted in Sawicki, 1997, p. 218). Additionally, in this rather dense quotation is embodied the rhythmic play of the jazz musical form. Stein's three elements of empathic understanding are operative in the creation of the improvisational jazz form. As constituted object, jazz is a musical art form embodying the African American call and response cultural idiom. Often in jazz the inimitable subjective meaning of an individual (i) instrumentalist or vocalist creates a unique musical expression. Other players (i's) understand intimately the musical meaning expressed by the instrumentalist and respond with their own distinctive expressions. Thus, an affirming response has been called forth constituting the unique empathic inner subjective musical expression of the participating players. The players follow through creating an instrumental chorus based on the group's intimate intersubjective contact with each other. Relatedly, Stein's theory introduces mutual recognition as squarely inferring motivated acts rather than blind actions of causality. Thus, as Sawicki clarifies, for Stein motivation was the objective correlate of acts of meaning.

Relatedly, the sociologist Crossley (1996) considers, from multiple disciplinary perspectives, an exegesis of intersubjectivity and meaning construction at a societal level. Crossley critiques intersubjectivity meanings within the realms of both macrosystemic and exosystemic societal levels—the physical environment, material culture, structural institutions, and their corresponding relationships with the individual. His critical analysis casts a wide net to include the commentaries of major thinkers within the intersubjectivist tradition, from Buber's philosophical I-Thou to Habermas's lifeworld. Ultimately, what concerns Crossley is citizenship in the universal world with its correlates of duty and recognition. Interestingly, Crossley distinguishes between the radical intersubjectivity of Buber's I-Thou face-to-face and communal relational subjectivity and ecological intersubjectivity, which operates at a level of generality, anonymity, and universality. Radical intersubjectivity, albeit operational at concrete communal levels, according to Crossley, is not enough for ethics and citizenship, since communal ways of relating condemn the experiential knowledge of the other. Apparently, citizenship is abstract and objectified, as is ecological intersubjectivity, and, consequently, is not needed in communal-sacred societies as inhabitants are governed by concrete subjective rules of behavior.

Crossley does concede, however, that radical intersubjectivity is primordial. I would argue, however, that it is precisely radical intersubjectivity that sustains communal living within African American neighborhoods and is, perhaps, more characteristic of communities that do not because of their inferior social status participate fully in the citizenry and are dependent on subjugated knowledge for self-definition. My reading of Buber's I-Thou intersubjectivity is that the experience of personhood as I allows the acknowledgment of the personhood of God. Consequently, the personhood of I can recognize the Godlike personhood of another. The second commandment, "Love thy neighbor as thy self," implies this mutual recognition of the personhood of God in each individual person—which makes it possible to love the others as one's self. Moreover, in my reading of Buber, I employ Stein's interpretation of empathy in that it includes the contextual experiences of the i. I reason that this reading gives a spiritual dimension to ecological intersubjectivity.

Notwithstanding, Crossley's primary contribution to his elaboration of intersubjectivity is the use of Mead's understanding of citizenship as founded on intersubjectivity. According to Crossley, the concept of citizenship permits us to think about intersubjectivity politically—it is a systemic property. The properties of citizenship are community membership, duty, and recognition. Complete citizenship is the political-social form of intersubjectivity. It is a role that must be learned, performed, and grounded in intersubjective praxis. A community is intersubjective space comprised of intersubjects. Duty (and its inverse attribute of rights) within the community suggests a sense of responsibility and respect for others that presupposes the understanding of belonging to a community vis-à-vis a recognition of that belonging or fitting in by another. Citizenship, argues Crossley, can never provide social integration because of its universal and abstract properties. Social integration is achieved in communal enclaves, and the task of citizenship is to link such enclaves while sustaining their stability and integration to participate in a universal pluralistic democracy. These enclave linkages are connected by way of intersubjectivity.

Relatedly, Crossley's propositions are, indeed, significant when we consider black adolescents who must engage in activities but are uncertain as to whether they can become fully citizens when they belong to an ethnic group that is viewed as a social

---

SOCIAL ECOLOGIES—A HIP HOP DRESS CODE: *"DRESSING IN LITTLE GIRL CLOTHES"*

In an inner-city middle school, teachers complain regularly about the faddish styles students choose to wear, although there is no official dress code. Generally, older students dress in a hip-hop style of dress. By the time they are seventh- and eighth-graders, students are keen on establishing their own dress codes and wear loose-fitting dress styles made fashionable by hip-hop rappers. Boys wear hip-hanging pants, sneakers, and oversized outer jackets. Girls experiment with various types of hairstyles (cornrow braids, curls, processed waves, and hair weaves) and from time to time set various dress codes for a given period. Girls dress in tight-fitting jeans, micro-mini skirts, or the fashionable hip-hop baggy look. However, not all girls fit this fashion mold. Girls who do not fit the mold are often excoriated, although in a playful manner. Teachers' complaints about the way students dress seem to mask worries and anxieties about safety issues in the school environment. To the students, hip-hop fashion is simply a context for flamboyant posturing, whereas for the teachers hip-hop dress is a portent of bad or violent behavior. Thirteen-year-old Renee, reticent and strikingly attractive, does not dress like her faddish fellow students. Renee sheepishly accepts the retorts of classmates about "dressing in "little girl clothes like the sixth-graders." After awhile, unable to manage feelings of shame and embarrassment about the way she dresses, Renee gets into scrapes and fights almost daily. Renee's fighting eventually results in a school suspension, and she is referred to the school social worker. Renee does not get support at home for trying out different kinds of dress styles. Renee's stepmother, a reserved stern woman, holds Pentecostal religious beliefs that are severely interpreted to set family standards for proper dress and behavior. Renee's father, employed at menial jobs, leaves the discipline of Renee and her 8-year-old sister to his wife (Renee's stepmother). At age 8, Renee's biological mother deserted the family because of drug (crack cocaine) use. *Study Questions and Issues:* (1) Identify and discuss what you consider to be the most salient issues that the social worker will need to address. Consider the varieties of intersubjective responses and their manifestations in the school and family contexts. In your discussion consider the contextual factors involved in the school and family ecologies. (2) What social ecologies will require social work intervention, if any? (3) Discuss the collaborative intervention context model (CICM), what core principals are involved, and how you would apply them. (4) Identify the contextual risk and protective factors operative in the particular case *See also:* Chapters 3 and 8 and Figures 2.1, 3.1, and 3.2.

pariah with second-class citizenship. Crossley concludes that power is a result of certain properties of intersubjectivities that are managed in a way that exercise control over their relatedness—their subjectivity, their desires as a way of controlling their actions. Black adolescents face tremendous obstacles in their struggle for recognition and the creation of a social identity. In American society, pubertal development is ambiguous. Adolescents are powerless due to their limbo social status. American society is youth oriented, and youthfulness is exploited in the marketplace. Thus, in many respects, adolescents receive attention from the adult world for the wrong reasons. In their transition to adulthood, adolescents receive minimal social recognition for the prosocial contributions they make to society.

Intersubjectivity, Developmental Domains, and Praxis

For the purposes of this text, *intersubjectivity is that domain of consciousness/ unconsciousness and perception through which the individual links the self to others and to the subjective elements of contextual experiences* (see Figure 3.4). Intersubjectivity suggests self-relatedness. In the proposed paradigmatic person-process-context construct, intersubjectivity represents contexting processes that, in turn, allow transactions of *motivated acts of meaning*. Motivated acts of meaning is used here as a term of health and adaptation. In adaptive or healthy responses, at both individual and structural levels motivated acts of meaning involve intentional empathic responses in the recognition of another and that other's contexting experiences. In maladaptive behaviors empa-

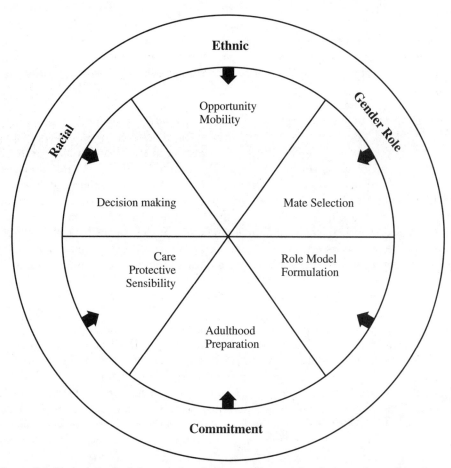

Figure 3.4. Domains of adolescent development. The racial, ethnic, and gender role commitment domain infuses all other domains.

thy is absent and behavioral responses are unhealthy or pathological. Contrarily, mal-adaptive behaviors occur in the failure of empathic affect accompanied by the denial of the contextual experiences of another. Simply put, I use the term "empathy" to in-fer a purposive reflexive appreciation of the other and the context of individual ex-periences. Accordingly, a phenomenological approach suggests the individual's ca-pacity to seek recognition and engage others empathetically. In so doing she then becomes an active agent of self-efficacy in her social environment.

Behavioral manifestations of empathic attunement become refined as the adoles-cent matures. Conjecturally, in the case illustration "Social Ecologies—A Hip-Hop Dress Code" it is likely that Renee's peers have not matured to the point that they can em-pathize with her particular familial situation. Classmates chide Renee for not being able to adjust to a peer dress code. Interestingly, the social context of the school is such that there is no structural empathic response to the way students dress. Instead, school staff members disparage students about how they dress rather than devise a school policy that would offer guidelines for appropriate school apparel. In this set-ting on a social structural level motivated acts of meaning regarding school attire are largely absent. The principle capacities in the self-relatedness of intersubjectivity are assertion and recognition, both of which can contribute to adaptive responses. Renee engages in maladaptive behaviors involving assertion and recognition by fighting (see Figure 3.1).

Moreover, assertion and recognition are companion capacities and suggest a re-flexive mode of interaction. A reflexive mode of interaction not only includes the as-sertion of "I am," but also how the self, once asserted, is recognized and confirmed by another, "yes you are" (Benjamin, 1988). A person-process-context model affords the study of how black female adolescents make meaning of their risk circumstances. Moreover, self-relatedness provides a standpoint from which to examine adolescents' self-development. In regard to the person-process-context model, one could argue that subjectivity and self-relatedness in responses of assertion, empathy, and recog-nition can be diminished when communal intersubjectivity is weakened or lost. Char-acteristics of empathy, assertion, and recognition can be reflected in maladaptive be-havioral responses if adolescents are unable to locate validating responses within their immediate social environments.

On this account, the case illustration "The Loss of Communal Intersubjectivity" dem-onstrates that a black girl's sense of beauty becomes distorted in her attempts to ad-just to the prevailing standard of beauty in a white suburban community. Clara's is-sues that relate to an ethnic/racial social identity could possibly lead to self-contempt instead of ethnic pride. Clara seeks validating responses for a beauty ideal from the appropriation of "white skin coloring" in her selection of makeup. Clara has lost the communal validation of black feminine beauty found in her former neighborhood. Developmentally, it could also be assessed that Clara is having adjustment problems in the racial, ethnic, gender role commitment domain. Notwithstanding that Clara's psychosocial predicament is a serious one, devastating and lethal responses can occur among adolescents for whom validating experiences of assertion, empathy, and recog-nition within the context of community are largely absent from their lives (see Fig-ure 3.1). In suburban communities, the rash of adolescent shootings and killings in school settings may speak to deficits in communal intersubjectivity. As well, inner-city adolescents who traffic in drugs among their neighbors and peers experience failure in this area.

It is uniquely relevant to focus on self-relatedness in studying the maturational development of minority adolescents. Female adolescents of color must synthesize varied and complex experiences, some of which are negative gender/race self-assessments (Stevens, 1997a). Thus female adolescents of color must learn to navigate hostile environments while developing personal and cultural integrity. Concepts of at risk, self-relatedness, and strengths, incorporated within a person-process-context model, provide a useful conceptual framework to explicate developmental struggles of black adolescent females. As Spencer (1995) has persuasively argued, minority adolescents develop the capacity to offset feelings of helplessness and powerlessness when confronting stereotypes and biases in a hostile environment. As a consequence, styles of coping must be developed in response to developmental issues, negative social appraisals, and societal inconsistencies that limit social and economic opportunities.

A person-process-context model considers social/personal processes within the dynamic interactional relationship of context. Despite similarities, the person-process-context model eclipses the elemental interactive risk model in significant ways. Foremost, the impetus for the interactive risk model is one of jeopardy or hazard. On the other hand, the person-process-context paradigm is singularly nonpartisan in its conceptualization of psychosocial functioning, therefore suggesting a more objective, inclusive, and encompassing perspective. The person-process-context model is bidirectional and includes risk, assets, and/or strengths, but assigns no particular value to any attribute. The significance of the model lies in the formulation of basic life processes as a reflexive mode of negotiation/interaction between person and context.

Moreover, the person-process-context model finds support in new and emergent theoretical perspectives of developmental transitions. In particular, the perspective of developmental contextualism has been termed by scholars to define a life-span framework that views "human development as "involving changing *relations* between developing individuals and their complex (i.e. multilevel) context" (Lerner, Ostrom, & Freel, 1997, p. 504). The formulaic phrase "person-process-context" and the term "developmental contextualism" are indeed comparable in that both attempt to describe similar phenomena. Visually, the figuration of person-process-context depicts mediating intersubjective processes as providing the catalyst for the uniform bidirectionality of person and context (see Figure 2.1). The developmental contextualism construct suggests that human development is contexualized equally by multilevel domains (e.g., family, neighborhood, and peers) and by temporality—historical phenomenon. Furthermore, female adolescents experience difficulty in the management of self-esteem issues in the school environment. On the other hand, black adolescent females at the onset of adolescence sustain self-esteem and relational connection with family to nurture and foster psychosocial development and personal identity (Spencer, 1995; Stevens, 1997b).

I have suggested elsewhere that the explanatory power of traditional adolescent theories when examining the development of black female adolescents is limited (Stevens, 1997a). In effect, traditional theories characterize adolescence as a period of storm and stress brought on by pubertal changes. Additionally, it is argued, this developmental turbulence is fueled by the adolescent's need for independence and autonomous functioning—emancipation from familial ties. However, recent theoretical perspectives suggest that adolescent angst as a normative phase is no longer tenable (Palombo, 1985). I argued in Chapter 2 that developmental maturation can occur without tumultuous upheaval and antisocial behaviors. Seemingly, there is conventional acceptance that adolescents will experiment with drug and sexual activity. As well, aggressive behavior or rowdiness is considered normal pubescent obstreperousness (Larson, 1983). Graff (1996) and McCord (1990) have argued that adolescents' antisocial behavior is considered both normative and deviant. Accordingly, contemporary youth receive conflicting messages about what is expected of them.

An ambiguous societal behavioral norm concomitant with profound differential developmental transition can reinforce adolescents' sense of self-estrangement. Equally important in promoting self-alienation is a consumer-driven market economy that creates and sustains a youth subculture. Treated as commodified objects rather than relational subjects, youth are likely to become alienated and dissonant. Thus self-alienation can become a fertile ground for the development of antisocial behaviors. The ecological domains of the media and the marketplace have profound influence on the psychosocial development of American youth (Boykin, 1994). The cultural meanings derived from these domains affect the daily praxis of contemporary youth.

How black adolescents carry out the struggle for recognition is examined in the interpretation of the developmental domains outlined at the beginning of this chapter and in each domain addressed in subsequent chapters. Grounded in qualitative research, the developmental domains constitute norm-modeling actions. The term "norm-modeling actions" is based on the work of Cancian (1975). Norms, according to Cancian, represent situated or social actions that cause others to validate identity. Norms are not objectified or externalized but are self-generated by those who want to project a particular identity. Cancian takes into account the valuative standard making domain of norms, and encompasses other related concepts, including membership norms and reality assumptions. Reality assumptions are those social actions that represent shared meanings and perceptions about the possible in everyday life. Ranking norms are social actions that represent the standard of conduct in a given community, which is used to evaluate the praxis of everyday life. For example, in the case illustration "Self-Assertions, Self-Efficiency, and Recognition" Mrs. Anderson ranks the behavioral norms for her neighbors by a rule that evaluates early sexual activity, adolescent pregnancy, and drug use and misuse as improprieties. These behaviors are considered outside the ranking norms of the community that Mrs. Anderson has historically known. So "those bad girls" are outside the membership norms of the community in which Mrs. Anderson resides. Yet the behavior of "those bad girls" may well represent the reality assumptions of many in Mrs. Anderson's community. Membership norms comprise both reality assumptions and ranking norms and are the valuative standards for including or accepting a person in a given group or community. Given such considerations one can well argue about shifting membership norms in a given community.

In consequence, norm-modeling actions, comprising reality assumptions, ranking norms, and membership norms, are those actions or behaviors that a person deems appropriate or inappropriate for the development of a social identity. Clearly, Mrs. Anderson's daughter, Anna Mae, does not believe that the behavior her mother attributes to "those bad girls" is behavior in which she herself chooses to engage, although this is Mrs. Anderson's fear. The developmental domains that I have delineated (see Figure 3.4) and are central to this text involve norm-modeling actions that constitute the norms and values that reflect a particular area of growth and development. I call these actions norm-modeling behaviors to suggest the transitional attribute of behaviors that adolescents practice. In other words, adolescents model behaviors that constitute the norms of the social contexts in which they seek to develop social identities. This reasoning suggests that when adolescents are exposed to various social contexts diverse opportunities can be provided to enhance development. Further, norm-modeling actions are those actions that a person has deemed appropriate or inappropriate for the development of the self that is sought to present to the world.

The adolescent is at a developmental threshold where norms and values are developing and developed within a set of negotiated actions and their intersubjective processes. Adolescents seek mutual recognition oftentimes in ways that are perplexing to adults as they embark on identity exploration. Mutual recognition, agency, and self-efficacy are sought by means of assertive actions. Adolescents model the actions of others as well as create their own actions that are reflective of the norms and values they are adopting. Ultimately, the limbo status of the adolescent years is completed and teens must enter into the social and political world of adulthood prepared to assume adult responsibilities of caretaker of the next generation. From a political and social perspective, adulthood preparation incorporates the empowered role of citizen. The quality of intersubjectivity, assertion, mutual recognition, and empathic understanding is central to all of the developmental domains.

Notes

1. I am indebted to the suggestions of Christine Fry, an anthropologist at Loyola University of Chicago, for pointing out to me the idea of the improvisational nature of people's lives. When I was conducting the PANSI study and reflecting on the norms that guided the lives of the girls of that study, Dr. Fry introduced me to Francis Cancian's (1975) text, *What Are Norms?* Dr. Fry explained that people make up standards of behavior and cultural meanings as they live their lives. Certainly, this idea is inherent in Cancian's theorization of self-generated norms. In subsequent years, I have come to appreciate how the concept of self-generated norms reflects the improvisational quality of life. As a jazz/blues aficionado since adolescence, it has occurred to me that the improvisational elements of the jazz/blues idiom captures the essence of what I hope to infer in the person-process-model that I have selected for this text. I use the term improvisation to mean, as Dr. Fry would say, that "they are making up the meaning of their lives as they go along." The person-process-context configuration, an ecological interactive model, extends the social work model of person-in-situation. In this section, I address blues/jazz as a metaphor for the person-process-context model and the adolescent developmental process. Jazz, an authentic and original American music created by blacks in urban cities, is the quintessential democratic experience. Jazz, according to Murray (1978) is simply no more than swinging the blues idiom. It is a celebration and consecration of both the individual and the communal, two attributes that become consolidated in adolescent de-

velopmental maturation. As creators of an original American art form, jazz/blues artists personified the soul of America. Moreover, African social patterns were firmly ensconced in jazz's improvisational form, which signified that the personal (jazz soloist) and the communal (jazz group) blended in such a way to represent an organic entity. Still, the musician-artist, usually male, represented what can only be identified as an authentic prototypical American cultural hero. The jazz/blues vocalist, most often female, reflected the spirit of the American pioneer women of the westward migration in that she was courageous, brave, and enterprising. The jazz/blues artist was the quintessential outsider for whom the American traits of independence, creativity, industriousness, and inge-niousness served to shape the musician's persona as well as the artistic expression of the music. The jazz artist represented the American trailblazer intent on exploring uncharted territory to realize his or her anima. Although jazz is an icon of a particular American period, its chronology is more often associated with F. Scott Fitzgerald and the flapper. The authentic artistry of the emergence of jazz subsequent to World War I is more cor-rectly aligned with the likes of musicians such as Louis Armstrong, Fletcher Henderson, Bessie Smith, Ive Anderson, Mamie Smith, or Alberta Hunter. America has, perhaps, until recently always been ambivalent about its authentic jazz originators. The com-mercial control of black music was always in the hands of white businessmen/entrepre-neurs. Further, the music was outside the mainstream of the concert hall. Although nour-ished by the cultural rituals and improvisational elements of black life, the music was often performed, in its early history, in speakeasies controlled by Italian, Irish, and Jew-ish gangsters. Ordinarily the corrupted sporting life of the night club café was the typ-ical setting where the jazz artist performed. As consummate artists in such environments they were at considerable risk to develop substance use/abuse and related problems. Of course all too many jazz/blues artist did acquire serious drug addictions, but many did not succumb to the devastation of drug abuse.

2. This period in American history has been identified as intensely racist because of the in-credible number of Negro lynchings that occurred during this time.

2

DEVELOPMENTAL DOMAINS

4 Racial, Ethnic, and Gender Role Commitment

Within black culture, and throughout African American history, overwhelming evidence can be found to support the claim that African Americans are "bilingual" in their abilities to navigate among differing cultural expectations.

(Brown, 1998, p. 107)

Introduction

As noted in the previous chapter, black female adolescents have unique identity issues that structure developmental tasks. The person-process-context model, in this chapter, considers how economically disadvantaged urban black teenagers, in coping with hostile environments, use cultural idioms to commit to gender, race, and ethnic identities. The *social identity* construct is introduced as the cornerstone of identity development in the adolescent's racial, ethnic, and gender role commitment (Figure 3.3). The processes involved in the construction of a social identity is considered within a three-dimensional view of race, ethnicity, and gender to accommodate an analysis of black female adolescents' maturation in a society that devalues both race and gender. Limitations of a gender analysis model of voice and connection are noted. I suggest that the black female adolescent experiences a relational crisis in both racial and gender identity development. Moreover, black female adolescents develop skilled, unique, expressive, and assertive styles of relating as a way to negotiate perceived hostile environments. The effect of white standards of beauty on African American female adolescent development is discussed more thoroughly in Chapter 5. This chapter offers an explanation of how black female adolescents began to evolve smart and sassy identities to resist controlling racist definitions of them.

I note the *family within a community* as the first contextual influence of human development. I emphasize the family not to diminish other influences, but to cast squarely the family as a context of major consequence in psychosocial development. Unquestionably, the family is the primary unit for the socialization of children. Moreover, I set forth the significance of the maternal relationship as ordering and directing the developmental course. I argue that the mother-daughter relationship is the crucible for maturational processes involved in the race, ethnic, and gender commitment domain. The discussion of family and the mother-daughter relationship should be considered as a framework for *all* the developmental domains that follow in subsequent chapters. The developmental domains delineated are pivotal areas of psychosocial growth during the adolescent period. Additionally, the term "kin-scriptions" (Stack & Burton, 1993) is presented as a construct to describe the patterning of psychosocial processes and critical events in the life cycle of the family. Certainly, in families, youth began to formulate a beginning commitment to gender, racial, and ethnic identities in social role performances. Adolescents commit to these performance roles with all the energy that pubescence allows.

The social location of women of color in American society is such that they experience the double jeopardy of racism and sexism. Women of color have a sociopolitical position of powerlessness in American culture (Gutierrez, 1990). Racial oppression and discrimination are endemic to American social institutions. Racist practices produce blocked opportunities, racial hassles, and hate crimes, all of which constitute stress and strain in the daily lives of racial minorities. Further, race intersects with the social locations of gender and class to produce powerful psychosocial determinants that shape certain family values and norms and, thus, the behavior of children. Sex typing and subsequent role assignments are initiated in families at birth. In families, females and males receive gender-based social prescriptions. More importantly, the configuration of sex typing generally is dictated by the convergence of multiple factors: by societal proprieties and constraints, by the commands of ethnicity, and by the particular injunctions of a given family. For instance, anecdotal narratives as well as scholarly treatises (Frazier, 1957) tell that many poor black families in the Jim Crow South saw that the formal education of females took precedence over the education of males. All too aware of the historical legacy of sexual violence perpetrated against black females, families sought to protect their daughters from the possible sexual harassment and sexual violence of white males.[1]

I address the role of the hybridity of African Americans in their socialization experiences. African Americans have been socialized in a Euro-American and Afro-American cultural ethos (Stevens, 1997a).[2] Enigmatically, the post–civil rights era has seen a profound shift from the goal of racial integration to one of racial separatism. Apparently, black youth's perception about the racial boundaries of American society is void of the social justice goals of full incorporation in American society, which defined the civil rights movement. I suggest that black youth see themselves as *separate from* American society rather than a *part of* it. Simply put, some black teens see themselves as strangers in America and as outlanders on their sojourn to adulthood. This attitudinal shift is reflected in the stigma black youth assign to scholastic achievement. African American adolescent academic achievers are labeled as "acting white" by their peers. Seemingly, this label is used opprobriously and occurs mostly in secondary education irrespective of class status (Fordham & Ogbu, 1986). The "acting white" label has a metaphoric connotation. The derogatory designation of "acting white" symbolizes the profound racial dilemma that confronts African American adolescents.[3] Accordingly, I argue that during adolescence, the bifurcated ethnicity of being African American, for black youth, is endured as a schizoid ordeal rather than as an experience of complementary cultural synthesis. The phenomenon of acting white is even more paradoxical when one considers the rise of multiculturalism and the demise of white Anglo-Saxon elitism with its concomitant social proprieties. The American ideal citizenry is no longer viewed as a "melting pot" reflecting Anglo-Saxon culture, but as a mixture of varied cultures and ethnicities. The stigma of acting white suggests that many African American adolescents perceive their lived experiences as un-American.

In other words, many African American teens see themselves as alienated from the "American experience." Or perhaps the term "acting white" represents a symbolic rejection of what is experienced as a white hegemonic oppression that dehumanizes. Thus, whiteness must be repudiated in order to claim black humanness. Apparently, a dilemma for African American adolescents is embracing American culture as one in which African Americans have a legacy of investment and ownership while sustaining positive ethnic identity. To participate in American culture with confidence, a sense of social investment and ownership must be experienced. In Chapter 7, I discuss social investment as a quality of resilient families. The challenge for African American adolescents is in perceiving their experiences as constitutive of American culture. On this account, this chapter addresses the nature of ethnic difference and resistance as integral to racial/ethnic gender resolution of African American adolescents. Resistance is seen as healthy opposition to oppressive racist practices and the stereotypical beliefs that denigrate African Americans. The family is the primary context for adolescents' first meanings of racial, ethnic, and gender roles. While the adolescent must reformulate and synthesize the meanings that these roles embody, the family represents the link to the adolescent's external social worlds. Black girls create a social identity that encompasses multiple meaningful identities to deal with the myriad complexities of coming of age in a racialist society.

Social Identity and Self-Presentation

Who To Be?

In Western societies, in particular, all adolescents are faced with the personal quest for identity resolution. This search for who to be implies agency, commitment, and freedom of choice (Keniston, 1965). Burdened by societal responses of inconsistency and opportunity limitations, the adolescent quest for African American youth is mostly defined by the social identity that will be developed. The creation of a narrative self via invariant role-playing performances that become self-owned and continuously self-created in essence is the making of a social identity. Obviously, such performances initially are grounded in familial interactional patterns, but take on new meaning or become pivotal during pubescence. Adolescents are natural and uncynical apprentices in learning the manners and morals of the social world of adults. To some extent the resilient adolescent is trying to train herself from the outside inward—so she seeks the idealized practices of the world in which she desires membership. Adolescents are engaged in activities of self-production that the adult has ritualized and customized as character; the adolescent is engaged in self-production as a performer in training who is learning the techniques of perseverance and sustainment in order to cope with her social world.

Generally, ethnicity refers to shared ancestral roots, historical experiences, and identity—the shared uniqueness represents a populace with distinct values and norms (Devore & Schlesinger, 1991). In a society configured by racial categories, race historically has been used rather than ethnicity to classify America's first Africans. Apparently, as the United States has become more culturally diverse, America's first Africans have favored, perhaps to become politically correct, an ethnic classification of African American. Notwithstanding, the the various change, in racial identity signification (Negro, colored, black) in the last 30 years possibly reflects the problematic placement of blacks in the social hierarchy in American life. Black Americans self-identify presently as an ethnic group—as African Americans. Without question, African American families socialized their offspring to cope with the daily hassles of institutionalized racism. Socialization into the ways and means of managing daily racial hassles occurs in families by explicit directives and by subtle cultural conventions.

During the early stage of adolescence, the adolescent commits to gender, racial, and ethnic values and norms to create a social persona—a presentation of the self to the outside world that embodies a social identity. The emphasis on gender, racial, and ethnic commitment, during this period, is not as secure as the process that will take place in the succeeding middle and late phases of adolescent development. The presentation of the self during the early period is largely one that is self-consciously presented. The intense sensitivity and acute vulnerability in self-experiences is responsible, in part, for adolescents' rather excessive self-absorption during this period. Commonly, the adolescent feels that she is acting a part, and while, at times, this play-acting may be pleasurable and exciting, for the most part it gives one a feeling of inauthenticity. Mainly, this is because she has not yet fully integrated those gender, racial, and ethnic values into a mature social identity. Tajfel (1978) has defined social identity "as that part of an individual's self-concept which derives from his knowledge of his membership of a social group (or groups) together with the value and emotional significance attached to that membership" (p. 63).

Principally, a social identity is acquired by way of reflexive recognition; a social identity is mirrored and then validated by others. Certainly, the adolescence female is aware of how she is perceived as a person in the context of family (see Figure 3.3). To a degree, she experiences idiosyncratic characteristics acknowledged by the family as integrated self-components. Notwithstanding, even in the realm of personal identity, she feels her world shifting since her social identity is so uncertain outside the family context. Mostly, the uncertainty experienced is because of an unconsummated social identity. While a social identity is emerging, it is not yet firmly validated by others. With untold pubescent fervor, the female adolescent confronts her social world with the hope of integrating the two selves, the social and the personal, so that self-experiences can be unified and integrated. Typically, the adolescent period lays claim to the adolescent's concerns for the ideals of social justice and social ethics, all of which require what I call meaning synthesis." Much of the turbulence and ambivalence seen in early adolescence is brought on by the internal struggle of achieving meaning synthesis in the varied developmental domains. Intensely ruminative, the female adolescent constantly engages in meaning synthesis. In adolescence, meaning synthesis represents the integration of diverse and consequential experiences that become organized into a coherent and consolidated standpoint of values and ethics. The integration of disparate experiences concomitantly with sound values and ethics makes possible an authentic self, and ultimately the smooth functioning of a social identity. Intrinsic attributes of the adolescent with a healthy social identity result in sound intersubjective processes of empathic caring, trustworthiness, attachment, and connection, to name a few (see Figure 3.1).

Without question, pivotal advancement in cognition exemplified by formal operational thought during this period facilitates meaning synthesis. Failure to acquire an organized ethical standpoint from which to appraise self-experiences and societal standards can result in moral alienation (Coles, 1997). The most difficult of all choices for youth is *who to be*—which essentially involves identity choices. A free decision must be made about one's social identity without the guarantees that one has made the correct choice. To make free choices about one's social identity is the strength of character (Keniston, 1965). Those who find commitment to a social identity difficult or nearly impossible drift afloat without being morally grounded. Adolescents without commitments are angry, alienated, and disconnected. Such youth employ maladaptive mechanisms of assertion (see Figure 3.1). With formal operational thought, the female adolescent has the cognitive wherewithal to consider both the consequences of self-actions, as well as the influential actions of others. For African American adolescents, the development of discerning cognition in confronting the social realities of American life cannot be overstated. The consequences of the environmental effects of social injustice and societal inconsistency on African American adolescent development in the particular domain of gender, racial, and ethnic commitment are enormous.

Developmentally, African American adolescents must achieve meaning synthesis in the face of societal deficiencies represented by unfair, unjust, and inequitable treatment of the social group to which they belong. Eventually, African American adolescents must perceive societal disparities without self-depreciation or self-blame. Moreover, they must learn to evaluate societal inconsistency without incorporating the relativistic morals and situational ethics used to view them as members of a stigmatized group. In the face of the pernicious evils of racism, African American adolescents must evaluate American society by its professed ideals—they must develop and sustain idealized transcendent values of fairness and justice. Commonly, during the early subphase of adolescence, moral proprieties that were learned in earlier developmental periods undergo a process of careful scrutiny, for reformulation and internalization and for self-ownership.

In late adolescence, this meaning-synthesis process is consummated. Its culmination signifies the resolution of a moral conscience for adulthood. Two significant psychological processes occur in this meaning-making scrupulousness. First, adolescents' perception of parents is profoundly changed. Parents are seen in a less powerful and idealized way. They are seen in the more realistic light of their imperfections and weaknesses. Simply put, parents are de-idealized. Second, adolescents develop an overidealized sense of social justice that causes them to critique social practices in absolute moral terms. Eventually as maturation progresses, these perceptions must be tempered by the realities of social life. Yet for African American adolescents, who are without privileged racial social status, this psychological dynamic takes a special developmental turn. Chestang (1972a) has elaborated on the development in African Americans of a conscience in a hostile environment. He asserts:

> The disparity between the black superego and that of the culture in general is not synonymous with the concept of superego lacunae. Rather, there is an alternative conscience, one which serves as a buffer against the immoral and conflicting expectation that blacks will be just and fair in the face of injustice and unfairness. (p. 5)

Because of the development of a buffer conscience, African American adolescents are less likely to de-idealize either parents or other significant persons in their proximal ecologies. Thus, African American adolescents, perhaps earlier than privileged white adolescents, develop a discriminating capacity for appraising the behaviors of others—a resilient quality. On the other hand, many post–civil rights generation African American adolescents are outraged, as evidenced in the misogynist and enraged music of rappers. For these volatile youth, the noble dream of a just and equitably integrated society espoused by Martin Luther King, Jr., represents nothing more than a dream permanently deferred.

Communal intersubjective spaces, such as religious congregations, family gatherings, or ethnic celebrations, are of inestimable worth to African American adolescents. These social spaces represent situations where validation and affirmation are acquired. As noted in Chapter 3, Crossley (1996) defines the primary, face-to-face relationships of communal-relatedness as radical intersubjectivity. He argues that the intimacy of communal relating lacks the objective and abstract standards and principles of conduct required for citizenship. Crossley correctly theorizes that communal intersubjectivity comprises emic experiences or concrete social discourses. But it is precisely in the familiarity and closeness of communal relations that African American adolescents learn to rely on established knowledge that will help navigate the situated locations where social inconsistency is met head on. African American adolescents require anchorage in communal relatedness to develop a sense of agency and self-efficacy. Collins (1990) argues that African Americans come to know themselves and the world around them by way of a four-dimensional knowledge standpoint. I contend that Collins's knowledge standpoint constitutes the mutual self-relatedness commonly experienced in healthy families and resilient community institutions.

On this account, I argue that disconnection from one's ethnic knowledge standpoint renders the individual more vulnerable to social inconsistency. In such circumstances, cultural or situational powerlessness can lead to aggressive acts of violence (Hall, 1977). Or, when the personal organized patterns of psychosocial experiences are culturally dislocated, the individual suffers psychological disassociation. Families too can become more socially disorganized when disconnection from a communal knowledge standpoint takes place. Accordingly, I propose that the four-dimensional knowledge standpoint discussed here epitomizes a cultural idiom and is a source of empowerment and self-efficacy for healthy adaptation in a hostile environment. Additionally, the four-dimensional standpoint provides grounding for building healthy resistance to racial injustices in order to realize a viable citizen role in a political community.[4]

1. *Concrete experience as a criterion of meaning.* The emphasis here is on the connected knowing that develops out of empathic shared experience and firsthand observation. Abstractions are derived from the praxis of everyday living. The category signifies the ability of astute discernment in dealing with life's praxis. In the cultural idiom, this perspicaciousness is commonly referred to as "mother wit."
2. *The use of dialogue in assessing knowledge claims.* This category signifies intersubjective reflexive discourse commonly experienced in the call-and-response oral preacher tradition of the black church. As an example, this dimension of knowing signifies the metaphor of communal voice in which the individual finds her personal voice within an affirming chorus of voices.

THE LOSS OF COMMUNAL INTERSUBJECTIVITY: *"WEARING FUNNY-COLORED MAKEUP"*

A private social work practitioner saw 16-year-old Clara for an initial interview. Clara was an attractive girl, thin, but not underweight. Mrs. Thompson, her adopted mother, accompanied her. Both Clara and Mrs. Thompson were well dressed. Clara's appearance was noticeable, however, in that she had ginger-colored skin tone, but wore powder about two shades lighter than her natural coloring that gave her a pasty look. Clara wore her hair long and straight. Mrs. Thompson, a 40-year-old single parent, had adopted Clara at 3 years of age. Clara's adoption, according to Mrs. Thompson, was never a secret, but was freely discussed. Mrs. Thompson complained that Clara was doing poorly in school and stayed in her room most of the time. She had made friends with some of the girls at the school and wanted to spend too much time at their homes. Mrs. Thompson worked long hours and often was not at home until late at night. She said that Clara often wanted to stay overnight at the home of friends. Mrs. Thompson thought everything had changed since she and Clara had moved to the suburbs a year ago. She thought she would try to get help for Clara because things didn't seem to be getting better. Mrs. Thompson had achieved some success, with little formal training, as the owner of a daycare establishment in the inner city. Prior to moving to the suburbs, Mrs. Thompson resided for 20 years, in a working-class and lower-middle-class black community. She and Clara had occupied a large three-bedroom rental apartment. Clara had attended the local high school and seemed well adjusted to the school setting. Mrs. Thompson saw herself as providing better opportunities for Clara by moving to the suburbs. She said that she thought that a new house and suburban surroundings would be a better environment for Clara. Mrs. Thompson was a new homeowner and pleased that she could now afford to buy her own home. She thought that she missed the old neighborhood and believed Clara did too as they had many friends there. Mrs. Thompson did not know any of her suburban neighbors. She said that of late, Clara had started "wearing this funny-colored makeup that made her look strange." Mrs. Thompson related that she didn't disapprove of Clara wearing makeup, but that she thought it should suit her skin coloring. Mrs. Thompson related that lately she and Clara argued a lot and that Clara seemed secretive and distant. Mrs. Thompson said that it's OK that Clara wears makeup, but she doesn't like the kind she wears. "It's much too light for her." Mrs. Thompson thought that Clara wore light makeup because she was trying too hard to adjust to her white friends. What made matters worse, according to Mrs. Thompson, is that the school had sent a letter home notifying parents of a special meeting about drug use on the school grounds. Mrs. Thompson said that she knew Clara did not use drugs, but she was afraid that the kids at the school might influence her. Since the move to the suburbs, Mrs. Thompson thought that things had gotten worse instead of better. Clara spoke little in the interview, but when she did comment her remarks were affecting and pointed. She said that she never wanted to move from their old apartment as she had many friends in her old neighborhood. She was lonely and wanted to have friends. She thought her new friends were quite nice to her and accepted her although they were white. She felt that her mother criticized her too much. Clara thought the schoolwork at the new school was more difficult. She thought that she could do the work, but needed more time to study. She admitted that she was spending less time doing homework and more time with friends. But she didn't like staying in the house alone and her mother was away all of the time. *Study Questions, Issues, and Exercises:* (1) Role-play the case to demonstrate how the practitioner would empathetically engage Clara and her mother for collaborative work. (2) Discuss whether Clara and Mrs. Thompson's natural strengths, needs, and interests were identified in the role-play and whether the practitioner and participants formulated the therapeutic and developmental issues to be worked through. (3) Discuss the impact of the family's move to the suburbs. In the move to the suburbs, do you think Clara and her mother are experiencing cultural dislocation or the loss of communal intersubjectivity? Explain. (4) Discuss what personal values and feelings the case might stimulate in the practitioner.

3. *The ethic of caring.* This category signifies the validation process that occurs in caring for another with affection and respect. It comprises three components: (1) a highly stylized personal expressiveness in the fashion of a cultural idiom; (2) emotionality that involves the integrated faculties of intellect and emotions, and (3) empathic caring that signifies the understanding and truth-seeking knowledge that emanates from the affectionate care given to another.
4. *The ethic of personal accountability.* Individuals are expected to be accountable for their knowledge claims. Thoughts and actions are believed to derive from an ethic belief system that is personal and moral. Individuals are respected because of their moral and ethical value.

Although the four dimensions coalesce when meaning synthesis is at its peak, it is the actualization of an ethic of personal accountability that makes integrity inviolable and social identity resolute.

As adulthood represents a social identity, it is expected that normatively adolescents experience a sense of privilege and empowerment in the anticipation of adulthood, especially if the developmental domains have been managed fairly successfully. Unquestionably, for members of a racially stigmatized group, the developmental domain of gender, racial, ethnic commitment signifies immeasurable difficulties for African American adolescents. In the preceding chapter, I argued that minority groups, because of their social stigma, must develop radical intersubjectivity in order to develop and sustain a sense of citizenship in the larger culture. Economically deprived African American youth, stigmatized both by economic conditions of class and race, become grounded in cultural idioms, at the onset of pubescence, to buffer unjust and unfair treatment in society.

Social Identity and the Ideal Image

During the early stage of adolescence, there is a growing awareness that the social self is inauthentic. This happens since the desired social image is not resolute, and thus not completely self-owned. Still, it is during this early phase that gender, racial, and ethnic values are brought to bear in the self-presentation that will eventually become secure as the declared social identity. Adolescent social ecologies, such as the school and peer group, provide fodder for the reflexive recognition of the pubescent self presented in this earliest subphase. Moreover, when adolescents are habilitated by institutional organizations, such as a church, the commitment to gender, racial, and ethnic norms and the doctrines, beliefs, and ideologies of the particular organization define values, by and large. This idea is especially illuminated when one considers the gender, race, and ethnic commitment of those black adolescent females who have membership, for example, in the Nation of Islam. In the Nation of Islam females are socialized to behave according to Islamic values and the norms of the organization. Additionally, racial identity, gender-based dress codes, and gender-defined social manners in the Nation of Islam are designated as behavioral proprieties.

Furthermore, the commitment to particularized gender, racial, and ethnic norms is, for example, clearly illuminated in the culture of military schools and Greek societies. In such instances, inductees are socialized to conform to a mythologized ideal image of a gender or racial/gender type of the particular subculture of the organization. Adolescent inductees then create an identity based on the mythologized gender/racial/ethnic types and the concomitant values and norms proselytized by the individual institution. Anecdotal evidence suggests, for example, that black sororities and historical black universities were noted for espousing a certain idealized female type that symbolized the desired beauty standard for black females. Unquestionably, the beauty standard upheld was modeled on the features of white women. The black poet Lucille Clifton, born in 1936, comments on her college experience and the discovery of the color code and beauty standard at a black university:

> At that time, at Howard, if you weren't light-skinned or had long hair you had to have something pretty strong going for you. Well, I was a drama major from New York. They didn't know that Buffalo is a long way from New York City, and for them that did not know, I could lay claim to Canada, so it worked out well enough. (1987, p. 269)

Clifton articulates the way certain resilient females cope with a standard of beauty that clearly constitutes self-rejection if internalized. Certainly, during early adolescence, the question of physical attractiveness poses a real dilemma for all female adolescents in a culture that comodifies the female body. Still, in American culture, the norm for physical attractiveness is whiteness. For African American females, the internalization of this standard can verge on pathology. In Morrison's *Bluest Eye* (1970) this subject is dealt with in its extreme ramification—the pathological condition of self-hate as evinced in the poverty-stricken tragic figure Pecola, whose desire for blue eyes symbolizes the desire for whiteness.[5] Employing some of Morrison's own language, Grewal (1998) brilliantly critiques Morrison's use of the novel as a metaphorical commentary on the construction of race and gender in American society:

> If the cultural production of gender is "to make the woman connive in treating herself as, first and foremost sight," the cultural production of race makes the black woman unsightly. Morrison makes it clear that while Breadloves' poverty was "stultifying, it was not unique" (34). What is unique is their *conviction* of their ugliness, which is not an essence but a political construct supporting slavery in the past and the status quo in the present: "It was as though some mysterious all-knowing master had given each one a cloak of ugliness to wear, and they had accepted it without question" (34). Morrison shockingly dramatizes DuBois' concept of "double consciousness," described as this sense of always looking at one's self through the eyes of another. (p. 30)[6]

Clearly, there is a psychological danger in only seeing oneself through the eyes of another, especially when the other has the power to suppress ways of seeing and knowing. Imperatively, African Americans develop their own ways of seeing and knowing as delineated in the four-dimensional standpoint previously elaborated. I argue that, for a healthy developmental outcome, by middle and late adolescence African American females have arrived at some meaning synthesis regarding the values of their cultural reference group; consequently, they feel supported and validated. Nonetheless, it is reliance on one's inner resources that fortifies acceptance of the self as physically attractive. Consider the case illustration "The Loss of Communal Inter-subjectivity," in which Clara appears to be ambiguous about her social identity. The makeup that Clara adopts seems to be a way of disguising or masking her darker-skinned complexion to fit in and be accepted. Commonly, inner-city black females develop unique styles of beautifying themselves, such as corn row hairstyles, that are distinct from those dictated by the fashion industry. Apparently, inner-city fashion fads are believed to be appealing by the fashion industry, as designers frequently adopt the styles of inner-city youth to embellish their own vogue creations.

Collins (1990) has clarified the way external standards of beauty affect the self-image of black women:

> This division of African-Americans into two categories—the "Brights" and the "Lesser Blacks"—affects dark-skinned and light-skinned women differently. Darker women face being judged inferior and receiving the treatment afforded "too-big Negro girls with nappy hair." Institutions controlled by whites clearly show a preference for lighter-skinned Blacks, discriminating against darker ones or against any African-Americans who appear to reject white images of beauty. African-American women who are members of the "Brights" fare little better, for they too receive special treatment because of their skin color and hair texture. (p. 81)

The GULTMC and PANSI research females were attractive young black women. Their appearance and demeanor demonstrated an individual and unique fashion style, typical of urban adolescents. Interestingly, most females, within both study groups, fit Collins's "Lesser Blacks" category. The college students who served as mentors for the GULTMC research displayed a diverse group of hues, which conformed to both of Collins's categories, "Brights" and "Lesser Blacks." All the GULTMC mentors were self-identified as black, middle class, and undergraduate students. The bonding between the two groups was undeniably less than optimal. The GULTMC females raised questions regarding the racial identity of a couple of the mentors who would have classified as "Brights"—they wondered about the mentors' racial ancestry, whether the mentors were black or mixed. The GULTMC girls defined "mixed" as being of interracial parentage. Further, the GULTMC females saw the mentors as having a superior attitude, whereas the mentors found the GULTMC females' behavior to be demanding and obstreperous. Undoubtedly, there were distinct class differences between the two groups. More importantly, in the GULTMC study class differences were reflected in the stereotypical perceptions of color-based behaviors commonly experienced within a black cultural reference group. Additionally, both groups represented two distinct subphases of adolescent development, early age and late age periods; consequently, the two groups' maturational needs diverged.

The Family as Ecological Nexus

The commonsense idea that the adolescent peer group is the cornerstone contextual domain of adolescent social identity has almost universal acceptance. Contrarily, it is the family that is the primary socialization unit for cultural adaptation. The beginnings of social identity development based on the intersubjective need for mutual recognition occur within the family. One wonders whether a sound grounding of social identity within the family can go off-track when social or cultural dislocations occur (see the case illustration "The Loss of Communal Intersubjectivity"). The family logically assumes the task of the socialization of its offspring to ensure its own survival. Notwithstanding that the family unit is indispensable to the development of adolescent social identity, social ecologies that extend beyond the nuclear family constellation have a variant and complex influence. Undoubtedly, in the future electronic virtual reality experiences of cyberspace will be a component of the social world of adolescents. Increasingly, adolescents of the information age will experience random exposure to variegated social contexts. Cyberspace social domains are another venue of cultural socialization. Conceivably, if this occurs, parental supervision of the social world of adolescents will be considerably diminished as the information age advances. Even now, scholars question to what extent parents ultimately determine maturational growth.

Recognizably, adolescents are exposed to consequential experiences outside the sphere of parental influence. Empirical documentation suggests that the social-economic organizational structures of neighborhoods, for instance, influence psychosocial behaviors (Brewster, 1994; Brewster, Billy, & Grady, 1993; Sampson, Raudenbush, & Earls, 1997). The significance of such studies is that they demonstrate the relevance of social experiences that occur outside the family context as influential in the adolescent growth process. Currently, environment now involves a nonphysical world of electronic informational discourse. Paradoxically, the proximal localities have become the world neighborhood via electronic communication. Speculatively, electronic communication systems such as email and the Internet make for proximally dense communications akin to those that occur in actual physical locations. Yet electronic communication is profoundly dissimilar in that it takes place in faceless sociometric spaces. Cyberspace discourse is free of the subtle nuances of oral dialogue that emanate from face-to-face encounters. Seemingly, intersubjective processes in electronic sociometric spaces will be stifled as the recognition of shared emotional experiences is likely to be diminished. Without question in order to ensure its continued survival, the family will create ways to adapt to technological-electronic ecological changes. The concern in such adaptation, nonetheless, is the formation and evolution of intersubjective processes that normally occur in families.

While it is possible that cyberspace environs will have far greater impact on the lives of future adolescents, the caveat is that these ecological domains will constitute a disparate and anonymous collective quite different from the organizing cohesive structures of family life that speak to affective experiences. Moreover, it is familial life that provides intersubjective experiences and mutuality in recognition. Evidently, African American urban economically disadvantaged families continue to maintain familial kinship networks. Ethnographic studies (Aschenbrenner, 1983; Stack, 1974) have documented the resilience of African American extended kinship networks in dealing with urban stress, while more recent scholarship (Wilson, 1987, 1996) chronicles its deterioration. The adolescent females from the GULTMC and PANSI studies had significant involvement with extended family members that suggested that despite the fragmentation of contemporary urban life induced by crime, joblessness, and structural dislocation, the strengths of extended family configurations was functional.

Still, using the family as the foundation from which to operate, youth reconstruct new identities based on relational interactions that occur in exofamilial contexts. This phenomenon, identified as the Cinderella effect, proposes that individuals assume different identities in diverse social contexts (Gladwell, 1998; Harris, 1998). Commonly narrated, the story of Cinderella tells of a reticent ordinary kitchen maiden who, because of a fortuitous shoe fit, is fated to marry a prince and assume the royal roles of princess and ultimately that of queen. The tale can be seen as a metaphor for the individual's capacity to embrace diverse social roles. Moreover, it suggests that individuals can meet the social expectations of multiple roles without undue stress or anxiety. Routinely, we see these phenomena played out in political life when elected officials take on the leadership roles intrinsic to government positions. Metaphorically, the Cinderella effect is an appropriate symbol for the empirical work of Cancian (1975), in which she theorizes that social contexts dictate the assumption of multiple social roles that prescribe an individual's social identity.

In psychodynamic theory, the significance of parenthood carries enormous weight. The nuclear family is essential to the theory's fundamental postulates of epigenetic psychosexual maturation, in which it is proposed that developmental pathologies are due to failed parental nurturance. New thinking suggests that the family is an ecological unit—a collectivity of kin engaged in transactional processes to ensure its own survival. The family represents a systemic process with its inherent rules, values, and norms. Implicit in this view is the idea of multiple contextual influences among kin, where the bidirectionality of intersubjective transactions takes place (see Figure 3.2). Historically, human development research has been individually focused. Typically resilience research has investigated the hardiness of at-risk individuals (Barbarin, 1993; Ford, 1994; Grossman et al., 1992; Haggerty et al., 1994; Masten, Best, & Garmezy, 1990), while the actual family processes that serve to mediate or to counterbalance risk have received less attention. Ecologically, the family serves as a bridge to expanding systemic structures.

The family is the female adolescent's connection to the nested contexts within ecological systems external to the family. Developed from studies of poor black families, ethnographers Stack and Burton (1993) conceptualized a *kinscript* framework to explore "how families as multigenerational [*interdependent*] collectives, and individuals embedded within them negotiate the life course" (p. 157). Although the construct has been conceptualized from the study of black families, the framework, according to Stack and Burton, is sufficiently abstract and hence germane to all families regardless of race. The kinscript framework suggest that the family life course is characterized by the praxes of daily living reflected in the specific cultural norms, roles, and transactional patterns that families use over time to ensure generational survival. The framework categorizes three multigenerational familial praxis: (1) the designation of work roles; (2) key life event timetables based on age of occurrence, such as birth and marriage; and (3) the relational power dynamics that members engage in to both conserve and develop family practices, customs, and traditions. Respectively, these family processes are identified as kin-work, kin-time, and kin-scription. Moreover, many kin-scriptions have developed over time in response to the structural strain brought about by racist practices. Historically, the entry into the labor market for working-class black women (even those with secondary education), for instance, was that of domestic workers, whereas for white working class women after World War II, clerical positions, such as telephone operators and sales clerks, represented admission to the labor force.

Certainly, black families carry out the praxes of their daily lives as other families do, but they do so under the weight of pernicious racist practices. Ultimately, black families must instruct offspring about survival in a society where because of racial stigma they are likely to be victimized or oppressed. Praxis for survival in racially oppressed societies is learned in families by means of socially prescriptive behaviors and attitudes that become integrated into the families' kin-scriptions, which inculcate a sense of worth and esteem. One could argue that the kin-scriptions of resilient families produce resilient youth. Poor families develop particular strategies to nurture resilient capacities in their offspring. Resilient familes have a strong sense of pride in the family's history. Many African American families migrated to northern urban areas after World War II to secure better economic opportunities. Resilient families tend to maintain ties to extended kin who remained in the South (Aschenbrenner, 1973; Hays & Mindel, 1973; Stack, 1974). Familial ties to the southern homestead and birthplace provide cultural anchorage and are a source of strength for such families.

Additionally, resilient urban African American families have a strong work ethic, are achievement oriented, and possess a sense of autonomy and responsibility (Hill, 1997; Williams, 1991; Willie, 1988). And, while birth and marriage life cycle events are deemed necessary to the family's survival, resilient families tend to postpone these events until after vocational choices are made and jobs are secured. Burton and Bengston (1985) have argued that a birth time kin-scription for poor urban African American families is often as early as the adolescent period. Some maternal grandparents sanction an early birth timetable for their daughters so that they can participate actively in parenting. On this account, I argue that an early birth timetable is likely to occur in families where the birth of children may be the only reward left for families who have experienced intergenerational economic depletion. An early birth timetable kin-scription may serve to counteract the generational despair and blocked opportunities that result from structural strain. African American families have a deep reverence for children, which are reflected in child-centered familial and communal values (Nobles, 1973; Nobles, et al., 1976; Wilson, 1989).[7] Rena, an 18-year-old pregnant PANSI teen, believed that being a mother would help her become a grown-up:

> Pregnancy is the first step in being a grown-up. Being a parent is the second step and taking care of yourself is the third step. Having a baby is a way of testing yourself so that your mother don't completely take care of you. When you are 18 years old you're grown up and can take on more responsibility. It is the transitional stage. After 18 you're a full adult. Between 15 and 18 you're growing up. My mother thinks that at 18 you're an adult. And, you're not a full adult until you have a job with your own bills in your name.

Moreover, relational power dynamics in resilient families often are such that successful family members are expected to make sacrifices to assist less fortunate members.

The institution of the family, concomitant with other ethnic social institutions, mediates psychosocial distress caused by hostile racial environments. Many families who are actively engaged in religious institutions, for example, find the emotional and social support needed in institutional fellowship to deal with the accumulated stress derived from hostile environments. Hence, for many urban black adolescent females, attachment to social institutions such as churches represents sanctuary from a hostile and threatening world. Thus, black adolescents who seek safe and suitable locations for identity exploration embrace social institutions that provide solace and communal self-relatedness. Clearly, black families are not monolithic, and as such their kin-scriptions will vary. Essentially, kin-scriptions are the means by which a family's identity is socially constructed. Such is the case that the reflexive image of the community reinforces family members' view of themselves as a distinct collective.

The Family: Mother-Daughter Relations

Is the mother-daughter relationship among economically disadvantaged girls developmentally more critical than of that of their more privileged cohorts? What is known is that poor girls are more likely to be reared in single parent households; hence, there is a greater dependence on the maternal figure. In the autobiographical text *No Respect*, Sister Souljah (1994) compellingly argues that the mother in the projects is the most central person in the life of the child:

> In the projects, somebody can call your mother a one-legged whore who does nasty tricks for men for five dollars and she will still be the most important and influential person in your childhood. She is the only one a child can depend on for survival and to interpret life. . . . But aren't all mothers everywhere the central figure in the eyes of a child? Mostly the answer is yes. But for children in the projects the answer is even more so. The difference is the "extreme complication of circumstance." The reason: Most children in the projects don't have a father to speak of. (pp. 3–4)

Ultimately, African American female adolescents learn the race, ethnic, and gender role commitment by means of the intersubjective connection of the mother-daughter relationship. Parents communicate to their children a sense of being and doing. Certainly, the father-daughter relationship is significant in the adolescent female's development. I say more about the significance of fathers in the maturation of daughters in the chapter on dating and mate selection. The emphasis of the maternal relationship is presented since this was the specific parental relationship that adolescent females in both the GULTMC and the PANSI studies stressed and identified as the most important of all relationships to them. The feelings, motives, and intentions that the race, ethnic, gender role commitment developmental domain demands are the core of the subjective self that comes into fruition in self-differentiation within familial female relations, especially that of mother. Armara, a 19-year-old nonpregnant PANSI respondent, realized that she, her mother, and her maternal aunt were both similar and different:

> Well as far as my mother goes, I would not be on public aid. And my aunt, well I wouldn't have all those people in my house not working; that would put too much stress on me. [Armara's aunt had adult children in the home who were not financially independent. Armara believed her aunt's children were dependent and exploitative.] I wouldn't take that, that's entirely too much. You can help people, but she does too much. I would not let

people take advantage of me. But, I'm like them. I'm strong, independent and courageous. I have a positive attitude and want a good education. I am very intelligent (laughs). I know I'm very intelligent. Well let's say compared to my friends. I look at them and sometimes think they're real dumb because they don't think about everything seriously in life.

The mother models the female identity that the daughter emulates. But before the subjective female self can be crystallized and differentiated during this period, the mother and daughter undergo a period of normative contention during the early adolescent period. The normative contention of this period is characterized by the mothers' defining behavioral parameters for the daughters' social conduct. Primarily, mothers during this period continue to see the maternal role as one of protection and discipline. Carrying out protective functions in parenting induces considerable psychological stress for African American mothers (Collins, 1990). Convention informs us that there are three primary socialization tasks that African American parents perform: (1) keeping children safe (physically and emotionally) from the dangers of street life, (2) protecting children from overt forms of racism and oppression, and (3) helping children develop bicultural competence. Seventeen-year-old Thelma, a PANSI respondent, believed that she was future oriented and bound for college because her mother was such a strict disciplinarian:

> Yeah. We live in the projects and it's a hard, but not impossible, life. My mother made it easier for me, believe it or not because she was strict and her being strict kept me out of things. There were rules and regulations. I could not stay out late at night, I had a curfew. The rule was that I had to go to school. She told me when you too grown to go to school then its time to be out on your own and you're grown when you're out of Mama's house earning your own income. I had responsibilities in the house, chores I had to do. My mother is everything. Now me and my mother we have had our troubles. Sometimes, I have felt like she is just pressuring me all the time. You know mothers have their ways! Sometimes when I didn't obey the rules, she put me out. I went to my boyfriend's house. At one point it was getting to be too much and I couldn't handle it—I went to a counselor. I got help from school. And you know it helped me. You know mothers have their ways and you go along with them cause you know they're for you 100%. My father—well he's somebody I just can't like, he's an alcoholic—never did much for the family.

Because many poor women bear parental responsibilities with minimal spousal support, parenting is an additional hardship. Empirically, little is known about male partner arrangements in female-headed households. What has been documented is that poor women generally choose not to marry. Poor black women view economic insufficiency among black men as a realistic barrier to marital formations and social mobility. Poor black women are more likely to have nonmarital companionable arrangements with the men in their lives (Jarrett, 1994). Nonetheless, how nonmarital partnered arrangements affect the psychosocial development of poor black girls, including their coital behavior, is altogether unclear, as little research has been done in this area (Keith et al., 1991). More will be said about this in Chapter 6.

Some of the GULTMC females shared narratives of mothers who were anxious and fearful in the performance of parental tasks. Some narratives told of severe and strict discipline regimens, while others shared stories of mothers who made every effort to listen to their daughters. Without question, the social behavior of the African

American female adolescent is under careful maternal scrutiny at puberty onset. The following narratives typify the anxious and the understanding mother-daughter relationship, respectively:

> My mother is the type, when I get in trouble, I can't say nothing to her. She don't wanna hear about it. I'll say, "but Mommy, let me tell you." She be like, "I don't wanna hear it, Caretha, I don't wanna hear it. Get upstairs, do your homework," and do this and this and this, and I be like, "That's dogged."

> My mother know how to talk to me. Like when it comes to stuff like my feelings or stuff like me getting a woman shape. She says stuff like, "How you feel, what's been going on with you today." My mother she says stuff like,"My little baby got a body." She says stuff like that. She said, "You're so cute, with your little waist," and stuff like that, she gives me compliments.

Early aged adolescent girls, because of where they are in the developmental trajectory, are more likely than older adolescents to resist parental disciplinary measures, especially those restricting neighborhood peer associations. Adolescents and parents experience discrepant as well as multiple and variant realities. Moreover, when parents are especially anxious, parental supervision and disciplinary measures can be labored, overdetermined, and insensitive to a child's maturational needs. When discipline becomes unduly harsh or strict, parents are more likely responding to unrealistic anxieties and fears. If parental supervision has been reasonable and sensitive the adolescent is more appreciative of parental supervision. Parental anxiety may be elevated at the onset of adolescence, as familial adjustments must be made to accommodate the developmental changes of puberty. Nonetheless, parents and their adolescent offspring eventually learn to accommodate each other.

Beset with egregious neighborhood conditions, resilient youth may embrace a family's positive identity as a means of protection. Anecdotal and empirical evidence suggests that neighborhood street gangs actively recruit members, but also have been known to demonstrate respect toward families who steer their youth away from the activities of street life. Paradoxically, socially mobile youth may receive protection from gangs against the hazards of street life. As is often the case, parents are ignorant of the codes of street life and hence are unaware of the safety measures peers use on the streets. Unsuspecting of the effective safety operations occurring in neighborhood streets, parental supervision, all to frequently, is overvigilant.

Commonly, among the GULTMC females mothers supervised their daughters by scare and intimidation tactics, especially after the onset of the menstrual cycle. During the early adolescent years, both GULTMC and PANSI females perceived parents as strict disciplinarians, especially mothers. Menstrual onset, maternal anxiety, and strict behavioral regimes appear to occur concurrently. Apparently, parental worries about early coital behavior and parenthood are expressed concerns about daughters. Eleven-year-old Ella, not yet interested in dating, reports that her mother seemed overly concern about sex and her future relationship with boys:

> My mother is just too worried about things that I don't think a lot about yet. One time I was on the phone with my girlfriend, talking about this boy. My mother picked up the phone and started screaming and calling us bitches. My mother makes me get off the

phone at night. I gotta be in the shower by 7:30. Everybody in my house gotta go to bed at 10:30. It's hard for me. I can't do the things I really want to do, like talk to my friends or hang outside. She said hanging outside makes you look like a hooker.

Certainly, the GULTMC mothers appeared to respond from a base of fear about what might happen to their daughters; parental anxiety at times was uncontrollable. As a consequence, parental discipline and supervision were often ineffectual.

Paradoxically, when racial/ethnic and gender role commitment appears to be settling, mothers become unduly anxious. Mothers become painfully aware of the daughter's reproductive maturity as signaling the loss of childhood attachment. Maternal anxieties, at this time, generate worries about premature parenthood and physical safety. Loss for the mother represents the loss of her daughter as child and loss of control over environmental events. Generally, in low-income neighborhoods, strict disciplinary methods are apportioned to girls during adolescence. At this time mothers believe that their daughters must earn their trust. Most mothers want to trust their daughters to make sensible decisions. Mothers, in such circumstances, are painfully aware of the social consequences of too early sexual initiation. And, while teenage daughters interpret their mother's disciplinary efforts as harsh and severe, mothers see themselves as protecting their daughters from the dangers of street life as well as the harsh realities of managing the social inconsistencies of a hostile racist environment.

Emergent among the GULTMC girls was the development of a free-spoken, independent, and spirited behavioral style I identify as "smart and sassy." This style of relating, characterized by assertive personal agency, was mediated through a colorful "slang" language:

Sometimes, I don't believe my mom knows what she's saying to me. I tell her, "Listen up! You need to learn how to talk to people, because you can't be like that. You can't be up and start screaming at me." I'm serious! You know what I'm sayin! She just starts yellin. But, I tell her. "Yo, just chill. You're making me and your self freak out." Like today I'm in my room and like anything can be out of order. She's a cleaning freak. And, she's like, "Marita, Marita, Marita, this and this." And I say, "Mom, hold up, chill out! Don't be yelling at me! I don't think you know what you're doin." She don't realize she yellin at me 'cause she's like, "I was yellin?" So I can't take it out on her. So that's what she really needs to do, change the way she talks.

While this relational style may have aggravated maternal anxiety, it certainly was not a style unfamiliar to mothers. Possibly, it was the mothers' familiarity with this relational style that caused concern. As noted in the previous section, Walker (1983) has noted that, in the black idiom, a female relational style of being "womanish," emergent in childhood, is generally curtailed. Here I provide Walker's definition of *womanish*:

From womanish. (Opp. of "girlish", i.e. frivolous, irresponsible, not serious). From the black folk expression of mothers to female children, "You acting womanish," i.e., like a woman. Usually referring to outrageous, audacious, courageous or *willful* behavior. Wanting to know more and in greater depth than is considered "good" for one. Interested in grow-up doings. Acting grown up. Being grow-up. Interchangeable with another Black folk expression: "You trying to be grown." Responsible. In charge. *Serious.* (p. xi)

Although the period for learning grown-up behaviors is a necessary part of the adolescent course, mothers understandably were anxious as they tried to balance responses to their daughters demands for grown-up treatment and their own fears about premature sexual activity. While the girls saw themselves skillfully engaging in arguments with their mothers, mothers saw their daughters undermining parental authority. Apter (1990) has suggested that in arguing with their mothers, adolescent girls become differentiated in their gender identity in that a sense of power and internalized controls are developed. Even so, the mothers of the GULTMC girls faced realistic fears about the social dangers of inner-city communities.

Since parents and adolescents experience discrepant social ecologies, parental perceptions about what adolescents do and how they spend their time are not altogether based on an accurate understanding of the activities that actually occupy adolescents' time. Commonly, parental perceptions about adolescent behaviors are often guided by the consequences of the parents' experiences and behaviors during their own adolescent period. Thus, the purpose of disciplinary prescriptions, for many parents, is designed so that adolescent children avoid the mistakes that were incurred during the parental adolescence period (Steinberg, 1990). Evidently, adolescent females know local neighborhoods as real, exciting, and familiar, despite recognition that there are "certain bad elements in the neighborhood, up to no good." For instance, the GULTMC girls did not see their neighborhoods or communities nearly as menacing and dangerous as parents. As communal ties to the neighborhood were mainly peer based, maternal anxiety was heightened. Still, during the early adolescent period among peers, parental lessons about safety and protection from neighborhood dangers are processed. At this time, peer associations are differentiated and neighborhood risks are evaluated. As meaning synthesis develops coherence and becomes crystallized, neighborhood dangers are realistically perceived, certainly by middle to late adolescence. Karen, a 17-year-old PANSI female, aptly describes the dangerous activities that occurred in her public housing neighborhood:

> There is something always going on that just makes you scared most of the time. It makes you shamed too, to know that these things go on in our black neighborhoods. I know of murders, rape, muggings, and there is drug use and selling. But, there is a boys' and girls' club gym and a lot of my friends, them that want to stay out of trouble go there. I guess, I think that if there were more parents' meetings things could be better in our neighborhoods.

Girls who develop core competencies of resilience make changes in their environments that will accommodate more beneficial peer affiliations. For instance, Karen saw her school environment to be as risky and dangerous as the neighborhood in which she lived. As a result, Karen made a decision to transfer from day to night school. She decided that the peers with whom she associated during the day school hours were negative influences. Karen was often suspended for fighting and truancy, which placed her at risk for school dropout. She thought she would do better in an environment with older, more mature students who were attending evening and night classes. Karen was in the eleventh grade when she made this decision. She was firmly committed to graduating from high school. By middle and late adolescence, realistic evaluations of environmental and peer hazards have been completed and have become integrated into a repertoire of competency skills that make it possible for resilient girls to navigate their social worlds.

On the other hand, early age girls are just beginning to sort out the meaning of their relationships with parents. The following excerpts from group sessions exemplify the temper of mother-daughter relations:

REASEE: My mother knows everything, it's hard to fool her. She's weird, she just knows everything.

JOHNETTA: My mother is just like me. She's quiet, no not quiet, she is a square. She's goofy.

MARIKA: The whole summer I didn't like my mother no more 'cause she used to make me stay at home. So I can't stand my mother. I hate her. So I can't stand my mother. I told her I hate her now . . . so I guess she's getting me back for you know now, trying to be strict on me still and I didn't do nothing.

ERNESTINE: You know, one thing I hate about my mother, she always wants me to baby-sit. The only time I get a high temper is when my mother does something that I don't like. But, she's mean. I try and talk to her. When she goes out and I baby sit, I say where you going? She says, "That's none of your concern. I'll be back."

The discord familiar to the mother-daughter relationship in early adolescence is quieted considerably, if not altogether passed, by the middle and late phases. Exceptions to the lessening of mother-daughter disharmony was when the intensity of the negative affect toward the mother was accompanied by the daughter assuming a parenting role in relation to her younger siblings. Ernestine, for instance, who often had to care for her younger siblings, avoided "baby-sitting" tasks by staying away from home—night, evening, and after school curfews were broken all too frequently. As Ernestine was unresponsive to parental discipline, the conflict between her and her mother only escalated. When Ernestine's home base was no longer a sanctuary, her street activities became more commonplace.

Moreover, for most GULTMC girls age-appropriate meaning-making behaviors ordinarily took place among peers where emergent new selves could be validated. But even as GULTMC females experienced emotional disruptions in maternal relations, they did not necessarily experience themselves as being disconnected from maternal care and affection. It is the identification with mother that seemed central for African American females throughout the adolescent period. The following GULTMC group exchange depicts feelings about relational connections and also about how peers help the girls arrive at meaning synthesis concerning maternal relations:

TERISA: My mother knocks me upside my head when I do wrong. You know one thing, I hate her because she is always wanting me to baby-sit.

GEORGETTE: My mother is so strict, she don't let me do nothin'.

JULIA: The whole summer I didn't like my mother no more because she made me stay at home in the evenings.

TONI: But your mother do that because she loves you. Mothers can't let you do just anything you want to do.
HARIKA: Yeah mothers are strict alright, but they do things for you that show you they care. My mother buys for us before she buys for herself.
TERISA: I don't know—Ummm. Maybe you're right.
HARIKA: Me and my mother we have a mother day so that we can talk about how we feel—sometimes we do some things that we . . .
TONI: Yeah! Like my mother she like my best friend, she tells me she loves me . . . and says when I get older she wants a lot of things for me.

Nonetheless, it is expected that the interest in the peer group during this early period will be outgrown as intimate but discretionary friendships develop in the middle and late period. During this period there is less need to utilize peers to synthesize and clarify meanings. Paradoxically, the fractious quality of the GULTMC's mother-daughter relationship was also common to relationships with peers, but took on a different meaning in the peer context. Typically, the quarrelsomeness of peer relationships, for the GULTMC girls, played out in a cultural idiom of humorous repartee that sometimes turned to hostile physical confrontations.

Peer relations also appear to undergo dramatic change as females become more selective in the choices of friendships. Developmentally, by the middle and late adolescence period, the adolescent occupies a different psychosocial space. She is less self-absorbed and has a more genuine empathic appreciation and acceptance of others. Simply, the late-aged female adolescent is more likely to seek intimacy in the domain of intersubjective relatedness than her younger cohorts are. Apparently, the dramatic relational change that occurs between mother and daughter is directed by the daughter's emotional developmental needs. The middle and late adolescent female wants validation as a woman, and when this shift occurs, the identification with the mother is consciously sought. Developmentally, the fact that the GULTMC females could tolerate a high degree of mother-daughter conflict while sustaining attachment suggested that they had achieved some level of self-coherence and synthesis that made self-differentiation possible. Moreover, self-differentiation while sustaining attachment suggests that adolescent girls can be empathically attuned to both their own developmental needs and the needs of others. Accordingly, this is the essence of a care protective sensibility or affective validation intellect, a component of intersubjective relatedness (see Figure 3.1).

In the PANSI study females did not report serious discordant maternal relations. PANSI females were older adolescents, in a different phase of development, and more likely to articulate an appreciation of their mothers' long-suffering circumstances as poor women who had the enormous task of taking care of families, often as single parents. Understandably, the PANSI pregnant females were likely to be sensitive about meeting the needs of their expectant infant and thus were sympathetic about the hardships of parenting, but nonpregnant females also expressed an appreciative sentiment for maternal responsibilities. For the PANSI females, mother was the most frequent person identified as the ideal person held in esteem and the most important older person preparing them for adulthood.[8] Rita, a pregnant 17-year-old PANSI female, spoke of her relationship with her mother:

> My mother works so hard. She is a certified nurse's aid, but she still doesn't make much money. She usually works in nursing homes. She is so considerate and responsible. Sometimes she tries to work two jobs even though she has high blood pressure—but she does this just to make ends meet. Now that I am 17, we have a better relationship because I have a better understanding of what she was trying to tell me about what not to do when I was 11. I think that I gave her a hard time then, when she be trying to talk to me, sometimes I would just leave out the house, go be with my friends. Then I just didn't want to be around her. Now we talk a lot. About the pregnancy, well she said everybody makes a mistake once. Now I have to be responsible. I'm willing to do what I have to do for my baby. If I let it happen again, the second time is no mistake. I don't spend so much time with my then so-call friends. I'm very careful now about who I associate with—who I call my friends.

Apparently, late-aged adolescent girls, both pregnant and nonpregnant, can arrive at a well-balanced sense of self with respect to sex-typing roles and sexuality once coital initiation takes place. Indeed, the transition from virginal to nonvirginal status is a consequential developmental marker and is contextually mediated (Brooks-Gunn, 1989). Most of the PANSI females did not believe that having sex made them feel grown-up, but once sexual initiation had taken place, it became a pivotal point for moving toward greater affective intimacies with mothers regardless of whether pregnancy had occurred. Apparently, from the female perspective, sexual intimacies place greater demands on relationships for affective connection. Subsequent to the sexual awakening that resulted from coital initiation, the PANSI females articulated a more empathic understanding of their mothers. This may well be because for the PANSI females, the mean age for sexual initiation was 16 years. Perhaps once sexual initiation has taken place parental remonstrance about sexual activity and accompanying fears of premature pregnancy are less threatening to both mother and daughter.

Additionally, it may well be that as girls mature developmentally, the shift in the daughter's perception of self and mother as two women bonded in sisterhood secures the mother-daughter relational connection in a way that was not possible before sexual initiation. Or it may be that maturation alone secures mother-daughter attachment. PANSI respondent 17-year old Alesha, a high school senior, was a virgin who had decided to use contraceptives because she wanted to be prepared in the event she decided to have sex. Alesha had been using contraceptives for approximately 1 year. She was ambitious and was planning to attend college. Alesha's relationship with her mother was intimate and open:

> I guess I just think my mom is wonderful because she helps me to think through things. She's someone I can just talk to. I think we have good communication in our family because we can talk about our feelings. We can share what we think about things. She was the one who told me that when I got ready to use birth control to come and tell her about it. I talk to her about my career goals and what I want to do with my life too. My mother tells me that the main thing in life is to be truthful and honest.

Smart and Sassy Behaviors

Developing Self-Efficacy, Recognition, and Social Competence

Obviously, the genus of racial/ethnic identity issues is dealt with early in relational connections that take place within both the family and one's community. In early aged adolescence, as the adolescent becomes aware of the biological and cognitive changes that forecast radical changes in the life course, racial, ethnic, and gender psychosocial issues surface for meaning synthesis and eventual resolution. Thus, adolescents are motivated during this developmental period to create a social identity that is contextually mediated. Erikson (1968, 1969) credited identity as anchored in social life as he postulated that the communal location of the individual is essential to psychological development. Although Erikson did not go too far afield from the postulates of psychoanalytic theory, his idea that the maturational process is grounded contextually was inventive for its time. While the Eriksonian thesis of the normative development of negative identity among American Negros cannot be fully accepted, there is something uniquely paradoxical about the social location of the African American in the very society that deems her or him somehow outside the American experience. Dill (1990) has argued that the African American experience in America is a dialectical one. She suggests that there is a "simultaneity of conflict and interdependence which characterize black-white relations" (p. 70).

The African American female adolescent must navigate her adolescent journey in a way that advances the settlement of her identity as an African American female. As was previously mentioned, the sense of being and becoming a black woman is derived from the maternal relationship. To develop self-efficacy, recognition, and social competence, cornerstones of sound mental health, racial identity resolution must be positive and self-affirming (see Figures 3.1 and 3.4). In American society, race has been constructed in such a way that certain undesirable characteristics are attributed to minority racial groups based on a social hierarchy of unequal power and privilege. Structures are then created to control, constrain, or eliminate those who are racially marginalized within the power hierarchy. Consequently, the least powerful or privileged (African Americans) commonly carry out transactions in oppressive and hostile environments. Indeed, the social geography of race is such that members of both minority and majority races experience racial identity problems (Frankenberg, 1993). Presently, scholars use various conceptual frameworks (assimilation, accommodation, multiculturalism, ethnicity, and dual perspective) to describe the adaptation and adjustment of racial/ethnic minority groups within a majority culture (Atkinson et al., 1993; Chau, 1991; De Hoyos et al., 1986; Devore & Schlesinger, 1996; Norton, 1978; Pinderhughes, 1979). Bifurcation, the sense of a double consciousness or the experience of living in two worlds, is one framework commonly used to explain adjustment (Chestang, 1972a&b; DuBois, 1903). The concept, however, suggests far more complexity than is commonly interpreted by scholars.

The internalization of oppression has been the most salient conceptualization of bifurcated adaptation when it is explicated as a model of duality/opposition. When interpreted in this vein, bifurcation suggests a deficit or victimized view of adaptation. Moreover, explanations of the African American experience viz a lens of oppression and victimization eschew explications of affirmative implications of African American history and culture. Simply put, such explanations leave out the ethics of African American resistance: what African Americans affirm about being black and what they affirm about being American (Cone, 1972; Murray, 1970). At best, the concept of a double consciousness represents identity as complex.

Actually, racial self-devaluation may be experienced as normative if it is considered as an integral feature of the bicultural self-development process (Boykin, 1983, 1986; Cross, 1991). As such, the development of identity in African Americans encompasses behavioral and psychological responses that mediate, negotiate, and repudiate oppressive conditions. I propose that negative and positive racial self-valuations may coexist while personal integrity is sustained. A strength perspective would clarify bifurcation as providing self-experiences for the development of bicultural competence or cultural flexibility. As a matter of fact, biculturalism may be a valid concept to explicate the experiences of African Americans' cultural flexibility, since cultural meaning systems define socialization experiences (Bruner, 1990; De Anda, 1984). Inherent in the notion of biculturalism is the idea that Euro-American and Afro-American cultural ethos are both constituents of the identity formation of African Americans. Moreover, both domains represent coherent realms of cultural integrity (Boykin, 1983).

Sustaining Connection to Family and Fictive Kin

Female adolescents experience a normative relational crisis at the emergence of adolescence, since awareness develops at this time that it is socially expected that one must separate or disconnect from family. Heretofore, self-development has taken place in relation to others, providing a sense of connection, care, nurturance, and mutuality. Society demands the severance of parental ties for adulthood adaptation. Thus, for adolescent females, the devaluation of gender relational values brings self-esteem considerations to the forefront (Gilligan et al., 1988; Surrey, 1991). To be sure, the African American female teen experiences this normative crisis, but her developmental trajectory is confounded by the fact that she undergoes a similar crisis because of her cultural group membership. A paramount issue for African American female adolescents is a perceived social expectation of, or demand for, separation from family and from one's fictive kinship group. Societal oppression of minority groups gives members a sense of shared experiences. Cultural dissonance is a core dilemma that comes to the forefront for the African American female at the onset of adolescence. Moreover, she perceives, in a new way, not only the societal devaluation of her gender, but also more importantly as a racial minority, her cultural reference group. On both accounts, this real and perceived devaluation is played out in the school setting, where cultural values are transmitted that are markedly different from feminist and Afro-American prosocial values. Thus, it could be argued that the accomplishment of bicultural competence is problematized in the school setting.

The female adolescent does not want to separate from what is valued. Rather, she seeks to change the content of her relationships in such a way that developmental changes are validated and her racial/ethnic group affiliation is supported. The self is formed and re-formed within the context of the cultural group, which is the matrix for the creation of personal meaning and self-narrative. Indeed, biographical narratives of African American luminaries document the observation that Afro-American group identity carries enormous meaning and purpose (Lawrence-Lightfoot, 1994; McClain, 1986). Hence, the experience of isolation/separation from the group can be problematic and painful and may contribute to poor mental health. Moreover, disconnection from one's cultural reference group not only generates guilt and shame and creates cultural dissonance, but also deprives the individual of psychological supports to cope with the stress of a racist society.

Developing Strategies of Resistance

Foremost, African American girls must develop strategies of resistance for self-liberation to counteract racial victimization (Ward, 1991) and gender devaluation. The development of healthy social identities must be anchored in social experiences that provide worth and value as an African American female. Also, the achievement of bicultural competence must take place. When African American girls construct ways to defy racial/cultural devaluation, are they at the same time asserting a diverse female identity? Do they in fact voice claims of self-affirmation of their difference? Do African American girls knowingly choose to project, in dress and hairstyles, a different standard of beauty? Is sassy behavior as negative as it appears on first examination? Or is sassy conduct (a willful, outspoken, independent, spirited behavioral style) a healthy evolving strategy of resistance? When considering how African American girls develop ways to resist racial/cultural devaluation such questions readily come to mind.

Black girls' sassy conduct is a central feature of identity exploration. The common inference of sassiness is defiant conduct. Notwithstanding considering a strengths perspective of sassy conduct, a counterpoint inference is candidness, courage, determination, and assertiveness—clearly, strengths needed to challenge racial/gender stereotypes and biases and to master bicultural competence. Hypothetically, sassiness can be a promising phase in the development of black girls, serving fundamental expressive functions for identity exploration. Foremost, it serves to offset feelings of helplessness and powerlessness when confronted with racial/gender stereotypes and biases, thereby fostering the development of self-efficacy. Moreover, sassy conduct is itself a strategy for resisting social devaluation. Ultimately, black girls must learn to discern environmental responses without attributing unwarranted self-blame. In the following narrative, a middle-school GULTMC early aged teen tries to discern a teacher's attitude about the learning expectations for black students. In other words, the student is making an effort to develop a coherent narrative meaning about the teachers with whom she must interact. She reflectively, but humorously, articulates:

> Sometimes I think the teachers are afraid of us. Like this one teacher kept asking me what kind of grade should she give this boy. Pl-ee-ase. So, it makes you wonder what teachers are, why are they there. I feel sorry for them. Once two girls were fighting and the teacher didn't do nothing. Just kept backing away saying stop. And then sometimes, they just don't do their job right because we would be on the same book forever. For me, I don't like staying in the same place. Kids want to be excited, kids want to be explorers. They'll give you an F if you talk in class. Pl-ee-ase, give us credit for work.

Similarly, the newspaper story that follows illustrates the burdensome task of African American adolescents trying to make intelligible meaning of socially denigrating situations.

> School administrators confronted Black teen females in a suburban school with expulsion because of the way the girls dressed their hair. School administrators, in a white suburban community, banned Black ethnic hair styles (i.e. cornrow braids). Although the school administrators had been informed otherwise, the hairstyle, they believed represented gang membership. Transgressions of the coiffure ban resulted in school suspensions. The situation invoked the following response from a 12-year-old girl. "They should be worrying about our education, not what we have in our hair." ("A Question of Style vs. Intention," 1996).

These illustrations speak to issues of mutual recognition, as well as unempathic and negative intersubjectivity on the part of school personnel. Equally important, the citations epitomize the problematization of bicultural competence in a school setting. In particular, the outspokenness of the teen's response to the school personnel's appraisals indicate not only attempts at meaning synthesis, but also healthy resistance to the negative attribution of their social identities. Negative affect and oppositional behaviors are likely to occur when one is feeling helpless and devalued, especially in instances of blamelessness or where one is falsely judged. Racial stereotypes are powerfully entrenched in American culture. The outspoken response of the teenager in the second passage indicates resistance to racial stereotyping and social devaluation. It is likely that this young girl became empowered in her resistance. Black girls learn early that they must demand respect—that respect is not automatically bestowed. The more common experience is that black girls are likely to feel socially denigrated once they come face to face with racial stereotyping (Collins, 1990). How to manage such situations requires meaning synthesis and sustaining self-relatedness while handling feelings of self-depreciation. Unfortunately this challenge of creating healthy resistance in a socially devalued circumstance is not only a burdensome task, but is an ordeal that many African American adolescents must learn to manage successfully. Consider 20-year-old Venus Williams's comments after winning the Wimbledon Grand Slam Tennis Championship in 2000. As an African American, Venus Williams is the third winner of the championship. Althea Gibson was a two-time winner Grand Slam winner in 1958, 42 years prior to Williams's win. Williams's comments are in response to a reporter's inquiry about how difficult it must have been for Althea Gibson:

> Yeah, it had to be hard because people were unable to see past color. Still these days it's hardly any different because you have to realize it's only been 40 years. How can you change years and centuries of being biased in 40 years? So, realistically, not too much has changed. But, I really appreciate how hard it was. You realize not everyone wants you to win, not everyone's going to support you—and that's O.K. (Rhoden, 2000).

Obviously, unwarranted social devaluation by adults should not occur at all. Adults should represent respectable authority role models in the lives of adolescents. Adults are expected to provide the mutual recognition and wise counsel that adolescents need, especially in the school setting, where adolescents are oftentimes first introduced to the meanings of social responsibility and citizenry. Evidently, black teens will find themselves in situations where they are expected to accommodate their own social devaluation. It is not surprising, when, that when black adolescents find themselves in such situations they will balk at such treatment through outright resistance. The illustrations depicted suggest that black adolescent girls will not collude in their own racial denigration. However, when resistance is destructive and unhealthy, black girls will likely engage in avoidance or oppositional behaviors. Tuning-out of the school environment by castigating successful school achievers as "acting white" may be a typical response toward those presumed to be in collusion with the oppressor. Resilience is operative when adolescents can meet racially devalued situations or social inconsistencies without feeling self-blame, helplessness, and powerlessness. Still, this is a lot to ask of teens. To deal with essential identity exploration issues of race, ethnicity, and gender requires of most black adolescents a level of maturity that many have not yet attained. In trying to cope with these issues it is no small wonder that many black adolescents are confused about who they are, where they are going, and how they will achieve maturational goals. Adolescents expect adult guidance, even if minimal, in dealing with fundamental identity exploration issues. The school environment, where adolescents must synthesize meaningful coherence about self, family, and society, is one of the most important contexts external to the family. It is in the school environment that social duty and social responsibility should become operationalized.

Plainly, healthy resistance is dependent on positive, understanding, and reassuring responses from significant others. African American girls' genuine predicament is the parallel need for resistance and connection and the social need to develop bicultural competence. They must capitalize on the strengths of sassiness while preserving kinship ties and developing and sustaining connections to social ecologies (e.g., schools, churches). The inherent tension here is that outspokenness and boldness may not be seen as strengths. Consequently, negative contextual responses to such behavior may cause black girls' disconnection from otherwise supportive systems.

Conclusions

The psychological stress of both racial victimization and gender devaluation is more keenly experienced in adolescence than in earlier developmental periods. Moreover, the felt demand, at adolescence, to move outside the confines of both one's blood and kinship group may be experienced as self-threatening. At the onset of adolescence, hypersensitivity to social devaluation, coupled with anxiety about meeting needs for connection and resistance and emotions of helplessness and powerlessness, comes to the forefront. Conjecturally, this profound vulnerability is outgrown as triadic meanings of race, gender, and ethnicity become synthesized; complex identities develop; and prosocial resistance is realized. Social victimization and devaluation may be consistently resisted and opposed in variant behavioral/psychological responses. When destructive behaviors (e.g., substance abuse, premature childbearing) are used to manage identity problems in oppressive environments, a survival existence is maintained, not a liberated one (Ward, 1991). Ultimately, the African American resilient female adolescent uses resistance for the self-evolution of empowerment and self-acceptance, healthy attributes to navigate the context of racialist environments.

Notes

1. Whether in the close quarters of households as domestic servants or as field hands in cotton fields, black families reasoned that the proximity to white males rendered their daughters vulnerable to sexual exploitation. Black females were often educated to enter professional occupations such as teaching to avoid employment as domestic or field hands. Not surprisingly, as professional employees in segregated institutions, black female relationships with white males tended to be more distant. Paradoxically, the social circumstances that led to the protection of the black female may well have contributed to lessening male leadership roles in family life. Moreover, as the white middle class proliferated, there was a high demand for domestic service jobs in northern urban areas. As a result, black women left southern sharecropping farms to secure employment in the northern cities. Franklin (1997) has persuasively argued that black women's migration north contributed to the rise of mother-only households in urban areas. She contends that women mostly migrated to the North alone, and when black male spouses subsequently followed, unable to secure employment, they sought jobs in regions far distant from the urban areas to which they had migrated. These migratory patterns weakened familial ties and strained male-female relationships.

2. A note of caution here should be registered regarding a European worldview in American society. Early in America's history much of what was considered an elitist class in American society was considered English or white Anglo-Saxon Protestant, as seen in both the early New York and Boston Brahmin upper classes during the era of Edith Wharton and Henry James. Commonly, America's upper classes spent extended periods in England and continental Europe. In the Colonial Period, both Benjamin Franklin and Thomas Jefferson were ministers to France. In particular, Jefferson was sympathetic to the French Revolution and influenced by the philosophical ideas of John Locke. Indeed, America's connection to an aristocratic European culture was well established. Moreover, the American Founding Fathers were learned men and as a result were exposed to European ideas and culture. Certainly Jefferson appeared charmed by the elitist sophistication of European culture of manners, food, drink, and furniture and brought this ambience to his beloved Monticello. Unquestionably the European sensibility has been integrated into American culture and has become the inheritance of all Americans. Certainly, this is the case especially of southern blacks, who lived in proximity to the aristocratic southern whites either as slaves or later as domestics. I recognize that some scholars have made a distinction between house slaves and field slaves (Frazier, 1957). While this dichotomy may have some merit, all slaves observed the manner of the daily life of the slave master whether in close or distant quarters. Moreover, this narrow and limited dichotomy omits the very valuable artisan class of black slaves who were the masonries, welders, carpenters, blacksmiths, and the like. While the distinction between European and ethnic culture is valid—I do not mean to imply here that the two are such distinct and disparate categories—they are distinct sensibilities informed by similar and uniquely dissimilar perspectives where both are enjoined as idiosyncratically American. Albert Murray (1970, 1978, 1996) argued that the Negro's cultural sensibility is indubitably an American one. As I have described elsewhere, the cultural orientations depicted are obvious comprehensive generalizations and are designed to be—they are similar in conceptualization to the cultural orientation constructs of anthropologists Florence and Clyde Kluckhohn. As America becomes more and more defined as a multicultural society, the demise of a sophisticated European continental upper-class consciousness as the idealized class sensibility to emulate is likely to occur.

3. In the era of legal apartheid—the pre–civil rights era, certainly in my elementary and high school days—similar labeling was attributed to high-achieving students. In those days students were likely to label the high achievers as "acting proper." It is likely that then issues of racial oppression were quite overt to signify whiteness and such labeling simply was not necessary. It is possible, however, that the meanings then as now were similar if not the same. Moreover, it may well be that contemporary black adolescents experience "historical dislocation." Nouwen (1972) has adapted this term. Nouwen borrows this term from Lifton (1970). Nouwen uses the term to define the "nuclear man," who represents a break with significant self-defining cultural traditions that cause him to adopt a nihilistic posture. I suggest that the struggle for civil rights and integration, for African Americans, was a cause that became the crucible for being. Once civil rights were achieved with the dismantling of Jim Crow segregation, it was as if the barrier for full participation in American democracy had been removed, while in fact racism continues to exist—the "dream deferred" remains. I believe African American youth are responding to what they perceive as a "dream deferred." It is likely that street youth have no connection with the idealism of the civil rights movement or the history of struggle for racial justice prior to the 1960s.

4. I used Collins's four dimensions as epistemological categories or ways of knowing in the construction of the instrument for the PANSI study, which made the instrument culturally sensitive.

5. Contemporary female adolescents are exposed to female images that appear to be quite different than those in earlier periods. For instance, the BET network promotes the recording industry through its televised music videos. The dancers and singers that appear in these videos perhaps will pose different kinds of issues related to beauty images, as the females shown have the benefit of makeup artists to create an image of beauty that uses a white beauty standard somewhat differently. Most dancers have fit slim bodies and, with the use of hair weaves, wear long, straight tresses. Spike Lee's film *School Daze*, in comedic storytelling, depicts the idealized beauty standard among black women as being light-skinned or near white.

6. Regarding Morrison's *The Bluest Eye*—in Grewal trenchant critique (1998) of Morrison's works she further elaborates on the cultural production of both race and gender, suggesting that woman is treated as a sight that is determined by the white male gaze, which promulgates the feminine ideal in the images of "Shirley Temple on cups, Mary Jane on candy wrappers, or Jean Harlow and Marilyn Monroe as idealized screen images" (p. 30).

7. The African proverb *"Children are the reward of life"* has historically been a supreme value of African American life, and certainly the African proverb *"It takes a village to raise a child"* is its corollary. While Hillary Rodham Clinton has popularized this latter proverb, the proverb among African American intellectuals was always seen as the consequence of placing the highest value and worth or the sanctity of life and the birth of children. Oppressive economic conditions often prevented families from improving the quality of life for their children. On the question of elective abortion, as noted nonpregnant girls were more likely not to have elected to have had elective abortions because of their family's strong disapproval of abortions.

8. The PANSI sample held their mothers in high esteem. When the girls were asked about the person they admired and respected most, 47.4 percent of the pregnant girls' responses were mother; while 50 percent of the nonpregnant girls' responses were mother.

5 Care Protective Sensibility and Role Model Formulation

Racism, gender discrimination, and economic exploitation, as inherited age-long complexes, require the Black community to create and cultivate values and virtues in their own terms so that they prevail against the odds with moral integrity.

(Cannon, 1996, p. 58)

Every ethnic group has a heritage of its own and is also heir to symbols of inspiration as different as Michael Jordan and William Shakespeare. All people are heir to everything of wonder that anyone has produced, regardless of race, gender, and place.

(Crouch, 1995, p. 32)

A central feature of the developing adolescent is the maturing capacity to modulate the surrounding environment and to select role models.

(Elliott & Feldman, 1990, p. 5)

Introduction

The person-process-context model (see Figure 2.1) incorporates a life span developmental psychosocial perspective through its emphases on the person as an active agent in the environment and on self-formation as a lifelong process. The model suggests that adolescents' multidimensional experiences be embedded in a broad social context. While I have argued that identity exploration is critical to the adolescent phase, the extraordinariness of this period, however, is primarily because of its transition from childhood to adulthood. Moreover, the period is pivotal since it represents the onset of self-formative consciousness reflected in a social identity. The salutogentic emphasis of the person-process-context model presupposes that self-formation is a lifelong process. In this chapter and in subsequent chapters, I address the remaining integrative developmental domains (care protective sensibility and role model formulation, decision making and dating/mate selection, and opportunity mobility and adulthood preparation) as paired spheres of experiences. The domains coupled in this manner reflect self-experiences as integrative correlates that embody age-typical tasks. In effect, all the domains indicate fields of self-experience in which the working through of maturational tasks occur. *As such, the maturational tasks of the developmental domains become organizers of identity, identity themes, and personal meaning systems.* Additionally, the domains reflect dimensions of experiences that build self-coherence—that embody the internal psychic core of the individual. Self-coherence, as discussed in the previous chapter, is seen as integral to healthy development. The developmental domains are the building blocks of the self-coherence that is eventually portrayed in a social identity.

Moreover, the model posits structural strain as representing adaptive challenges at any given point in the life span. Additionally, the adolescent period is seen as a "zone of proximal development" (Vygotsky, 1978, p. 87) desirably facilitated by social interaction with able adult individuals with whom one can identify in order to realize the upper limits of one's abilities. This is representative of a developmental reserve capacity allowed in maturational growth (Heckhausen, 1999). In the person-process-context model the values of connection, care, empathy, and mutuality, as previously indicated, are core African American ethnic values. These ethnic values shape the coping strategies that give meaning to life and therefore are critical in the development of moral agency.

Perhaps more than any other developmental domains, the care protective sensibility is grounded in the spiritual heritage that characterizes much of African American life. The care protective sensibility domain refers to the affective and behavioral expressions of care, loyalty, and nurturance in relation to others. Learning to care for others evolves over time during the adolescent period. This evolving sensibility of care and nurturance is central to the adolescent's self-view or social identity. It becomes a self-defining personal-communal view for adaptive living (see Figure 3.1). The essence of the care protective sensibility is the *self-relatedness* to others embodied in personal and communal life-affirming meaning. The African American church community is the most common social context for the developmental of this empathic connection sensibility. Paradoxically, since their migration to northern urban areas, African Americans are more dependent on the church community for the expression of the care protective sensibility. In rural southern communities where the church was the center of communal life, empathic connection practices dominated daily life. In urban communities, the church competes with many cultural institutions for the attention and involvement of inner-city inhabitants. The care protective sensibility domain grows out of the four-dimensional standpoint personified by an ethnic-cultural idiom of caring and personal accountability of intersubjectivity, as identified in the previous chapter. When black adolescents incorporate this ethnic idiomatic value, they develop personal virtue and enact ethical values. Moral agency is especially needed for undervalued youth coming of age in a hostile environment of ambiguous choices and relational estrangement. All youth as they mature along the life span must learn to develop the capacity to make commitments to personal goals *without* assurances of outcomes. This evolving capacity is a prime symptom of strength of character that is nourished by the construction of meaningful identities (Keniston, 1965). However, in a society of deeply embedded racist ideologies, African American youth have an added burden, as they must develop the capacity for care, nurturance, and moral commitments despite disempowering structural conditions that communicate a devalued self. Moreover, structural strain may overlay pathological family circumstances that can deepen the personal suffering of a black girl. Obviously, a black girl chooses neither of these processes or contextual conditions, but they must be contended with as she moves along life's course.

Undeniably, the human condition is ambiguous and suffering is a dynamic existential ingredient of living. African Americans did not choose mental and physical suffering engendered by racist ideologies. Nonetheless, African Americans can and do exercise choice in the manner in which suffering experiences are responded to. Inasmuch as adverse social economic conditions resulting from racist ideologies have persisted in varying forms over time, African Americans have had to develop moral wisdom from their anguish and misery as an oppressed minority (Cannon, 1996). It is not uncommon for individuals to develop resilience in oppressive conditions. In effect by exercising the will to struggle in miserable circumstances, individuals become resilient by finding life-affirming meaning in the praxis of suffering itself. In this way, the misery of the situation is transcended (Frankl, 1985). For example, American cultural icon Oprah Winfrey, an African American woman, is the consummate inspirational individual living out the protective care sensibility ethnic values. She has interacted with the public concerning her anguished adolescent trauma of rape, pregnancy, and abortion for transcendence and moral agency. Winfrey personifies the protective care sensibility, which has, in turn, enabled her to create intimacy, care, and personal accountability with television audiences. This translation of protective care sensibility values to a medium that is remote and public is the genius of Winfrey and, perhaps, is largely responsible for her phenomenal media success.

The protective care sensibility is linked to role model formulation in that the protective care sensibility represents those affective qualities demonstrated by an individual that communicate emphatic connection without which a role model could not be selected. Role model formulation suggests the capacity to create from one's experiences an integrated ethical and social value system to inform personal decisions. Specifically, the adolescent must learn to assess behaviors of persons in their environments and to reach decisive judgments about these behaviors. This formulative process about the behavior of others occurs concomitantly with the development of a value system. Equally important, role model formulation is greatly influenced by what the ethos defines as gender prototypes. This has enormous implications when one considers that gender roles have undergone tremendous change in contemporary culture in the last 30 years. While this culture shift in gender roles has been influenced greatly by the feminist movement, the movement itself has changed as gender roles themselves vacillate. Consequently, idealized gender roles have yet to solidify with constancy. Although empirical research regarding media influences on adolescent development is relatively recent, social scientists suggest that American adolescents, and particularly black adolescents, may be negatively influenced by media culture, namely television (Boykin & Ellison, 1995).

Media Culture and Self-Relatedness in Social Context

The television media consistently fabricates and markets role models by means of dramatic and comedic storytelling and spectator sports. The power of the television media to project story characters as gender prototypes is enormous. After all, the strength of fictional characterization is directly related to the intersubjective (empathic) qualities the character portrays. For example, an anti-hero or anti-heroine

character is readily identifiable as a role model if the character is drawn sympatheti-
cally. The power of the *Godfather* films was the sympathetic characterizations of its
central characters despite the fact that they were murderers, drug profiteers, gam-
blers, and the like. Interestingly, Oprah Winfrey has commented that television is
not a source of substantive narratives. Favoring a preference for reading with the creation of book clubs, Winfrey has commented that she views television programming
as far removed from profundity and erudition. Yet it is likely that contemporary youth
have greater exposure to media culture than to literary works.

The media is a socialization agent that instills values of "materialism, in the form
of the urgency of material consumption, the status-determining efficacy of material
possessions, and the life affirming virtue of material well-being" (Boykin & Ellison,
1995, p. 115). Common opinion is that television impacts the developmental trajectory of youth, especially in the domain of role model formulation. While the impact
of the television media on the lives of young people cannot be denied, an apparent
strength, however, in inner-city black girls is to idealize and emulate persons that are
personally known to them. I postulate that inner-city black girls select adults from
their proximal environments to model because of the need to affirm mutual self-
relatedness, which underscores the care protective sensibility values of nurturance and
empathy. Two GULTMC narratives are illustrative:

> Before I came out here to Boston, I had not seen my aunt since I was 5 years old. When
> I came out to Boston me and her got back into contact with each other. I admire her be-
> cause she is the only person in my family who really did something with herself. She went
> to Yale and Harvard and now she has some kinda big position with the state board. I ad-
> mire her because I think to myself, God, she did this on her own and stuff. I admire her
> for that.

> I like Mr. Bolden. He's a good teacher. He's the type of teacher you go to his classroom
> and you know he respect you. He's a real person. He won't let you fall back on your work
> and stuff. He's white, but he is not prejudice. See, what I'm saying. At the beginning of
> the school year he told us, "Just because I am white, don't think you can't ask me stuff."
> There is like two white people in our class, but mostly everybody is black, Spanish, and
> Haitian, and some other races. He told us, "I'm everybody, I'm white, black, Spanish."
> He learned spanish. He's honest and don't push things under the rug.

One of the sessions of the GULTMC social skills intervention curriculum specifically addressed media images. Clearly, the GULTMC girls were making every effort to arrive at some level of meaning synthesis about the images portrayed in the
medium of television. The GULTMC girls seemed perceptively sophisticated in their
critique of media culture. The girls' discussion of media culture and role model formation was candidly articulated:

DOREEN: I think they do commercials that I call abusive to blacks. I saw a com-
mercial last night, you know, and the white lady was all happy and stuff talkin about
"we're family." And the black lady was all mad and stuff didn't have no family just
staring in the camera. That's what you call stereotyping or—something.
NIECEE: Yep!
SW: What about Oprah Winfrey? Do you think she's a positive role model?

Rose: Do you like Oprah Winfrey?
NIA: I don't like her. She change too much. You see her eyes now? She got blue eyes.
CLARICE: Naw! She got green eyes.
NIA: Yeah, like green-blue. Ehhhhh.
TERISA: Yep! She's like I changed my eyes to blue. So you can change your eyes to any color you want. She tries to change herself to make other people happy. She should just be herself, not change for nobody, just be who she wanna be.

The GULTMC girls were equally perceptive in their evaluation of entertainment celebrities:

ZORELLE: You know that Snoop Dog? [Snoop Dog is a West Coast rapper.] I saw him on this program on MTV. Well, he was talkin' about how in California there is a big rip between New York rap and California West Coast. And he was saying he don't get involved in that kinda stuff. If they [other rappers] want to do that, they can do that, but it's all about the music and doin' what you need to do. Then I saw him on his video and he was definitely in New York with all those skyscrapers and everything. I thought, I was like for me that sent mix messages. It's not about East Coast, West Coast—really it's all about making money anyway.
LEAH: Can I say something, not to be against you, but in a sense it did look like that, but how do you know that's what he was trying to portray?
[Everyone speaks at once]
ZORELLE: That's what I saw and it didn't match what he said. I could be wrong, but that's the way I perceived it. That's the thing, if they want to have rip between the two, that's OK. But don't say one thing to me and do another thing. That's contradiction, that's inconsistent. I can't stand that! That's manipulators!

Winfrey's biographical history shows that role models are available to persons throughout the life span. I argue that role models are readily available to black teens as idealized persons can be found in both near and distant environments. Or, as Crouch's quote at the beginning of this chapter suggests, we are all inheritors of the countless role models the human race produces. Certainly, role models can be discovered and formulated from the written word regardless of race. When derived from literature, role models are as plentiful as the imagination can conceive. To illustrate this point, consider the role model formulation of Winfrey. For Winfrey, her traumatic ordeals were authenticated at the age of 16 upon reading the celebrated African American poetess and writer Maya Angelou's well-known autobiography, *I Know Why the Caged Bird Sings*. Oprah's relationship to Ms. Angelou is atypical in that she is now a personal friend and mother figure. This is an interesting trajectory for a role model found by a 16-year-old teenage girl in the pages of a book. Self-discovery through literature is significantly relevant to the idea of the immediately availability of role models by way of the written word. The significance of Winfrey's moral self-awakening, at age 16, is that role model formulation and selection was experienced through the written word.

PATTERNING ONE'S FUTURE SELF–CARE PROTECTIVE SENSIBILITY AND ROLE MODEL FORMULATION: *"SHE'S JUST HOT"*

Vonnie Sterling sought help at Catholic Charities for substance use. Her family and the parish priest supported Vonnie in seeking help. Seventeen-year-old Vonnie lives with her 37-year-old mother, Mrs. Sterling; two brothers, Mark and Robert, ages 19 and 20, respectively; and 58-year-old Mrs. Williams, the maternal grandmother. Mrs. Sterling was married at 17 years old when she was 2 months pregnant. Mr. and Mrs. Sterling were both high school graduates. Mr. Sterling was seasonally employed as a construction worker and had a drinking problem. A year ago he was killed in an attempted street robbery in the neighborhood. Vonnie was especially close to her father. However, she had demonstrated no outward signs of grief since his death. Mrs. Sterling is employed as a daycare worker. Mrs. Williams works as an attendant in a ladies lounge in a hotel. Mark and Robert both work as hotel waiters. Vonnie is a junior in a public high school and is a B student. The family has hopes of Vonnie attending college. Vonnie dates occasionally, but has no steady boyfriend. Three years ago she was an active participant in the parish teen groups, but she no longer attends these activities. Her older brothers are very protective and discourage her from dating neighborhood boys. She works after school in the parish rectory. The family is Catholic. Mrs. Williams attends Mass regularly, although other family members only attend Mass at religious holidays, such as Christmas and Easter. The extended family occupies a three-bedroom apartment in a working-class and lower-middle-class black neighborhood in a large metropolitan northern city. In recent years the neighbor has been ravaged by drug misuse and drug trafficking, especially in crack cocaine. The family's other kin reside in the rural South. Two weeks ago Mrs. Sterling found a bag of marijuana in Vonnie's bedroom dresser drawer. When Vonnie's mother confronted her, she became angry and belligerent and accused her mother of prying and refused to speak of the matter. Several days later, Vonnie tearfully admitted that she had gotten the marijuana from a neighbor, Ruby Goldson, and that for the past 6 months she had been smoking marijuana regularly, at least twice a week. She mostly smoked it with some girls at school at one of their houses. The girlfriends with whom she "smoked weed" were of recent acquaintances. Vonnie confessed that she thought that smoking weed was beginning to interfere with her schoolwork. Vonnie said that she smoked weed because it made her forget about missing her father so much. Ruby Goldson is a 27-year-old woman who occupies an apartment, with her 30-year-old boyfriend, Charles, in the same building in which Vonnie and her family resides. Ruby is employed as a buyer in a downtown (upscale) department store. Charles is a computer operator. Vonnie claims that she admires and looks up to Ruby because "she's smart, educated, has fine clothes, and has a fine man. She's just hot." She said that Ruby had told her that smoking weed was not bad, like smoking crack, and that a lot of people did it. According to Vonnie, Ruby had started smoking marijuana at age 17. Ruby thought it would ease the pain of missing her father. Vonnie had always spent a lot time visiting Ruby since the couple moved into the building a couple of years ago. Most of the time the two looked at television and fashion magazines and talked about the soap operas. According to Vonnie, Ruby had never mentioned smoking weed until she was crying one time and couldn't stop. She had told Ruby how losing her Dad hurt and how hard it was to talk about what she was feeling with her family. She could talk to her grandmother sometimes, but talking to her always ended up with a sermon about going to Mass. *Study Questions and Issues:* (1) Discuss how you would assess Vonnie's marijuana use, e.g., experimental, dependent, addicted. Also consider whether Vonnie is at risk for use of other substances. Consider risk and protective contextual factors that impact Vonnie's substance use. Explain. (2) Discuss how you would apply the person-process-context model, especially concepts of community bridging, kin-scriptions, and nested contexts to strengthen your assessment and intervention. (3) Discuss the developmental domains of role model formulation and care protective sensibility in relation to Vonnie's relationship with Ruby Goldson. (4) Discuss the application of the collaborative intervention context model (CICM) in the case. Identify the intervention principles you think would be most helpful in working with Vonnie and her family. Explain your choices. See also: Chapters 3 and 5 and Figures 2.1 and 3.1–3.3.

"I read it over and over. I had never before read a book that validated my own existence." Oprah's story bears a haunting similarity to Angelou's: raised in a tiny town in the South by her grandmother, shuttled between her mother's and her father's big city lives, surviving such horrific experiences as being raped at a very young age, finding comfort in books. (Johnson, 1997, p. 53).

The self-validation experienced by Oprah is the result of reflexive mutual recognition. Maya Angelou, in her autobiography, asserts a sense of being and doing to which the reader (Oprah) offers a confirming response of self-discovery. As Benjamin (1988) has insightfully stated, "Recognition is . . . reflexive; it includes not only the other's confirming response, but how we find ourselves in that response" (p. 21).

Role model formulation-protective care sensibility processes are much more than this mutual recognition. The selection of a role model involves deliberative and evaluative internal processes that the adolescent undergoes subsequent to this mutual recognition of likeness. Deliberation and evaluation are internal dynamic processes that require varied interactive feedback within different contexts. Consider the case illustration "Patterning One's Future Self." Vonnie Sterling is emotionally vulnerable because of unresolved grief over the death of her father. Consequently, Vonnie is limited in her capacity to engage in deliberations that will enable her to evaluate Ruby's life. Additionally, the vignette suggests that Ruby and her companion Charles are socially isolated, which makes it impossible for Vonnie to evaluate the reaction of others to Ruby. Vonnie is not in social relationships to get feedback from others about what their thoughts are about Ruby. Normally, the weighing of the esteemed person is a process that will continue throughout the adolescent's relationship with the role model. In some respects this interactive feedback evaluation is quite necessary for role model formulation because it makes the role model accountable. In this regard, one could argue that the arts have limited influence on the imagination of youth.

In particular, one of the reasons why a literary novel or biographical story is experienced differently when translated to film is that cinema minimizes the subject's (viewer's) internal dynamic interactive connection with the subjects (actors/characters) projected on the screen (object). Consequently, the moviegoer has a relationship with the object (film) rather than to subjects (story characters). Moreover, the technological artistry of postmodern films creates a visual imagery that, in effect, overwhelms the senses, thereby weakening the viewer's relational connection to the narrative. How movie audiences respond to the estranged and almost hostile feature of contemporary films varies. Anecdotal evidence suggests that inner-city black adolescent movie audiences engage a film in dialogue, creating a cacophonous environment that the average moviegoer perhaps would find unsuitable for viewing. Thus, if black youth do engage film characters as role models they do so on the basis of the strength of the film narrative. While all adolescents have public access to literary works, exposure is largely determined by interest. Certainly, not every adolescent will be intrinsically motivated to seek the pleasures of reading. Contemporary adolescents are overexposed to the media culture of television.

Boykin and Ellison (1995) argue that media enterprises, television in particular, are a source of mainstream socialization for America's cultural ethos represented by materialism, rugged possessive individualism, mastery, control, and competition. These expressive cultural values, the authors contend, are conveyed in television narratives and advertisements that are populated by persons who are "contented, happy, and well adjusted [as well as by] persons of high status who possess power, influence, and resources" (p. 115). The authors argue that the social learning imparted by the television media is especially problematic for poor black youth since the means (instrumental values) by which end goals are accomplished are rarely, if ever, conveyed. Moreover, Boykin and Ellison assert that since television is not an interactive medium, black youth require feedback to correct misapprehensions about what they view. Youth are more likely to see movies and the like with peers rather than adults. Importantly, for the first time songs are being marketed primarily through a synthesis of simple narrative, dance, and music lyrics, commonly known as music videos. Basic television networks such as Black Entertainment Television and MTV market music videos for the adolescent consumer. Music video programming is likely to have a significant impact on the behavior of all teens. The impact that the dramatization of song lyrics through visual images has on contemporary black female adolescents' role model formulation has not been sufficiently researched.

Interestingly, there is a striking uniformity to all the female images projected in music videos; the women have ultra-thin bodies, silken-long coiffured hair, and glamorously made-up faces. The videos relate heavily laden sexual messages in both song lyrics and choreographed dances. It is not altogether clear what impact such images will have on the development of adolescent females' role model formulation. However, pop culture that encourages young girls to engage in sexualized behavior is likely to influence them negatively (Anderman, 2000). Conjecturally, the least of this is that they are likely to become prematurely sexual active or see themselves as sexual objects. Given that popular culture is dominated by visual media imagery, the idealized virtues of females are likely to undergo change since music videos are geared specifically for an adolescent market. Thus, it is not altogether clear whether earlier arguments by scholars such as Collins (1990), concerning the asexualized images of the black mammy and the matriarchy as controlling effigies of black female oppression, will have relevancy for postmodern culture. Clearly, these are areas that seem worthy of investigation and reconceptualization. Historically, differences in the social circumstances of black and white women have been used to control the oppression of both. This has been accomplished, nonetheless, in ways that white females can experience the privileges of racial superiority while depreciating their black sister cohorts.

I have stated that role model formulation suggests that valuative judgments about valued and nonvalued behaviors are personified by persons both within proximal and distal nested contexts. Moreover, role model formulation is a complex process that constitutes the mutual recognition and evaluation of the person one has chosen for patterning one's future self. The process involves that measure of identity exploration that allows the adolescent to temporarily relinquish parts of the self for self-appraisal or self-examination. In the case illustration "Patterning One's Future Self," Vonnie's sharing of her emotional hurt to Ruby is a kind of self-surrender, but it is responded to inappropriately. One could rightly argue that Ruby's response lacks personal integrity. The self-appraisal in which the adolescent engages involves the evaluation of the similarity in one's self with the older idealized individual, including the futuristic projection of the self as the now idealized person is. While likeness or sameness brings mutual recognition, the esteemed other will also possess some material effects or some personal trait that the adolescent admires or holds in esteem that she experiences as different. Thus, experienced differences are the perfect foil for admiration, awe, or esteem. The integrity of the adolescent is sustained throughout the formulation process by constant decision making that involves the application of the adolescent's developing and evolving ethical-social value system. This ethical-social value system is reflected in a care protective sensibility of intimacy, care, and personal accountability (or empathic intersubjectivity). The adolescent's empathic and idealized attachment to an admired individual (adult role model) must be regulated by the personal integrity of that adult. As is often the case, the adolescent's idealization of a role model is exaggerated. The trustworthiness and uprightness of the adult can temper the adolescent's overidealization, however. If the adult is without integrity, involvement with the adolescent becomes shallow and narcissistic and can be developmentally injurious, despite the adolescent's emotional dependence on that adult. Undoubtedly, reflexive recognition, essential to the intersubjective nature of relationships, occurs in the role model formulation process, but for healthy development it must be adaptive recognition (see Figure 3.1). Healthy role model formulation requires not only the reflexivity of mutual recognition, but also interaction that involves the sharing of self-reflections.

The Moral Agency of Sassiness and Role Model Formulation

Black adolescents are heirs to an African American legacy of moral integrity developed within the context of a socially unjust structural system. In the previous chapter, sassy behavior as willful forthrightness was referred to as a form of healthy resistance when confronted with racially denigrating circumstances. I have suggested that sassy behavior during the adolescent period emerges as an expressive function of identity exploration. Certainly, as sassiness emerges during the adolescent period, it will serve diverse functions in identity exploration (Stevens, 1998a). However, as sassiness becomes a conscious solidified expressive style of liberated resistance, I propose, it is presented as an integrated, affirming self-mode. *Sassy behavior as resistance can be viewed as resolute racial/ethnic identity characterized by moral agency. It is moral agency that provides the psychic energy to confront the dialectical condition of embracing a black identity in America with personal and communal life-affirming meaning.* Sassy behavior, seen in this light, surfaces in adolescence, but eventually becomes crystallized as a special meaning experience wherein a racial, ethnic, and gender identity is integrated and consolidated concomitant with a care protective sensibility. As the consolidation of this particular self-affirming meaning experience takes place, it enables the adolescent girl to integrate positive role models.

"Moral" is used here in the sociological sense of Goffman's (1961) concept of moral career. Moral career, according to Goffman, relates to the study of a social persona that includes an examination of the periodic sequential changes that occur within the self as well as in one's framework of reference for judging self and others. A trajectory process (career) develops in the life of a person and serves as a turning point for the individual. This turning point can serve as a transforming experience where a new identity or social persona emerges. The transforming experience has a sense of rightness and integrity about it; hence the designation of the term "moral." The concept of moral career is a way to theorize about sassiness in the development of adolescent black girls. It suggests an evolving sense of self based on historical ethnic lessons and imagery that are self-integrated to provide an affirming ethical framework for judging self and others. Historical ethnic lessons and imagery are symbolized in their concreteness and specificity in the occurrence of familial traditions as well as in the broader sense of the legacies of a people. To strengthen this point, recall the case illustration *"Historical Legacies and Self-Narratives,"* in which a specific clinical intervention was used that embodied historical narratives of brave and courageous women. In this regard the role model formulation domain is directly correlated to protective care sensibility values. Role model formulation is linked to the empathic virtues embodied in a protective care sensibility if healthy and positive role models are to be selected. The moral agency referred to here will be rooted in the spirituality of the black church, which provides ethical standards of behavior. Certainly, in the church setting, role models are convenient and accessible.

Because of America's racial apartheid, the black community developed parallel institutions for self-maintenance and self-development, the most important of which was the black church (Hamilton, 1972). Importantly, social and political resistance was modeled in the leadership of the black preacher, who not only sermonized about survival with dignity, but also preached the value of a faith filled life in the here and now. The church offered a lifeline of hope to its members (Cone, 1972; Brown, 1998). Evidently, from its inception, the black church was an institution of structured social organization that responded to the social and political needs of the community, whether as part of the Underground Railroad that aided the escape of slaves or as a leader in the organization of a bus boycott in the civil rights movement. Foremost, the church became a place where members could acquire the social status prohibited in the larger society.

Arguably, the black church represents a social context for the engagement of youth in prosocial activities. The social organization of the black church is such that special programs and committee structures are developed for youth participation and thus socialization in the church culture. This carefully constructed youth substructure is designed to promote social development and to prepare youth for adulthood. Special programs, modeled on those of church elders, provide youth with opportunities to learn social and leadership skills. Young people may sponsor fundraising activities, have usher boards, and organize special program activities for liturgical celebrations. Moreover, urban churches currently receive public funding for special youth programs designed to address the social service needs of their communities.

These programs are formulated to service teens with special needs, including those who may be at risk for premature parenthood and substance misuse and abuse. Rubin, Billingsley, and Caldwell (1994) have argued that given the multiple social and economic problems in black communities, black churches could do more to the serve their respective communities. However, black teens that do attend church and participate in congregational or parish activities feel that church involvement is significant to their lives. Yolanda, a nonpregnant PANSI teen, thought that her religious background played an important role in helping her learn to become a morally responsible person:

> I went to Catholic school all my life. Education was stressed. We would go to church every Sunday. Catholics teach you how to be responsible to yourself and to others, how to act in public; how to respect elders, how to care about others, how to act like an adult. And the church does a lot of social things me and my family are involved in.

For healthy prosocial engagement, the adolescent must master environmental regulation to achieve some sense of self-efficacy. A significant and primary mode of environmental modulation is the selection of appropriate role models. The choosing of role models, whether fantasized or actual, reflects the underlying formation of the adolescent's striving to formulate coherent principles or standards that will guide present and future behavior. Oprah Winfrey presents a countenance of sassiness and empathic caring. Additionally, she seems forever young in her willingness to idealize African American women such as Toni Morrison and Maya Angelou as ever-constant role models. Role model formulation represents a domain where developmental self processes take place that create a shared perspective for the growth of empathic intimacy in meaningful relationships. This sense of the moral agency of sassiness is rooted in a historical legacy of oppression. Maya Angelou (1994) in her poem "Still I Rise" articulates the earthy and bold manner of African American women. The timbre of the poem symbolizes sassiness.

> You may shoot me with your words,
> You may cut me with your eyes,
> You may kill me with your hatefulness
> But still, like air, I'll rise
>
> Does my sexiness upset you?
> Does it come as a surprise?
> That I dance like I've got diamonds
> At the meeting of my thighs.
>
> Out of the huts of history's shame
> I rise
> Up from a past that's rooted in pain
> I rise
> I'm a black ocean, leaping and wide,
> Welling and swelling, I bear the tide.

Leaving behind nights of terror and fear
I rise
Into a daybreak that's wondrously clear
I rise
Bringing the gifts that my ancestors gave,
I am the dream and the hope of the slave.
I rise
I rise
I rise.

The Adolescent Girls' Social Network

The Family, School, Neighborhood, and Peers

The struggle for self-definition among African American adolescents is profoundly consequential. To achieve maturational identity successfully, the black adolescent girl must overcome the cultural limits of racial-gender stereotyping. Despite the personal stress involved in managing this dilemma, a social network of support can assist a girl in transcending such stereotyping. Organized self-experiences are, in part, influenced by others' view of one's self. However, the adult to whom the adolescent girl is emotionally attached and from whom she seeks self-affirmation is critically influential. As previously discussed, the mother-daughter relationship is the primary instrumental-expressive relationship to guide the adolescent girl in achieving meaning synthesis related to gender, ethnic, and sexual role commitment. In the PANSI study, findings related to role model formulation suggest that the girls' mothers were most consistently identified as the singularly idealized and admired person. It is worth noting that a mother-daughter relationship, although primary, is still subject to emotional turbulence. Essentially there is no self-experience that is not an intrinsically social or intersubjective experience. While particular abilities, talents, and temperaments may be innately determined (e.g., musical talent), it is not until such biological capacities are given social definition that they become a basis for a sense of identity (e.g., to think of one as a gifted musician). There is empirical documentation that black adolescents look to their proximal environments for identity affirmation. Black adolescents are more dependent on their immediate social network for self-definition than they are on the broad distal social context (Spencer, 1985). Similarly, Rains's (1971) now classic sociological study on adolescent pregnancy indicated that black pregnant adolescents were less dependent on mental health professionals (e.g., psychiatrists, social workers) for explanations of their behaviors than their white counterparts were.

Ecologically, the microsystems of nested contexts (Figure 3.2) are apparently more momentous for black adolescent socialization than for white adolescent socialization. One explanation for these phenomena is that black adolescents because of historical structural strain are less likely to identify with those perceived as powerful oppressors of blacks. One could argue that black adolescents ultimately must identify with an abstract mainstream culture to experience belonging—that is, they must learn

to embrace democratic principals of social justice, equality, and fairness without necessarily having experienced these practices in daily life. Granted, because adolescents
developmentally have the capacity for abstract thought, democratic principles can be
integrated. Nonetheless, for adolescents, theoretical principles are perhaps best
learned when they can be put into practice. Moreover, words have structured cognitive meaning (Greenspan, 1997) and are learned by way of intersubjective experiences
that eventually become specific discriminate feeling states.

Notwithstanding, to reason in this manner has enormous implications for role
model formulation among at-risk black female adolescents. One focal implication is
the need for school environments that will promote a contextual educational environment of learning. Common opinion is that black youth are educationally poor
achievers. The worth of academic performance is assessed outside the context in which
it occurs. The onus is on the student to achieve irrespective of environmental conditions. Moreover, empirical research seems to support this conventional observation.
At-risk adolescents could benefit enormously from educational institutions that have
pedagogical processes where the locus of learning is contextual. The heart of contextual pedagogy is to highlight the interactional aspects of learning and the environment. Pedagogical processes that stress contextual learning differ from traditional
pedagogy in that (1) contexts are scrutinized for learning opportunities both within
and outside of the school environment and (2) learning goals are defined by talent
development rather than talent assessment (Boykin, 1994). School reform policies that
incorporate contextual pedagogy are more likely to assist at-risk students in role model
formulation processes by providing environments where students readily identify with
school personnel as idealized individuals or desirable ego ideals.

How a social network influences developmental process relative to the care protective sensibility and role model formulation is concretely elaborated, in one way,
by contrasting and comparing girls whose social networks differ in respect to exposure to varied environments. The concept of social network is quite congruent with
an ecological perspective insofar as individuals' social networks span ecological spheres
that provide a microanalysis of their embedded contexts (see Figure 3.2). According
to Barnes (1954) a social network is egocentric in that it is seen from the self-
perception of the individual who is at the center of a web of interpersonal relationships. The network, then, is mapped and described only from the median viewpoint
of the individual (Flanagan, 1999). Social networks seen in this way represent personal social capital (Eames & Goode, 1977). Viewed in this way, the autobiographical narratives of the PANSI and GULTMC girls provide a personal vantage point
from which to view the influences of social institutions, such as the family and church,
on the care protective sensibility and role model formulation spheres of development.
I contend that the ethic of caring and personal accountability is practiced and learned
in the social ecologies of family and church in time-honored ritualized socialization
experiences.

Billingsley (1992) has made a compelling argument that the generative African
American family has historically embraced a moral code of virtue that advanced the
resilience and social mobility of their offspring. He considers his own family legacies
of moral virtue as typical of the African American familial experience:

My parents had a reverence for learning second only to their reverence for the spiritual. And they passed this along to their children. They were not isolated. . . . There were other values too by which my parents lived that helped to prepare their children for upward mobility. . . . As for my mother, long before we would discover the African moral code embodied in the seven cardinal principles of virtue, and long before Spike Lee would encapsulate these principles in the title of his movie, my mother was the living embodiment of the moral code, "Do the Right Thing." . . . My family story is not an isolated case. (p. 278)

Billingsley has captured here the soul of the traditional African American family both in agrarian southern communities and northern cities in the early 1900s. In these familial households, the families' spiritual, moral, and educational values were the life blood of familial life. Moreover, the institutional affiliations of church, social clubs, and activist organizations embodied the life blood of communal life in a social network of densely integrated interpersonal relationships where the upbringing of children was central. Moreover, the extended family supportive network contributed significantly to intergenerational social mobility patterns (McAdoo, 1997). Thus an integrated ecological system was created that reinforced spiritual and moral values. Black families were anchored in reinforcing integrative nested contextual systems of self-relatedness. Children in such families were the bona fide heirs of the strength and integrity characteristic of systems of reciprocal care, commonly found in the "nested contexts" of school, church, and family (Nobles et al., 1976).[1]

According to Staples and Johnson (1993) Billingsley's, in his now classic work, *Black Families in White America* (1968), was one of the first scholars to argue against the prevailing view of the black family as pathological. Billingsley's work stressed the strengths of black families, noting in particular that the southern African American family was embedded in a network of supportive interpersonal relationships. Certainly, the adoption of care, loyalty, and empathic values in relation to others helps develop moral virtues. Billingsley has identified such families as traditional generative familial constellations. Despite notable strengths of African American families, a few scholars question whether the integrity of the black family can be sustained. This point is argued given the historical chronological structural crises of poverty and racism and the present social catastrophes of black male homicide and incarceration and single female-headed households (Gibbs, 1988; Madhubuti, 1990).

It seems important to note two major demographic shifts that profoundly affected African American communal life. This communal life was anchored in an agrarian generative traditional family of a care protective sensibility: I propose that this care and nurturance sensibility was first changed by the two mass migratory movements of African Americans to northern industrial urban areas occurring in the early 1900s, the 1940s, and 1950s. The second demographic shift occurred with the geographical relocation of the black middle class from black inner-city neighborhoods to racially integrated suburban communities in the 1960s and 1970s. The street culture of many inner-city communities, characterized by violence, drugs, and criminality, represents the antithesis of the traditional ethnic values of empathic care and personal accountability described here. Similarly, others have cogently argued the demise of relational mutuality and caring in inner-city communities (Anderson, 1990; Wilson, 1996). Certainly, the drug subculture of inner-city communities is antithetical to traditional African American social and ethical values.

Anderson (1990) and Wilson (1996) persuasively argue that the devastation of inner city communities is due, in large part, to the withdrawal of work opportunities and the departure of black middle-class leadership. The exodus of middle-class habitants created homogeneous neighborhoods of poor, unemployable, and permanently displaced inner-city residents. Moreover, Anderson (1990) argues that the integrity of black urban communities of the 1940s and 1950s was fairly stabilized. I suggest, however, that despite measures of stabilization in city life, black communities possessed a distinctive preponderance of urban properties, including spatial density, marginal labor, unemployment, erosion of private life, and illicit lifestyles, all of which contributed to the erosion of a protective care sensibility among inhabitants. For example, during earlier periods, before the pervasive infiltration of illicit drug trafficking in black communities, illicit lifestyles were maintained by illegal gaming systems such as numbers betting, illicit gambling enterprises akin to contemporary legalized state lotto games. Illegal gaming enterprises created an underground employment infrastructure that included numbers runners (distributors), collectors, accountants, and printers.[2] Perhaps this type of recreational infrastructure has been less toxic in its effects than the drug trafficking existent in contemporary black communities. Still, black families have historically engaged in strategies to defend their offspring from the onslaught of social dangers. Empirical research documents that the strengths of African American families rests in learning skills needed to clarify and manage the concrete realities of daily life (Nobles et al., 1976).

Social Contexts and Community Building Strategies

Psychosocial gains are netted when individuals skillfully manage the concrete realities of daily living not only in their immediate environments but also in distal environments. Regarding distal environments, a social mobility enhancement strategy, according to Jarrett (1995) involves investment in prosocial activities outside of one's proximal environment, identified as *community bridging*. When black youth are afforded participatory exposure to external macrosocial worlds, they not only become culturally bifircucated but also become active cultural contributors and participants. Simply put, youth are cultural shareholders in American society when they contribute knowingly as active societal participants. Moreover, according to Jarrett, families who exercise specific social mobility strategies are considered *defended families*. These strategies protect and enhance family strengths.

Poor families, Jarrett contends, use five strategies to promote adolescent social mobility. The strategies (all of which are fairly self-explanatory) are a supportive adult network structure (i.e., relational connection with adult role models both within and outside of the kin network), restricted family-community relations, stringent parental monitoring strategies, strategic alliances with mobility-enhancing institutions and organizations, and adult-sponsored developmental activities. While all of the mobility-enhancing strategies place restrictions on relational connections, the restricted family-community relations strategy is perhaps the most circumscribed. According to Jarrett, families that utilize social mobility-enhancement strategies restrict interpersonal relations among both kinship and community residents. Socially mobile families erect both symbolic and physical barriers to defend themselves from actual and

perceived threats to their lifestyle. Moreover, the social mobility strategies are contextually grounded in the domains of family or community institutions. The significance of the resilience of the family as a collective unit renders Jarrett's analysis especially noteworthy. The view that community bridging and kin-scripts are
complementary constructs finds support in the idea that community bridging can be
thought of as that family characteristic that depicts particular kin-scriptions. As noted,
kin-scriptions are simply specific practices that affirm, over time, a family's way of
doing things. Moreover, kin-scriptions can be thought of as the particularized social
norms that the family constitutes for its daily operations and generational survival.
Family identity within a community is established by way of distinct and observable
kin-scriptions. Simply stated, in the community or neighborhood a family becomes
known by its unique quotidian practices.

The community-building strategies suggest that poor inner-city parents are well
aware of the kinds of support that their children need to become socially invested in
American society. To be sure, defended families seem better able to resist the many
dangers of hazardous environments. Moreover, defended families are buffeted both
by prosocial investments and by familial codes of moral and ethical behavior. Apparently, family propriety is taught by way of adults' persistent pronouncements of the
impropriety of those in close proximity—offspring learn correct behavior by examining the behavior of others in their immediate environments. The proprieties or in-
discretions of kin and non-kin alike are presented as a way to define exemplary and
derelict individuals. At the same time, however, youth are instructed to respect others, regardless of imprudent behavior. Children learn how to accept and respect others while at the same time grasping the necessity of being discriminate in relational
connections. The following comment by a PANSI girl is illustrative:

> Well, I try and respect everybody. That's the way I was taught. Everybody is due respect
> no matter how they talk or behave 'cause they are human beings, you know what I mean.
> Now, I may not admire them, but you see I respect them. You can be low down and I
> will respect you. That's why it makes you so mad when others don't respect me. Even if
> I see people doing things I don't like, I still respect them. There are drug addicts around
> my house, they are my neighbors. I don't like what they do but I respect them. They do
> a lot of things that is just plain nasty and they are not good parents, believe me—know-
> ing this, I still don't disrespect them.

Seemingly, young black female adolescents develop a discriminating capacity in
evaluating the behaviors of others. One could argue that this remarkable perspicuous
ability is refined, in part, because of the complexities of at-risk environments. In a
group session aimed at the development of confidence in body image, the GULTMC
girls inadvertently began a discussion of neighborhood events involving drugs.

ZORELLE: Did you hear about the man, the wife, the brother, and the sister—
they were all dealing drugs. All in one place. But listen at this! They each had their
own way to get in. And, they each had their own cars. And they lived somewhere different all in there own houses. They was raided. Fifty-two thousand and five hun-
dred stars a day.
GEORGETTE: See, I hate drugs. They not doing nothing but helping people kill
themselves.

NIA: Okay! Hello! You don't see no drug dealers doin' drugs.

BELLA: But, most drug dealers think like, "You don't use your product you selling." And they just killing other people. Killing people's babies and stuff.

NIA: Naw! Drug dealers not stupid.

TERISA: But still, they're wrong in doin' what they do. They're helping people kill themselves, but the people are doing it too. Nobody makes you take drugs. You decide to take drugs.

MARIKA: Yeah. But, a lot of people feel they can't get a sense of pride, then that's who they go to, the drug dealer. I guess the drugs make 'em feel better—but it's oh so sad—pitiful. But, you're right it's a decision you make.

Arguably, adolescents living in high-risk communities must make decisions that will aid in the successful negotiation of adverse surroundings. At-risk environments are likely to be inhabited by characters that openly engage in disreputable acts, such as drug trafficking, prostitution, stealing, and the like. As previously noted, strength in resilient youth is the capacity to identify an adult role model or mentor with whom positive attachments can be made. Certainly, in order for a girl to identify such a person, she must be able to discern the strengths and weaknesses of those persons to whom she is exposed. While at-risk environments have their hazards, resilient girls develop the strength to navigate this environment. This rather remarkable trait bolsters the maturational development of resilient youth. Unquestionably, shrewdness in environmental navigation is developed to handle daily hassles.

Armara, a nonpregnant 17-year-old PANSI respondent, evaluates the behavior of a neighborhood:

> She's a bad example of a person to be like and a mother. All of her kids are grown; but she's a two-faced person. She's one of those persons who try to totally control their children's lives. She put her son out of the house at Christmas, because he would not give her all of his check. She's money hungry and only care about what's on the outside; about how people dress and look. I would never want to be like her. She's not a good person or a good mother.

Armara casts a discriminating eye on kin and non-kin alike. In trying to formulate a standard for proper and improper behavior she is not prejudiced by blood kin. The following comments refer to an uncle: "He's not responsible. He has no job and he has a Drinking problem. He's lazy. I just hate men who won't help their women out, who won't get a job."

Positive intersubjective processes (see Figure 3.1) nurture resilience. Healthy development of the care protective sensibility and role model formulation domains need the support of balanced familial processes. Expectedly, maturational development for the adolescent girl is a dynamic process of unparalleled proportion. At the outset, early aged girls must learn to minimize egocentricism, sustain a positive belief in self, and modulate the environment for the selection of gender prototypes. These tasks are tempered for all girls by the realities of daily life. The inner-city poor black girl, however, is likely to be exposed to too much too soon—that is, she is likely to experience exposure to toxic social situations. At age 10–14, biological changes are the most profound and developmental issues the most intense. It is an awesome task for a 10-year-old girl to deal with the attendant issues of sexuality, including the capacity for reproduction.

Moreover, contemporary adolescent girls have untold decision-making liberties. Virtually limitless opportunities for consequential decision making leave little room for preparatory learning. In particular, early aged adolescent girls in at-risk environments are likely to confront many life experiences realistically. However, idealization is thought to typify this developmental stage. Expectations of self and others are tempered by the raw experiences of daily life. Resilient girls examine the personal tragedies and triumphs of family, friends, and neighbors microscopically. Early age-graded characteristics of self-centeredness and grandiosity are regulated by the development of self-protective strategies needed to lessen risk and harm in chaotic environments. Modulating the environment for self-protection affects the domain of care protective sensibility and role model formulation in significant ways. First, for the resilient girl, empathy and respect mean commanding self-respect and demanding that others respect themselves—the resilient girl will not suffer fools gladly. Second, resilient girls look to adults for character traits that embody principled standards rather than material status (Stevens, 1994).

Age-Graded Developmental Issues and Their Influence on the Care Protective Sensibility and Role Model Formulation Domain: Peer Relationships

Because of the multiple stresses of transformative puberty changes, girls during early adolescence are especially vulnerable emotionally and physically. Girls typically reach puberty a few years before their male counterparts. At this age, girls experience mundane occurrences intensely. In the previous chapter, it was noted that adolescents experience a feeling-state of inauthenticity as they evolve a social identity. Such feelings are compounded when confronted with the developmental task of regulating and organizing behavior and affect. Generally, a consequential task of adolescence is to utilize formal operational thought to change impulses into affects and mental representations, to pattern new internalized object relationships, to form new self-structures, and to enhance capacities for self-observation. Adolescent transformational organizations of self include the capacity for shared meanings, empathic communications, and the development of new ego ideals, all elements that speak to the care protective and role model formulation. Clearly, then, adolescents must learn not to act out their needs but to rely on differentiated representational elaboration (Greenspan, 1997)—that is, they must rely on elaborate symbology rather than behavioral enactment to distinguish emotional states. Typically, adolescents use language to characterize affective understanding of their social-emotional worlds. Adolescents are, without parallel, exemplars of the use of vernacular expressions. Adolescents employ unique behavioral practices and vernacularisms to deal with daily hassles. Both behavioral practices and colloquial linguistic coinages separate adolescents from adults. Generational separation makes possible a social hiatus that adolescents require to manage their social worlds. Yet this gap paradoxically must be bridged at critical intervals if adolescents are to be developmentally successful.

Historically, African Americans have used a vernacular lexicon to express aggression and power in social interactions, such as the ritual repartee games of signifying or playing the dozens. These games, often carried out in a humorous or joking manner, are meant to discredit or embarrass another. Playing the dozens, in particular, has been defined as ritualized or spontaneous insults directed most often at another's mother (the dirty dozens) or at an opponent (the clean dozens). More importantly, signifying conversational repartee represents rhetorical understatements and can be seen as a metaphor for black language skills (Ellison, 1964; Folb, 1980; Gates, 1988; Goodwin, 1990). The GULTMC girls were well rehearsed in the verbal insult games of clean dozens, in which they were constantly engaged. Regardless, care protective sensibilities and the sought-after ideal prototypes for role modeling did not go unnoticed by the GULTMC girls, but they apparently took a circuitous route in their normative development.

Relatedly, what was remarkable about the GULTMC girls was the quality of their peer relations. Typically, for early aged adolescents, peer group belonging is critically important during this phase. The GULTMC girls were passionately competitive in their relationships with each other. They were rival cohorts for the attention of male peers. The girls seemed to be in a constant state of fury and rage when relating to one another, which, in turn, brought about explosive arguments and physical fights. School suspensions were mainly because of fights, and most fights were about boys with whom girls claimed romantic interests. Competitive aggressive behavior among the GULTMC girls often aroused feelings of general distrust and disrespect. Fourteen-year-old Reese described such a fight:

> She tried to jump me because she thought I was going with her boyfriend. But that boy started talking to me first. I don't even like him. Yeah, I called her a 'Ho too. She hit me and then we was fighting and then she got me on the ground. She got me on the ground and pulled my hair and another girl came over and tried to take my jewelry and I had taken it all off except for my rings. They was trying to take my ring and this girl punched me in the back of my neck. The next day I was coming off the bus and she just looked at me and her sister had missed the stop so she was on the bus and she started yelling get that bitch, she's right there go and get her. The next day after that we were back at school and she didn't say nothing to me. She walked down the street, she didn't say nothing to me. She looked straight past me. Then, that same day, this other girl comes up to me and she said: "Your name Reese," and I said: "Yeah." And she said: "You had a fight with my cousin." And, I was like yeah. "I heard she kicked your ass, is that true?" I said: "I don't know, it wasn't a long enough fight."

Reese's comment "I don't know, it wasn't a long enough fight" displays the skillful, stylistic, idiomatic, and often humorous repartee in which these girls would engage.

Moreover, GULTMC girls tended to engage in fights when attempts to achieve meaning synthesis faltered or when peers, especially in the presence of adults, shamed them. At such times, the girls were contentious, quick to show anger, and took the offensive. Interestingly, bellicose behavior among the GULTMC girls was individually focused and did not result in clique or gang activities. Girl gangs are more likely to evolve from warring cliques. Girls are more likely to form cliques during the middle adolescent period, generally around ages 15 and 16, after they have entered high school. Generally, cliquish girls in inner-city schools are disengaged from authentic relational connection with adults. Warring girl cliques become solidified as gangs when they join companion boy gangs for safety and protection ("Gang Girl," 1998).

Contrarily, the GULTMC girls continued to look to adults for support despite the fact that oftentimes they felt such support was not forthcoming. Combative behavior among the GULTMC girls would result in "talk" or "gossip" among school staff members, who saw fights only occurring among the girls, not the boys. In turn, the GULTMC girls thought that teachers seemed unwilling to help them resolve conflicts and believed that teachers were too frightened by their rowdiness. In turn, GULTMC girls saw teachers as inadequate adults since they could not depend on them to help resolve quarrelsome disagreements. Nonetheless, truculent encounters among the girls were not easily managed and the girls often ignored adult authority. Generally, the girls did not automatically defer to age—adults did not automatically warrant respect; they had to earn it. Actually, the school provided a few structured opportunities where adults "proved themselves." The girls responded positively to such adults.

Resilient girls seek out honest, trustworthy, and caring adults in their immediate environments, irrespective of gender, to support them in the management of developmental tasks. Chosen adults are admired for instilling confidence and for demonstrating respectful trustworthiness. For the GULTMC girls such a person was the school's music teacher, a black woman who set behavioral limits, expected "proper" social conduct, and genuinely liked the girls. According to the GULTMC girls, the music teacher was a "good listener and someone who cares about us." Developmentally, the girls' choir participation enhanced self-esteem and fostered cultural pride. The choir's repertoire included contemporary and ethnic-based musical selections. Inadvertently, then, school choir activities helped achieve cultural meaning and cultural synthesis. The school choir had a reputation for stellar gospel performances. Frequently, the choir performed for political dignitaries and at special municipal celebrations.

The girls' choir membership and participation demanded a flexible cultural style, as they were exposed to various citywide community (municipal and cultural) institutions. According to the girls, they had to learn "how to act proper." The girls believed that they were learning such social decorum as sitting, speaking, and dressing properly. But the demand for high behavioral standards and the distinctive social exposure were appreciated and valued by the girls, as they felt supported by the music teacher in developing bicultural competencies and improving social skills. Still, choir productions were exceptional and not routine school events. Illustratively, a PANSI girl found a caring and esteemed adult in her high school principal, a black male who recognized her scholastic and intellectual abilities. Thelma relates the positive and supportive relationship she experienced:

> He's an ideal man because he cares about the school. He respects the students. He had faith in me and he has a positive attitude about all the students. He help me see that I really was a good student and could go to college if just applied myself. At first I didn't really see in myself what he saw. Now, I'm on the honor roll. He's pushing me to go to college.

Eventually, the GULTMC girls used their daily peer interactions to evaluate the quality of their relationships. Clearly they sought to develop trustworthy female peer relations. Apparently, the girls' impetuous frays were linked to evolving complex so-cial identities. More importantly, the girls sought to clarify the meaning of friend-ships and began to differentiate various types, such as associates, hangers, ace friends, or soul mates. The girls' demonstrable skills in classifying relational connections, stim-ulated in part by peer conflict and competition, indicated creative meaning-making activities that involved an ethic of caring.[3] The girls' developing sense of sisterhood was fostered by care protective sensibilities and role model formulation processes. In-terestingly, as the GULTMC girls became less competitive, they were more empathic and tended to recognize qualities in each other that represented ideal traits embody-ing developmental tasks, including a sense of agency and autonomy, self-differentia-tion, and individuation. In this way, peer relationships serve to advance role model formulation processes. The girls' various commentaries reveal their attempts to eval-uate their interpersonal relationships:

> Ella is quiet, but very outspoken. She's my girl, you don't have to try and figure out what's on her mind. Besides, she's quiet so you know she's about being serious. She's my girl. An another thing, she's polite and speaks with an educated voice.

> Well Resse looks like an independent person, but careful in what she says to you. You can tell her what's on your mind and you know it's safe.

> Awright! How would you feel if your best friend, or just say your friend liked somebody you really, really liked but she never told you how she felt about him. And you told her everything about how you felt about this boy you liked. And she went out with him be-hind your back, and she wasn't the one to tell you, he was the one to tell you, that she—that he go with her—well—I—no shit, it really, really sucks—you feel hurt.

> People think, because of how I feel, and I'll say just how I feel and don't hide things—that I'm being rude and nasty. And, cause I wasn't all that different in my dress, but tried to dress like everybody else—well, I musta been rude. Now, they're like, "I didn't know you was like that—nice and everything." Like Ella, when Ella first saw me [meaning the first year at middle school], she was like, she said, "You're all rude, I didn't like you at first." And, I was like, "I wasn't sure about you either."

Clearly, early aged adolescent girls begin to recognize model traits in one an-other. And, as girls' developmental growth proceeds, intense friendships are forged. For the GULTMC girls, intimate peer attachments occurred during the last year of middle school and continued through postsecondary school.[4] Relatedly, GULTMC girls resembled the PANSI girls in their evolved capacity for sustaining intimate friendships. Marion, a 19-year-old PANSI girl, speaks of a cherished friendship that was developed during the high school years. The two friends experienced the tragedy of their mothers' terminal illnesses. Marion poignantly describes this special rela-tionship:

> Me and Laura went through high school together. We were going away to college in Florida together. I couldn't go because my mother was too ill. She went away but had to come back because her mother got ill. We went through our mothers' illnesses together. After her mother died, she immediately took to my mother. And, her father is just like my father too. We are all very close. When my mother died, her father told me that there would always be a place for me at his home. But then her father died. When we are to-gether we talk about life in general. Lots of times we just cry together. But we are always

each other's support. When I need someone she's right there. We talk about the future if we are going to make it. We go to the movies, bowling. I really believe we are the best of friends two people could possibly be.

Without question, girls' social contexts afford opportunities for meaning-making processes that can either foster or frustrate their developmental course. In the Prologue, it was noted that the PANSI study indicated that nonpregnant and pregnant girls differed significantly in care protective sensibility protective theme occurrences. The study's care protective sensibility theme was reflected in the girls' affective and behavioral responses of care and loyalty. While the differences between the two groups occurred across thematic categories, remarkable differences were seen in the occurrences of peer relations and male role model questions. Possible explanations for this rather puzzling finding is that an aspect of resilience in inner-city girls is the capacity to modulate the environment for the selection of both female and male adult role models. Evidently, the need for the nurturing presence of adult males is critical in the lives of inner-city female adolescents, since females head most inner-city families.

Because of economic restraints, poor inner-city African American women adopt family formation patterns that include varied partner arrangements. An adaptive strategy of poor urban African American women is to extend the parental role to nonbiological fathers as a means of involving men in childcaring activities. Despite demographic surveys that document the absence of males in inner-city households, ethnographic data indicate that males have a sustained presence in female-headed domiciles. When males are present they are in either partner or extended kin relationships with the women who head the households (Aschenbrenner, 1983; Jarrett, 1994; Stack, 1974). Consequently, the variable family formation of inner-city African American girls may well provide male role models. Early feminist theorists' emphasis on the consequences of differentiated gender development tended to overlook the essential significance of adult males and/or father figures in adolescent girls' lives. Although more recent literature conveys a less divided adolescent developmental view, there is a paucity of literature regarding paternal influences and adolescent coping, especially related to ethnicity. Clearly, parental figures are the first prototypical gender models for children and youth. Girls require nourishing, affectionate care from fathers or father substitutes for healthy development. In the PANSI study, the nonpregnant girls were more likely to live in a household with the father present. Additionally, over one-half (60 percent) of the sample GULTMC girls had an adult male figure present in the home.

By late-age adolescence, resilient black girls have appropriated social conduct from esteemed persons found in their immediate family or community. Hauna, a 19-year-old pregnant PANSI participant, lived with her maternal grandmother. Ray, the 21-year-old expectant father, had recently joined the grandmother's household as the couple had plans for marriage. Hauna and Ray wanted their own household dwelling and had hopes of securing an apartment. Hauna left her mother's home to live with her grandmother when she was a sophomore in high school because she could not tolerate the chemical dependency problems of her mother and stepfather. At the time, Hauna was a college sophomore at a city junior college. Hauna thought that she would model her life only slightly differently than the family friend whom she held in esteem:

> Hattie is a self-made businesswoman. She keeps pushing herself harder and harder for more and more. She never quits. She's always coming up with something new. She owns her own trucking company. She's a real hustler. That's my grandmother's best friend. She's in her 50s too. She's like a godmother to me. My grandmother is 53 and Hattie is 52. She has trucks for construction. She has different trucks that go out through the city and spread salt during the winter. She's been in it for three years now and doing quite well. I would use my education more than Hattie. She finished high school and some college; but she's missing something like 2 credit hours from being a certified public accountant. I would go to school one day or a couple times week or something. But, I would want to be like her; maybe not own a business, because it's too much responsibility, but to run the business. I would want to be successful at doing that. And, I would want to be ladylike, to be respectful. To finish school and make a decent paycheck.

Obviously, the parents of some inner-city girls do not exhibit behaviors their daughters find exemplary. Hauna identified her mother as someone she did not admire or respect.

> [My mother] upholds her husband in wrongdoing. She lost everything for nothing, her job, and her children. [Hauna had younger elementary school age siblings.] She worked at Spiegel for 13 years. She makes up excuses for him, lie for him. She's always on his side. And she won't listen to the family. I'm not depressed about it, but the whole thing just makes me mad. She met him at the job. I believe it's him that got her hooked on drugs.

Finally, while both early and late-age adolescent girls seek appropriate role models within their proximal environments, older girls develop a unique dress style, are less competitive with female peers, and have committed to friendships characterized by mutual caring and nurturance. As was mentioned in Chapter 2, black girls must deal with the monumental developmental tasks of synthesizing coherence from triadic experiences of socialization that affect racial/ethnic/gender identity. Positively, the care protective sensibility and role model formulation domain is vital in this identity exploration and development. Intersubjective qualities of assertion, self-efficacy, and recognition strengthen the nurturing and empathic intersubjectivity of friendships. Developmentally, friendships deepen as girls' attention shifts to concerns about future goals, vocational and career choices, committed dating, mate selection, sex role identity confirmation, internalized morality, and the integration of personal standards of beauty. Select friends become soul mate companions, those with whom the vicissitudes of life can be shared.

Role Model Formulation and Personalized Beauty

One of the most challenging developmental tasks for adolescent girls is the integration of unique and personally owned standards of beauty; that is, girls must learn to develop a sense of comfort and acceptance about their physical bodies—their general appearance. The failure to settle an identity involving a positive incorporation of the bodily self can lead to serious emotional problems. In particular, eating disorders and their sequelae are grave psychological problems that are commonly associated with female adolescents. Anorexia nervosa has been documented as widely diagnosed among white teens. Nonetheless, there is some anecdotal evidence[5] that suggests that black girls, like their white cohorts, experience eating disorder problems. The PANSI study did not specifically address the subject of physical appearance or body image. Nonetheless, because of the naturalistic setting of the GULTMC study, I learned that for the GULTMC girls, body image was a topic of special importance to them. Additionally, one of the sessions in the social skills intervention curriculum was designed to deal with this particular issue. The GULTMC girls seemed most aware of a corporeal self when they were observed or approached by males. Ordinarily, in such circumstances the girls experienced ambiguous and shameful feelings, but above all they were self-conscious when confronting a male gaze:

> Yesterday, I was walking down the street, right. And like I said, I had on a body suit and baggy pants. And this dude walked by, I guess he was drunk, I don't know what was wrong with him. He said something like, I looked very pretty and he said something about my body. He said that I got the body and the boom, something like that. And he was like, I don't know, he was like, he was acting real stupid, and at first I wanted to laugh. He was like, "Whoa-oo, you gotta body like a grown woman." He said, "Go-o-damn!" Everytime a man looks at you, why they gotta look at somebody's body? I wish they could see what I was like, but they never give me a chance to show them. Seem like all they see is my body. They don't see nothing else. It's like, "Oh-h, her body this and her body that." Men say my body is growing, and boys say I look like a little girl.

Moreover, the GULTMC girls seemed overly concerned about skin color and the texture and length of hair. Typically, worries about skin color and hair seemed ethnically determined, as girls' criteria for "good looks" were based on whether someone was light-skinned or dark-skinned or had good hair or bad hair. Equally important was the fact that the girls used the "good looks" criteria to judge nonphysical traits. Notwithstanding that early aged adolescent girls are clearly competitive in their judgment of peers, comments about physical attributes also conveyed a banal understanding of appealing "good looks" for African American women. Some notable comments about "good looks" follow:

> I don't believe he's right for you. He all light-skinned, so you know he be conceited.

> She think she all that, cause she got long hair—she got all them braids and earrings on her hair. She think she better 'an everybody.

> [The comment here refers to a discussion about Ophra Winfrey:] She lost the weight on her own, it wasn't like somebody was like, "You're too fat." She lost the weight, cause she chose to. Then she gained it. Maybe she chose one day to be that big. It's not like you're supposed to do this and that and change for other people, because as soon as you look at somebody, and they are like 160 pounds and then they go down to 122, you be like, "She on drugs." That's the first thing they say.

Obviously, early aged adolescent females are self-conscious about their body image. Seemingly, early aged adolescent girls have overdetermined responses to the negative aspects of their physical appearance. At the same time, girls at this age experience an intense emotional struggle in trying to develop a signature style. When women learn to fashion their own stylized self-presentation they embrace themselves as attractive and appealing. Self-acceptance of the physical self is a manifestation of resilience. It is likely that young girls look to their immediate context to modulate personalized beauty standards. Inner-city black women fashion creative and signature fashion styles. Commonly, fashion styles are known to be uniquely elaborate, such as cornrow braids, marcelled waved hair, naturales, and head wraps of colorful fabric. Erykah Badu, the 28-year-old pop singer, created a beauty signature of regal head wraps:

> When I was growing up, all we had for fashions of beauty were fashion models or Barbie. I grew up being told it is not normal to look the way I do [*according to mainstream beauty standards, it is not normal to be black and beautiful, despite the slogans of the 1960s*]. No one taught me to do head wraps. One day, I just took three yards of fabric and started wrapping and it was like second nature. Once I saw how beautiful I was, I felt comfortable and grounded. I was adorned with my culture effortlessly. (Trebay, 1997)

More than 30 years ago, psychiatrists Grier and Cobbs (1968), in their psychological treatise *Black Rage*, concluded that kinky hair was at the root of shame and self-hate in black women. All too frequently this interpretation epitomizes explanations of why black women straighten their hair (Dance, 1998). Unmistakably, the Grier and Cobbs explanation ignores the anthropological perspective of ritualized self-adornment that women undergo to beautify themselves. Interestingly, Grier and Cobb join a list of other notable scholars in the attribution of poor self-concept and felt inferiority among black women. The self-hate explanation is exceedingly inadequate in clarifying social adaptation and coping among black women. White and White (1998) suggest, for example, that the straightening of black women's hair is not necessarily motivated by the desire to be white:

> [I]t is possible to see other meanings in the early twentieth-century vogue for hair straightening. Straightening of the hair, which is to say, removing the knots and some of the kinkiness from it, was nothing new in African American life. It had been an important part of African American, indeed African, cosmetic activity long before Madame C. J. Walker or any of her rivals in the cosmetic industry were born. Whether accomplished by traditional or modern methods, straightening was a practical necessity if some sort of styling were to be accomplished, a preliminary to styling, not its end point. Once that point is recognized, advertisements for hair-straightening compounds appear in a different light. (pp. 71–72)

Without question, multidimensional developmental theories are needed to explain the complex life of individuals. A one-dimensional psychological view will not accomplish this. To illuminate this assertion, one need only to examine the life of Madame C. J. Walker, a woman of exceptional courage and ambition credited with introducing the cosmetology enterprise of straightening hair to black women. Motivated to more than a washerwoman, Walker had become, in 1910, America's first black millionaire. Common opinion is that she invented the straightening comb. While she adapted this technology for her own purposes, the straightening comb was a European invention. In fact, she invented hair products to improve the health of black women's hair. Her first product was a hair preparation to prevent the loss of her own hair. It was so effective that she begin to sell her merchandise door to door to other women (Giddings, 1984). How do we account for the extraordinary success of this woman born 2 years after emancipation of slaves? How do we explain her remarkable ambition, her desire to improve the appearance of black women? Further, we wonder about the equally remarkable young women (most of whom were poor and in their late teens) recruited by Walker to become beauticians. Trained to be hairdressers and employed to market the beauty of black women, these young women were instructed in fashion, graciousness, and good manners. Madame Walker's hair products were marketable because they were exceptionally effective—hair was healthy, well groomed, and grew to new lengths. According to Giddings, Madame Walker's enterprise (i.e., training of and employment for black women hairdressers) had a rippling effect. In the employment of beauticians she improved the appearance of other black women, thus making them more employable.

Importantly, black female fiction writers consistently oppose the devaluation of black women in their writings. In her novel *Betsey Brown*, Ntozake Shange (1985) defied a cultural stereotype by setting the denouement of the novel in a beauty shop. The older black women customers in the beauty shop confirm Betsey's beauty. A black beauty shop is actually a setting where women transmit shared meanings (value and norms) of folk culture. Similarly, Dancer (1998), appropriating the African American idiom "honey hush" as the title of her collection of black women's writing, effectively captured the setting of the black beauty shop:

> Doing their hair has offered women in the black community another opportunity for socializing, whether it be in families in the home . . . coeds in college . . . or women in a beauty parlor getting a professional do. . . . In such settings African American women truly let their hair down and engage in some of the freest and most hilarious repartee to be found outside their kitchens and front porches. (p. 137)

A point can be made that a beauty shop offers contextual experiences embedded in an intersubjective field. A hairdressing visit to the less chic parlors, according to Dancer, is a social experience for black women, an occasion to gossip, eat, drink, and interact socially for hours as customers converse in a folk idiom of humorous repartee. More importantly, these gatherings present opportunities for relational sustenance. Surely, girls will overhear the stories, humorous lies, and gossip that happen when the women gather. In Dancer's *Honey, Hush*, she recalls her own early childhood experiences listening to black women converse with each other wherever they happen to gather.

> When I remember being the fly on the wall during gatherings of my mother and her friends (which was a bit later in my life, when I was an adolescent and teen), their sessions were a bit more scurrilous, the language a bit more obscene, the subject matter often risqué. But their hen parties were always marked by a constant stream of comic tales, outrageous anecdotes, new jokes, naughty sayings, and comic retorts. (p. xxv)

In the comic and risqué bantering that engages black women is an implicit philosophical outlook about life. Apparently, girls' exposures to such gabfest sessions were grist for the developmental mill. Again, Dancer eloquently states this fact:

> When I reflect on these sessions. . . . I'm happy that my daughter and her peers are sharing this tradition which is an education in life, in being black women, in dealing with the

world, in deflecting the threatening blows, in relating to men, and loving (or at least not hating) themselves as blackbrownbeigecreamedamnnearwhitewomenwith straightcurly-bushykinkylongdammnneardowntothewaistmediumshorthai r and breasts and hips of varied and sundry descriptions. I am happy that she is learning that laughter is not simply funny; it's serious medicine; its righteous therapy. She who laughs . . . lasts. (p. xxvii)

Adolescent girls are presented with varied contextual opportunities to create new meaning systems for the development of coherent self-narratives. Self-narratives guide and direct operations of self-experiences for the present and continued development for the future. Cognitive maturation is believed to take place in adolescence; consequently, introspection and recursive thought processes can be engaged in meaning making and meaning synthesis—critically important developmental tasks during this period (Spencer, 1995; Stevens, 1997a). Commonly, adolescents engage in role model formulation cognition and behaviors. Adolescents seek out model adults with whom idealized attachments can be made (Stevens, 1997b). Harris (1998) suggests that like Narcissus of Greek mythology the adolescent falls in love with the reflection of her own image. Implicit in this argument is the idea that adolescents look to their peers for mirroring and self-validation. Notwithstanding the consideration that the narcissism of adolescents is not a novel idea, developmentalists regard the occurrence of self-centeredness as concomitant with the emergence of formal operational thought. Hence, it would seem to follow that the adolescent's advance cognitive capacities can give rise to an exaggerated sense of self-involvement and self-preoccupation that allows for recursive thinking.

At the same time, however, adolescents' engagement in voluntary prosocial activities also suggest that they have the capacity not only to model adults, but to view persons from an empathic perspective (Stevens, 1997b). Clearly, in the case illustration "Patterning One's Future Self," Vonnie's grief exacerbates normal proclivities for an exaggerated sense of self-involvement, which is not helped by Ruby's prescription of marijuana use to ease painful memories. Moreover, consider how Vonnie managed her grief as compared to Ramara in the case illustration "Nested Contexts." As was previously noted, it is important that shared experiences serve as interactive feedback in modulating the adolescent's evaluation of others. In some respects Harris's (1998) observations constitute a kernel of truth in that in contemporary culture adolescents seek to mirror one another. Such mirrored validation makes for a unique subculture dependent on conformity to faddishness in dress, mannerisms, food, and language. Still, adolescent subculture is bolstered by a mass media whose aim is to create a demand, among a targeted population, for particular consumer products. It can be argued that the media represents a social ecology, among several, that influences the adolescent's identity construction (Boykin & Ellison, 1995). Yet, adolescents are great improvisers. Like jazz artists, adolescents are poised to compose lives that comprise spontaneous creative social actions.

Conclusions

Unquestionably, adolescents require healthy mentoring relationships with older individuals. The maturity and wisdom of elders aid the role model formulation process.

Commonly, mentoring and role model relationships were readily available to youth
in school environments as well as the family. In the previous chapter, the difficulty
that many black female adolescents experience in relating to authoritative school personnel was observed. Individual efforts to make sense out of the denigrating conditions found in school environments require interpersonal management skills that many
adolescents simply take time to develop. Despite the social outcry of role model deprivation for economically disadvantaged youth, civic leaders ignore the fact that traditionally the school was the primary socialization context outside the family where
role modeling formulation transpired. Evidently, after the historic 1954 school segregation decision, schools have, in unprecedented ways, become a battleground for
warring political and civic conflict. This effect on the maturational development of
youth is unclear. In the case of the GULTMC girls, the incorporation of a social
identity that included conformity to school norms was a difficult process. Clearly,
PANSI girls who were successful in educational settings had by secondary school embraced the social role of student.

African American families, as most families, teach their offspring about proper
social conduct by way of doing and being. Moreover, generation and intergenerational variability in class mobility patterns exist among poor urban black families.
Seemingly, when class status is in transition, socioeconomic status (SES) variability
is common to poor families (Stevens, 1993). Commonly, kin who have made the transition to middle-class status are included in the adult supportive network of defended
families. Kin who are successful SES achievers serve as role models to offspring. Kin
achievers serve to strengthen the mobility aspirations of defended families (Jarrett,
1995; Stevens, 1993). Reliance on inner resources and the supportive relations with
older women in their environments make it possible for most black females to develop appreciation of their strengths and beauty by middle or late adolescence. Low-
income black adolescent females locate significant, caring, and supportive women
within their kinship networks. This was certainly the case for the PANSI females who
discovered role models close by. All PANSI females, with one exception, were able
to find near females who earned their respect and admiration. The one lone PANSI
female who was unable to locate a female in her immediate environment identified
movie star Julia Roberts as someone she believed warranted her admiration. When
asked whether there was a woman in her environment she admired, 19-year-old Er-
ica had this to say:

> I don't know anybody in my own environment, because everybody I know could be bet-
> ter. The people I know are OK people, but they are not the best people they could be.
> Maybe I just have high standards. Well, let's see. Nope—can't think of anybody. Women,
> I know could just be better, not let folks take 'em for granted.

Indeed, this young woman did have standards, but they were idealized to the point
that she brooked no weaknesses in the women she knew. Moreover, a celebrity such
as Julia Roberts is literally someone unknown. Precisely because she is unknown, however, an idealized attribution can be projected. Perhaps for this adolescent the de-
preciated view of those with whom she interacts regularly represents her de-idealized
view of significant adults in her environment, an attribute developmentally more characteristic of early age than late-age adolescence.

Early and middle-aged adolescent females self-consciously begin to develop a sense of self that incorporates gender and ethnicity. During this time, they are quite competitive with their female peers. Ordinarily, competitiveness is centered on clothes and male friendships. Dress codes come into play and romantic attachments develop during this period. An inordinate amount of leisure time is spent in either talking about these interests or engaged in activities where such interests can be pursued. In the middle and late phases of the adolescent trajectory the commitment to gender, racial, and ethnic values and norms takes on new meaning. The female adolescent moves from uncertainty to assuredness of gender, racial, and ethnic commitment—to resolution of this developmental domain. In middle and late adolescence phases, social identity undergoes solidification. Adoption of social values and behavioral norms come together and form a coherent social identity of femaleness. Still, even this sense of womanness is buttressed by Afro-American cultural values that define her as an African American woman.

Accordingly, the adolescent female engages in idealized role-play performances. These performances comprise behaviors that reflect the values and norms that she wishes to incorporate into both personal and social identities that become self-owned. The adolescent female learns her role performances from observation and the inter-subjective experiences with which she is mentally attuned. In late adolescence, the adolescent female arrives at a cohesive self-presentation, with the least ambivalence and anxiety in her commitment to a gender, racial, and ethnic social identity. The creation of a social identity is brought about by engaging in routinized interactional role-playing performances that become self-owned and continuously self-created. Obviously, such performances initially are grounded, in familial interactional patterns, but they take on new meaning or become central during pubescence. Adolescents are natural and uncynical apprentices in learning the manners and morals of the adult social world. The adolescent, to a large degree, is trying to train herself for a social identity from the outside in, so she seeks the idealized practices of that world (adulthood) in which she desires to become a member. Adolescents are engaged in activities of self-presentation that an adult has customized as character. Unlike an adult, the adolescent is engaged in self-presentation as a performer in training who is learning the self she wants to become—that is, to make real the self that occupies interior psychological space. Paradoxically, black teens themselves are cultural role models. When the media projects a black style of dress in music videos and other commercialized venues, it may become universally fashionable without racial stigma. It is likely that cultural appropriation will occur more and more as technological advancements make the world truly a global village. Repeatedly the media reports global trends of cultural borrowing. A news release from Tokyo, Japan, is illustrative:

> They're bouncing to hip-hop music at health clubs and boogying all night to rhythm and blues at Soul Train Cafe. Women are curling their hair into Afros—called "wafferu" (waffle) hair—while their boyfriends are growing goatees or frequenting tanning salons to darken their complexions. Suddenly black is very beautiful for some of Tokyo's trendiest youth. [A Tokyoan, Akiko Togawa, is quoted:] In Japanese society, you don't have many options; society is inflexible. So when young people see black people who have made it, despite the discrimination in America, they see people who have successfully asserted their individual identity." ("Japan's Youth," 1998, p. A19)

Notes

1. I use the term "nested contexts" here as defined by Bronfenbrenner, which suggests that ecological systems, such as family, schools, and neighborhoods, are successive nested ecological systems and their effects are bidirectional. I contend that in racially segregated communities prior to the 1960s, in both northern and southern regions, these nested contexts were characterized by mutual recognition, care, and empathy, which was a recognizable strength in black communities. See Figure 3.2. Note the inclusion of the constructs of kin-scriptions and community bridging.

2. Illicit gaming industry continues to thrive in some Northern American cities. One can easily engage in betting numbers in New York City boroughs, especially those where people of color are majority residents. The 1998 film *Hoodlum*, featuring Lawrence Fishburne as a New York gang leader, depicts aspects of this illicit enterprise.

3. While the social skills curriculum was designed to foster interpersonal development, the intervention simply built on girls' existing strengths.

4. The 3-year posttest follow-up occurred when the girls were juniors in high school. Relationships that the girls developed in middle school were maintained once they entered high school. While I did not maintain contact with the GULTMC girls after the 3-year follow-up, in the fourth posttest year, newspaper accounts reported a tragic accident involving three GULTMC girls, two of whom were fatally shot and the third wounded.

5. Personal communication with mental health workers suggests that an increasing number of black female adolescents seek help with eating disorders.

6   Decision Making, Dating, and Mate Selection Expectations

She had loved him; she had begged her parents to let her see him.
When they had denied her permission, for the first time in her life,
[she] had defied them and snuck off to see her boyfriend.
But eventually she had bowed under the pressure from her parents

(Lawrence-Lightfoot, 1994, p. 79)

The lore of the streets says there is a contest going on between the boy and the girl
even before they meet. To the young man the woman becomes, in the most
profound sense, a sexual object. Her mind and body are the object of a
sexual game, to be won for his personal aggrandizement.

(Anderson, 1990, p. 114)

Introduction

Societal responses to adolescents are fairly inconsistent. Common opinion is that adolescents will be normally rebellious. At the same time, however, adolescents are repudiated and punished for defiant behaviors since a prevalent view is that rebellious behaviors are a sign of maladjustment (McCord, 1990). Moreover, adults typically characterize adolescents as poor problem solvers or decision makers. Such practices lead to paternalistic attitudes that serve to protect adolescents from the consequences of their flawed judgments (Santrock, 1998). Unfortunately, how adolescent decision making is affected by the confluence of biopsychosocial factors, especially social structural elements, has not been well defined in the scientific literature (Langer, 1996). I contend that in order to realize efficacious decision making and promote healthy choices, adolescents require social supports and opportunities that test personal strengths. Conversely, when adolescents lack supportive social structures, decision making is less efficacious. Paradoxically, minority youth are stereotypically socially maligned for rebellious behaviors, while at the same time limited social programs are available to them to address such behaviors. Indeed, while the adolescent's decision to smoke, drink, engage in sexual activity, or use licit/illicit drugs is reason for adult concern, adolescents need opportunity venues that reward the adoption of healthy prosocial behaviors. Notwithstanding, as practice wisdom suggests, when adolescents do become entangled in a cycle of negative decision making, seemingly deficient coping patterns develop and problem behaviors culminate in antisocial activities. Largely on the basis of age at onset and the frequency of antisocial behaviors, scholars (Dryfoos, 1990; Ensminger, 1990; Furstenberg, Brooks-Gunn, & Chase-Lansdale, 1989; Jessor & Jessor, 1975; Rosenbalum & Kandel, 1990) define adolescents as experiencing problem, deviant, or delinquent behaviors.

Fundamentally, the adolescent must decide "who to be" (Keniston, 1965). This rather pivotal decision underlies the identity exploration to which youth commonly commit themselves. Reasonably, the intense cognitive, biological, psychological, and social transitions common to this period can precipitate and exacerbate mental stress. Moreover, during this period, stress could well become unmanageable, resulting in poor decision making. There is agreement among scholars that as puberty brings about complex and expansive changes in cognition, decision-making skill is affected (Byrne, 1997; Keating, 1990; Lewis, 1981). Cognitive processes in adolescence involve elaborate changes in an individual's thought, intelligence, and language (Santrock, 1998). Normally, decision making is accommodated by developmental modifications in cognition typified by expansive abstract thought. Empirical findings from new cognitive research offer more comprehensive explanations of how adolescents think than Paiget's earlier conceptualization of the development of the capacity for abstraction embodied in formal operational thought that occurs at approximately 12 years of age. Piaget's theory has been critiqued as limited in its explanation of the cognitive changes that take place during the adolescent period (Santrock, 1998). New developments in biological research document the fact that the adolescent brain differs from that of the adult. The development of the frontal lobe of the brain is initiated at adolescence and is not fully matured until at least 18 years (Seltz, 2000). The frontal lobe of the brain controls cognition, involving planning, organization, and emotional control, all activities important to decision making. Expectedly, older adolescents are believed to be better decision makers than their early cohorts are. From a psychosocial perspective, the decision-making styles of adolescents differ uniquely from those of adults, as decision making in adolescents is more reflective of their development (i.e., the transition from child to adulthood status); in adults, decision making is more reflective of personality or ideology (Langer, 1996). Clearly, cognitive processes are instrumental in decision making, but other processes are equally significant, such as the social ecological contexts of the individual's physical world.

Conceivably, it can be argued that social ecological influences seriously impact the cognitive mechanisms so critical to decision making. This chapter will address psychosocial processes involved in two developmental domains: decision making and dating and mate selection. Decision making refers to the development of problem-solving strategies that are practiced and carried out in the proximal social contexts of family, peers, and school. The decision making domain includes the development of competencies in managing immediate problems in living, including anticipation, preparation, and planning needed for the realization of future goals. The inclusion in this chapter of the dating and mate selection domain with decision making is not incompatible. Is decision making essential to choices that must be made about dating or courtship, love and romance? Sternberg (1986, 1988) has theorized that intimacy, passion, and decision/commitment are central to the understanding of romance and love. I use the dating and mate selection domain to refer to valuative judgments about girls' perception of the behavior of males within their immediate environment, including perceptions about romantic attachments. Perceptions of male behavior are derived from a girl's personal experience and firsthand observation. Most important to dating and mate selection are the choices girls make about becoming romantically involved with male friends. Early romantic and emotionally intimate attachments during the adolescent period are thought to be influential in later decisions about mate selection and marriage in adulthood. Adolescent maturational changes thought to be directly associated with decision making and dating and mate selection, such as cognition, sexual desire, and sexual activity, are discussed. Challenges to decision making and dating and mate selection for inner-city girls are addressed within the social contexts of family, peer, and community. The case illustration *"Deciding on the Future"* raises critical issues about developmental dilemmas related to decisions, mate selection, and futuristic goals.

Social contextual challenges are presented as a framework for the reflective consideration of the person-process-context model of the text. The interactionist viewpoint of the person-process-context model suggests that psychological and sociocultural challenges to decision making, including decisions about romantic interests, can be effectively met through interaction with skilled individuals in one's environment or social contexts. In previous chapters, I argued that mutual recognition, self-efficacy, and assertion were intersubjective attributes that were central to the development of self-relatedness, a connective element of the person-process-context paradigm. The attributes of self-relatedness are used by resilient girls to mediate exposure to risk factors as well as to promote social behaviors intrinsic to the specific developmental domains of decision making and dating and mate selection. An interactionist view is supported by Vygotsky's (1978) theories with a strong emphasis on culture in the lives of people, suggesting that maturation interacts with environmental experiences. In this view, cognitive processes and mechanisms are enhanced through social interaction with skilled others (Santrock, 1998).

Pubertal Development: Overall Considerations

Maturational changes during the adolescent period affect decision-making abilities and dating patterns. Importantly, age is consequential in decision-making competence and in the onset of other-sex partner attachments that make up dating patterns. Conceivably, decision making is inextricably connected to maturational development that involves key age-related transitions, including cognitive processes, socioemotional processes, and reproductive maturity. Certainly, when decision making is effective, self-efficacy is experienced. Adolescents commonly embark on a search for meaning and purpose in life. The adolescent's quest for being can lead to effective decision making about present and future dilemmas in living. New thinking among theorists and researchers is that the potential for developing personal meaning and wisdom is unhampered in adolescent development. It is inferred that wisdom is not just an attribute of elders, but is built up, during the adolescent period, from efforts of identity exploration and self-evaluation (Fry, 1998). Fry eloquently states:

> [T]he potential for developing personal meaning and wisdom is unrestricted in adolescent development. Whereas some aspects of wisdom entail knowledge about the fundamental aspects of life (i.e., knowledge about important and difficult matters of life, their interpretation, and management), there are equally other aspects of wisdom that relate to and reflect the adolescent's understanding of everyday routines (i.e., knowledge of common

activities and events, experiences of everyday uncertainties and doubts about difficult choices and decision making, inasmuch as these are difficult matters specific to this stage of development). (p. 95)

Is the development of natural abilities unfettered, as Fry eloquently suggests? Or does Fry speak to the enduring nature versus nurture debate? Is the idea of unrestricted freedom in meaning and wisdom construction useful for an exegesis of adolescent decision making? Regarding a reflective pragmatic discussion of resiliency and coping in adolescence, the second question posed here necessarily invokes an affirmative response. The point of posing this query is to elevate, for examination, the centrality of decision making in adolescent development. Arguably, the ability to cope competently with life's daily hassles promotes self-efficacy. Most teens eagerly anticipate autonomous functioning and enthusiastically embrace decision-making opportunities. On the other hand, some teens are overwhelmed by the multiple choices independence grants and are reluctant to exercise decision-making abilities.[1]

Studies suggest that puberty timing effects are found on social adjustment measures. For instance, early maturing females are more likely to experience rule-breaking behaviors and poor adjustment outcomes than late-maturing females. Early maturing girls experience drunkenness and school truancy. Also, early maturing girls tend to date early (older boys) and have more social popularity. There is some evidence to suggest that early dating, frequent dating, and single-partner committed dating are associated with early sexual activity (Magnusson, Stattin, & Allen, 1985; Stattin & Magnusson, 1990; Stevens, 1993). Despite early menarche, body development, and elevated testosterone levels, empirical evidence suggests that variability in adolescent sexual patterns is more likely attributable to contextual social factors than to hormonal changes (Brooks-Gunn & Furstenberg, 1989; Gargilo, Altie, Brooks-Gunn, & Warren, 1987; Hayes, 1987; Katchadourian, 1990). Notwithstanding, the consideration is that the pivotal marker of reproduction maturity will occur even when socioemotional maturity is lacking. Van Gennep theorized that adolescence is a well-defined transition from the asexual world of childhood to the sexual realm of adulthood. Arguably, reproduction maturity is the pivotal marker for this transition.

In traditional societies, tasks, skills, duties, and responsibilities that defined social maturity accompanied the rites of passage that demarcate the transition from childhood to adulthood. Unlike adolescents in traditional societies, the modern Western adolescent is without sociocultural maturity markers and is dependent on biological markers for this transition, which in the case of girls is ordinarily viewed as menarche. Recent developments in puberty research clear up many myths about adolescent sexuality. As a matter of fact, only within the last decade has there been serious research about pubertal processes and their effects (Brooks-Gunn & Reiter, 1990; Dubas & Petersen, 1993). Principally, the essential contribution from this empirical research is that puberty is not a single event. While common opinion is that menarche signals puberty, it is arguably a critical marker, but it is only one event, occurring fairly late in a prolong and complex process involving endocrine and somatic changes. This process of physical changes will end with reproductive maturity. Actually, in industrialized countries the age of puberty onset has dropped because of improved nutritional status. Ordinarily, puberty begins, for girls, between age 8 and 11 and takes between 4 and 5 years to complete (Tanner, 1962).

The teen years are typically distinguished by independent strivings and dependent longings (Blos, 1967). Self-esteem regulation coupled with the socioemotional needs of independence and dependence complicate the acquisition of competent decision-making skills. Adolescents are more likely to experience high levels of self-esteem when the consequences of decisions are positive social rewards. Emotional support and social approval from others enhance self-esteem (Harter, 1990). Moreover, adolescents make cognitive self-appraisals about what information is needed to improve decision making. Additionally, social approval is likely to be forthcoming when adolescents demonstrate competent decisions. Thus, self-evaluation is associated with cognitive processes. Researchers refer to the self-evaluative function of cognitive processes, in part, as social cognitive monitoring. Social cognitive monitoring involves both cognition and intersubjective elements. Apparently a regulatory function, social cognitive monitoring involves how an adolescent thinks about, explains, and orders her social world, including the relation of herself to others (Santrock, 1998). Inferred in social cognitive monitoring is the notion of perspective taking, that is, the adolescent's capacity to take the viewpoint of another, to understand the feelings, thoughts, and attitude of another (Selman, 1980). Additionally, while perspective taking focuses on cognition, it can be considered as empathic understanding, an intersubjective quality associated with the care protective sensibility domain discussed previously. Social cognitive monitoring is, to a degree, contextually dependent, as it involves contextual processes.

It seems reasonable to assume that for poor decision making to have an unequivocal effect, poor decisions must be protracted or cumulative with consequential outcomes that are detrimental to self and others. For example, once an adolescent has initiated a delinquent career, pragmatic decisions are necessarily made within the framework of the particular trajectory in which she has embarked. To be sure, resilient youth will demonstrate healthy decision making in adverse environments. Certainly, the coping skills of resilient youth can become refined in meeting challenges of environmental jeopardy, such as drug trafficking, gang-related behaviors, sexual harassment, and racism. It is important to note, however, that personal coping and decision making are not complete antidotes for the eradication of stress engendered from environmental conditions. Generally, it is assumed that effective coping brings about stress relief and modification of a circumstance, however, there are particular life pressures embedded in social structures that are resistant to individual coping efforts (Pearlin, 1991). Similarly, I suggest that particular conditions existent in inner-city communities are unaffected by individual coping efforts. I use resiliency here not to demonstrate that adolescents who cope competently or make sound decisions necessarily experience significant stress reduction or changes in their neighborhoods; the term is used to exemplify both the vulnerability and the strength of the girls living in these environments. In short, resilient inner-city African American girls do make competent decisions and execute healthy coping strategies despite environmental conditions. Yet there are many challenges to girls' skilled decision making related to dating and mate selection within the contextual spheres of the family, peers, community, and neighborhood. In the discussion that follows the GULTMC study findings are used primarily in the analysis of childrearing practices related to early maternal concerns on dating. In subsequent analyses of the topics of romantic attachments and neighborhood influences, findings from both the GULTMC and the PANSI samples are considered. The selective considerations of the findings in these analyses reflect age-graded developmental differences.

Challenges of Decision Making, Dating, and Mate Selection

Family Vulnerabilities

Related to considerations of family vulnerability are societal factors and family process factors. Generally, the African American family has been depicted as an extended kin constellation, the members of which occupy the same domicile (McAdoo, 1993; Taylor, 1996, 1997). The strength of the extended family unit is that it provides multiple parental surrogates or allomothers through which varied relational connections of emotional, social, and economic supports are available to offspring. In some respects, the African American extended family represents social capital since its extensive instrumental and expressive role functions have aided intergenerational survival. Social capital mediates social-environmental risks or structural strain effects. Yet increasingly among African American inner-city dwellers, extended kin, including grandparents, aunts, and uncles, reside in separate households. I propose that it is likely that the physical breakup of the extended family has made the kinship network less influential in the rearing of children. That is, kin have less of an ongoing influence in childrearing practices. The unraveling of the African American extended family unit may have been hastened by longstanding social welfare policies, which obstructed fathers' occupancy in indigent families and aided adolescent mothers in setting up separate independent households as emancipated minors (Jewell, 1987). Additionally, the loosening of the extended family network has been attributed to major changes in the American economy, involving the shift from manufacturing jobs to service and high-technology occupations and to the unparalleled concentration of wealth. It is argued that these changes have adversely effected all American families (Staples & Johnson, 1993). Moreover, a profusion of anecdotal evidence and empirical documentation suggests that drug misuse has ravaged black communities, dismembering the extended family. Such accounts suggest that the family itself may represent an ecology of risk when extensive drug misuse and drug trafficking occur among family members, including offspring and elders (Fullilove et al., 1993).

The GULTMC and PANSI sample girls were residing in single-parent households headed by women. However, among these sample girls, kinship connections were such that they were sustained by family members residing both in nearby neighborhoods and in distant rural regions of the southern United States. Still, for contemporary adolescents, the family has become less consequential in decisions of peer social activities, especially dating. Indeed, the contemporary nuclear family, as the chief generational collective of functional roles, responsibilities, and obligations, seems uniquely vulnerable in meeting adolescents' social needs. Seemingly, the contemporary American nuclear family is less capable of protecting youth from negative outside influences. Modern nuclear families compete with myriad societal influences for adolescents' time and attention. For example, commercial recreation, including TV, music, movies, and video games, is designed for isolated consumer markets, such as teen markets, adult markets, urban markets, and so on. In turn, this segregated division of consumer goods creates separateness in social, leisure, or recreational activities.

Dating, a term used to describe modern courting patterns, initially appeared in the 1920s. Modern life was reflected in the remarkable cultural changes brought on by the social effects of the automobile, coed education, the telephone, and films. Such transformations hastened the change in traditional patterns of courtship in which the family habitually dictated social transactions and social arrangements (Hine, 1999). The social invention of dating distinguished matchmaking as exclusively the responsibility and choice of the two individuals involved. The demise of the power of the family in decisions concerning courtship indicated that matchmaking was no longer a collective undertaking by parents and chaperons. Modern courtship patterns meant that parental control no longer reigned, and thus parents were no longer singularly responsible for orchestrating social arrangements so that their daughters could meet eligible men. In earlier periods, parents knew with whom their daughters shared leisure activities and they knew where those activities occurred. This was no less true of the nineteenth century American Negro as it was of whites.

The Negro, too, was a participant in the social and cultural fabric of American life. The free Negro liberally embraced American cultural values and courtship patterns despite legal and social mores to restrict venues for social gatherings. In the daily tabloids, the social activities of African Americans were commonly reported with mockery, as African Americans were seen as parodying American European culture rather than authentically embracing the culture as part of their heritage as Americans (White & White, 1998). Interestingly, derision by whites of the Negro's cultural adaptation indicated that the Negro was damned for both her or his African and American cultural heritages. First, the Negro's unique folk expressions, culturally different from those embodied by the dominant culture, were considered odious. Second, the Negro was ridiculed when the majority groups' cultural expressions were embraced to express her or his Americanism. Illustratively, White and White cite a report in New York's *National Advocate* as early as the 1820s of African American men and women leisurely promenading on Sunday evenings after attending Sunday worship services. Importantly, the reportage offers a glimpse of the Negro's adaptation to an American lifestyle:

> Attempts by African Americans to establish alternative venues for sociability, especially anything more upmarket than a tavern or a dancehall, met with white opposition and hostility. Blacks were, for example, excluded from all of the ice cream and tea gardens in New York. In 1821, however, a new venue, designed exclusively for an African American clientele, opened at the African Grove, behind the hospital on the west side, a development that the *National Advocate* attributed to the increase in the number of blacks in the city. The African Grove was a place where "ebony lads and lasses could obtain ice cream, ice punch, and hear music" and where "black fashionables saunter up and down the garden, in all the pride of liberty and unconscious of want." (p. 93)

The public social spaces in which dating occur today are much more varied than in earlier times. All things considered, economically disadvantaged youth are isolated in urban ghettos and have limited access to recreational social spaces suitable for dating. Still, movie establishments, skating rinks, dance halls, institutional assembly halls, sport events, pop music concerts, shopping malls, and the like are social spaces where contemporary adolescents commonly gather. Moreover, given technological advances, social spaces for relational connection may be created electronically via cyberspace, where the mode of relating is isolated and acontextual. It is likely that adolescents will make increasing use of cyberspace as a means of communication. Compared to earlier periods, one significant difference today is the absence of adult supervision in those social settings that adolescents frequent or construct for relational connection. More importantly, dating among contemporary adolescents is likely to involve sexual activity. Unfortunately, adolescent sexual activity often results in premature parenthood. Adolescent parenthood contributes to the socioeconomic vulnerability of the family. An adolescent girl's maternal status compounds the initial disadvantages of being poor, although her economic, educational, and social impoverishment before she gives birth is the primary reason she is poor later in life (Alan Guttmacher Institute, 1994).

Courtship configurations, whether traditional or modern, embody the societal recognition of the adolescent's biological and social metamorphosis. Additionally, dating patterns appropriate the adolescent's transformation in self perception. Relatedly, a girl's view of self-changes to accommodate reproduction maturity, believed to occur at the time of menarche. Ordinarily, the expression "coming of age" suggests this eventful time. The adolescent girl no longer sees herself as a child, but as a blossoming woman. The self-view that one has the biological capacity to give birth informs decision making and self-construction during the adolescent period. For instance, a girl undergoes cognitive restructuring as she perceives herself to be changed biologically. Significantly, contextual factors are also attributed, as the girl "coming of age" is treated differently by parents and family members. Still, the transition from virginal to nonvirginal status is socially and contextually mediated (Brooks-Gunn & Furstenberg, 1989; Ensminger, 1990; Gibbs, 1986). Ultimately, learning decision-making skills during this period seems to be pivotal in modulating sexual desire and emotional intimacy.

The ways in which low-income African American inner-city families negotiate their daughters' social-recreational needs, including dating, vary considerably. Seemingly, inner-city African American parents' disciplinary responses range from exceedingly stringent to overly permissive. Fordham's (1996) ethnographic study, for example, documents that parents of high academic achievers (girls) exercised stringent parental control of their daughters' activities, whereas parents of low academic achievers (girls) permitted their daughters unlimited freedom in decisions about both academic and social affairs. The high academic achievers, at best, made decisions to adhere to parental controls. Also, girls who were high academic achievers were not allowed to date until the late teens, whereas girls who were low academic achievers were permitted to start dating in the early teens. Additionally, high academic achievers were ambitious and had futuristic goals, whereas low academic achievers had modest goals for the future and were less likely to be ambitious. These findings are consistent with other works that suggest that rigorous parental supervision during the teen years can advance social mobility and promote the development of resilient characteristics in African American adolescents, such as academic success (Jarrett, 1995; Sampson, Raudenbush, & Felton, 1997). More will said about this topic in the next chapter. However, an alternative explanation for resilient girls who achieve without authoritarian discipline is that resilient girls are motivated to achieve precisely because they lack structure and discipline in their environments.

There has been limited investigation of black parenting practices among family researchers (Aschenbrenner, 1973; Billingsley, 1968, 1992; Hill, 1972, 1997; Ladner, 1971; McAdoo, 1988, 1997; Nobles, 1973; Rainwater, 1970; Staples & Johnson, 1993; Willie, 1988). One of the most important contributions of Fordham's (1996) study is a finding related to the gendered specificity of parental controls concerning the interrelationship of dating and decision making. Still, severe parental controls aimed at the regulation of dating behaviors may not be actually helpful to the adolescent girl. Developmentally, dating can be viewed as that practice of social intersubjective processes by which adolescents learn to relate companionably to other-sex partners. Learning emotional intimacy and empathic ways of relating to other-sex partners prepares the adolescent girl for the eventual selection of marriageable mates (Feiring, 1996). Tellingly, the literature is scarce related to dating, sexual desire, sexual activity, and mate selection among African American female adolescents. Albeit limited in its generalizability, there is some evidence to suggest that urban girls' exposure to violence, both sexual and environmental, is a significant factor in the inability to experience sexual pleasure (Tolman & Szalacha, 1999). But sexual desire and sexual pleasure are only components of a much larger pattern of male and female relationships, involving the modeling of functional relationships that take place in the family. The family is the context for learning perspective taking of the expressive and instrumental roles assumed by family members. Studies of black families suggest that black fathers embrace the expressive nurturance of the parental role eagerly and value companionship with children (Staples & Johnson, 1993). Certainly, males as well as females model girls' self-expectations of partner behavior in romantic relationships. However, what is largely absent in the research literature on black families are studies related to parenting styles and adolescents, especially about African American females and their relationships with fathers and father surrogates. Although the GULTMC and PANSI respondents resided mostly in single-parent households, most girls could speak of extended kin or father surrogates who were relationally connected in their lives. However, it was not clear how these males were involved in the disciplinary controls of the girls.

The GULTMC and PANSI findings indicate that adolescent dating is a cause of worry and concern for inner-city parents, especially mothers. Inner-city mothers experience the family unit as expressly vulnerable during the "coming of age" of their adolescent daughters. Consequently, many mothers become fearfully overprotective when girls begin to attract the romantic interest of boys. In such circumstances, early age adolescent girls are given narrowly defined prescriptions and broadly defined proscriptions for relating to males. Among the GULTMC girls, mothers in the supervision of their daughters' social activities carried out vigilant and punitive disciplinary measures. While mothers viewed their behavior as expressions of "tough love," early

age adolescent daughters rarely understood or shared their mothers' outlook. Tough
love restrictions among a couple of the GULTMC mothers proved so ineffectual that
institutional measures were sought. In one particular instance, a GULTMC mother
filed a Children In Need of Supervision (CHINS)[2] juvenile justice report to augment
disciplinary control of her daughter's behavior:

NIA: You should have seen how my mother was acting in court. She kept saying to
the judge, "Take her to jail. Take her to jail. I don't care nothing about her. She ain't
coming back to my house cause she didn't tell me where she was staying at last night."
ELONDA: Do you really think your mother wants you in jail?
NIA: I don't know. Later, she said she did it because she loved me and she really
didn't want me to go to jail. But she just really gets to me, it's like I can't be a separate person. She has to know everything I do. I guess I just don't like it.

What was especially compelling about this particular mother was her persistence
in marshalling whatever forces available to her to achieve her goal of disciplinary control. Although most GULTMC mothers did not resort to such extreme measures of
controls, mothers were similar in their desires to exercise control over their daughters' behaviors. These study findings contradict Fordham's findings, since the
GULTMC girls were not high academic achievers and their mothers were making
every effort to be authoritarian disciplinarians. In such situations, girls are likely to
learn inadvertently fear and distrust of males. In a discussion of dating, the GULTMC
girls spoke of doubt and seemed to have a lack of confidence in the evidential trust
possible in male-female relationships:

HARIKA: All boys are dogs, whether you know it or not.
SW: Really!
NANETTE: They'll mess with somebody else regardless of what.
CARETHA: It's true, they are dogs.
SW: They're all dogs?
CLARICE: When they fall in love, they use somebody else as a rebound. To get
both of them, if one fall apart.
SW: Ohhhhhh, so you're saying—[interrupted].
CLARICE: They just cheat a lot, they cheat girls like it's anything.
SW: That sounds like a pretty painful place to be in. If they are dogs you must get
used a lot. I think that's what I'm hearing. Is that right?
ELONDA: Yeah! Most women think that.
ANGEL: Yeah! It's a man's world and ain't nothin you can do about it. Even our
teacher, Ms. Barton, says it's a man's world.

Adolescent girls require particular intersubjective skills that demonstrate care, nurturance, protection, and empathy (see Figure 3.1) to relate to males with whom they
will become romantically involved. Girls can confuse qualities of caring romantically
and becoming emotionally overdependent at the expense of their self-development.
Notably, for some inner-city girls, with the absence of a father figure in the home
environment, the irregular presence of father figures, or the existence of severe psy-

chological difficulties in adult partnered relationships, maturation of emotional intimacy, empathic caring, in other-sex relationships can become compromised. Conceivably with the absence of the father or male presence in the home, girls can mature with overromanticized notions about male female relationships. Alpha Smith's poignant exclamation *"I guess I didn't know what I wanted to do with my life"* (see the case illustration "Deciding on the Future"), embodies this kind of emotional overdependence and signifies a relinquishment of personal agency or self-possession. Perhaps what would have been helpful to Alpha would have been involvement in community institutions where female role models were available with whom she could have a personal relationship. Female role models with rewarding and rich lives as persons in their own right might have aided Alpha in solidifying future goals and ambitions. Equally important for girls like Alpha is to have healthy male-female relationships modeled in contexts outside of the family, such as the school setting, churches, or community institutions. It is likely that adolescent girls begin much earlier than 18-year-old Alpha to try to make sense of their feelings about committed other-sex relationships. The camaraderie of same sex-peer relations can be an aid in meeting the romantic challenges of other-sex relationships. Girls can use their relationships with each other to make sense of their romantic feelings about boys. When girls engage in the process of decision making with their friends during early adolescence, particular skills are formulated for later use. Thus, by middle and late adolescence girls can use their mental and emotional energies to focus on their social ambitions and goals.

Clearly, the GULTMC girls were trying to sort out feelings about committed other-sex relationships. Field notes demonstrates the ambivalent feelings the girls were struggling with about female-male relationships:

> Many of the girls seemed to be more forgiving in their attitudes toward men than women. At the same time, they often ascribed a lot of power to women. Women they said have the power to leave or fight back. They don't expect men to change so the responsibility for change is a woman's. They seemed to have an understanding of the need for a woman to take care of herself and protect herself. However, some of them didn't have compassion for the "victim" or an understanding that people get caught up in destructive situations that might be hard to get out of. When one of the girls was having trouble with boys pushing her around, they blamed it on her, but also tried to help by telling her how to fight back or offering their assistance in fighting back.

The GULTMC girls seemed to be learning perspective taking while at the same time sustaining a relational connection to one another. The adolescent girl must resolve identification issues with each parent, both father and mother. Even in the case of an absentee father, a girl must come to some understanding about the meaning of the loss of the father in her life. Intersubjectivity refers to synthesis of meaning consciousness, not just within individuals but between individuals (Benjamin, 1988). The mutual recognition of self and other that occurs in self-relatedness carries with it attunements, feelings, motives, and intentions (see Figure 3.3). The affective responses about the father's absence that results in the deprivation of mutual recognition can be the source of mourning or depression for the adolescent girl. In the father or father surrogate, the adolescent girl learns intimacy and femininity based on sexual and

DECIDING ON THE FUTURE: *"I GUESS I DIDN'T KNOW WHAT I WANTED TO DO WITH MY LIFE."*

Eighteen-year-old Alpha Smith, at 3 months gestation, presented at a university hospital's prenatal clinic for care. Alpha told the doctor that she was uncertain about carrying her pregnancy to term. She was referred to the hospital social worker. Alpha was a high school senior and expected to graduate in 2 months. Alpha resided with her 45-year-old mother, Mrs. Smith, and her 15-year-old sister, Tonya. Mr. Smith, a heroin user, deserted the family shortly after the birth of Tonya. The family resided in public housing near the hospital campus. Alpha's 30-year-old brother, Arnold, employed as an automobile mechanic, was married with two preschool children. Arnold and his family resided in a working-class suburb many miles from the city, but visited Mrs. Smith frequently. Mrs. Smith received SSI disability benefits. She had recently been diagnosed with degenerative spinal arthritis. AFDC benefits and earnings from Mrs. Smith's employment had supported the family for many years. Mrs. Smith, along with her husband, had migrated to this urban northern city when she was 18 years of age. Both Mr. and Mrs. Smith had extensive kinship networks of siblings, nieces, nephews, great aunts, and uncles in rural Georgia, from where they migrated. In recent years Mrs. Smith only saw extended family members at funerals. Both of Mrs. Smith's parents were deceased. Alpha's pregnancy had only been shared with the expectant father, fellow classmate 18-year-old Larry Sanders. Alpha and Larry had been in an emotionally committed relationship for two years. The two became sexually active 6 months after they began dating. Alpha seemed emotionally overly dependent on Larry. She had no close girlfriends, but spent time, during school hours, with a couple of female classmates. Larry shared a class upbringing similar to Alpha. He was employed after school in a medical laboratory. Larry had given Alpha money to get an abortion. She had spent the money on clothes, toiletries, and graduation fees. Larry, now angry at Alpha, had refused to see her and refused to take her to the Senior Prom as planned. Although Alpha was a good student, her future plans were vague and ambiguous. In contacts with the social worker, Alpha spoke often of how she loved Larry and wanted to marry him, although the two had never made marriage plans. Alpha had used birth control pills effectively until her senior year. She told the social worker that in the second semester of her senior year, she discovered that frequently she forgot to take the pill. She seemed puzzled about "forgetting to take the pill." However, as the clinical work progressed, she explained that she thought she was fearful about her future plans after graduating from high school. "Larry seemed so sure of himself and had real plans about what he wanted to do with his life. I guess I didn't know what I wanted to do with my life." Larry was a merit scholar and had plans to attend a prestigious out-of-state university in the fall. Larry attended one clinical session along with Alpha. It was difficult for Alpha to accept the fact that Larry had terminated their relationship. At 3 months gestation, Alpha considered that she would carry the pregnancy to term and disclosed the pregnancy to her family. Alpha's family supported her in the decision to carry the pregnancy to term. Although Alpha's immediate family were not churchgoers or church affiliated, religious beliefs seemed prominent in her decision to have her baby. Family members agreed to help in providing childcare. A maternal aunt in Georgia agreed to have Alpha and the baby live with her and her family until Alpha could become settled about her future. Larry had agreed to support Alpha by legally acknowledging paternity. He wanted a relationship with his child. Larry had never known his own father. Alpha began to think seriously about how she would support her baby and considered the possibility of attending business school. Overall, once Alpha made the decision to carry the pregnancy to term she was quite frightened about her impending maternal responsibilities. She asked that the social worker be present at labor and delivery. She was frightened to go through the experience alone. It was the social worker's first birthing experience. Alpha gave birth to a healthy 8-pound-baby boy that she named Dwayne Sanders. She continued to see the social worker for several weeks after her 6-week postpartum check-up. At the birth of Dwayne Larry was away at school, but he did follow through with acknowledging paternity. He had his name entered on Dwayne's birth certificate. Larry's mother, Mrs. Sanders, was actively involved with Dwayne, providing child-care on occasions. Alpha and Dwayne made plans to move South temporarily to live with her aunt, secure employment, and take business courses at a small historical black college in a community near her aunt's home. Alpha planned to have Larry and his mother maintained their involvement with Dwayne after her move south by sustaining contact with them. *Study Questions and Issues:* (1) Alpha's chronological age suggests that she has reached a level of cognitive maturation that would enable her to make effective decisions regarding birth control, abortion, and future career goals. Discuss why you think Alpha discontinued birth control use and was unable to plan for her future. (2) Discuss how you think the concept of kin-scriptions might be operative in Alpha's family. (3) Discuss the various developmental domains that you think are salient in Alpha's situation. Explain. (4) Discuss how you think Alpha's connection or disconnection from communal institutions affected her developmental trajectory. (5) Apply the collaborative intervention context model (CICM) principles that you think are the most salient for Alpha's situation. *See also:* Chapters 3, 4, and 6–8.

gender differences. Self-differentiation takes a different turn with a father than with a mother, insofar as a father represents difference; concomitant with the recognition of difference, however, is a sense of shared thoughts, feelings, and intentions. When girls' development is compromised in this regard, they are not likely to make dating decisions based on the affiliate qualities of companionship, intimacy, and empathic caring.

Ordinarily, the GULTMC mothers saw neighborhood male youth as potential threats to the integrity of the family. For example, maternal anxiety was exceedingly high among the GULTMC sample about males in the neighborhood with whom their daughters might become romantically involved. The maternal anxiety among GULTMC mothers seemed centered mostly around fears of sexual activity and pregnancy. The anxiety of mothers about premature sexual activity appeared to be reality-based; the possibilities of early sexual activity and pregnancy were real-life concerns, as many of the mothers themselves had been adolescent mothers. Mothers powered by long, discouraging ordeals of partnered relationships or failed relationships saw themselves as protecting their daughters from similar experiences. Equally important to the GULTMC girls were instances of gender bias in maternal concerns about their social activities. The girls believed that their brothers had unlimited freedom in the pursuit of their social activities, including those that involved romantic liaisons. Clearly, the girls saw mothers' responses to boys as being overly permissive. The GULTMC mothers did not discourage their sons from early dating. Fordham (1996) claims that the rearing of black males in a racist society is much more complex than the rearing of black females. She compellingly argues:

> The dicta for successfully rearing African American males are more complex and complicated than those used by the parents of females. One reason for the difference is that parents of males are compelled to take into consideration not only the racialist nature of

America as a nation but also the patriarchal principles that exist in both the larger society and the imagined Black community. African American parents are thus compelled to
teach their sons to embrace a twofold contradictory formula: to concurrently accept subordination and the attendant humiliation (for survival in the larger society) and preserve
gender domination (for survival in the Black community). (p. 148)

Although Fordham's argument is a compelling one, there are no signs that this
aphorism is succeeding. Nor is it clear that male domination is necessary for survival
in the black community. Recognizably, it is difficult for black parents to rear their
children in ways that will foster pride in their ethnicity while at the same time teach
them survival strategies for dealing with racial practices, which for black males can
be lethal. Straddling this tightrope of childrearing practices, black mothers (Anderson, 1990; Fordham, 1996; Williams & Kornblaum, 1985) tend to support a patriarchal ethic in the rearing of sons. This occurs by the attribution of premature manly
behaviors with the assignation of the "little man of the house" or through discourses
that infer value and esteem to patriarchal status. What effect gender discipline has on
girls seeing their brothers disciplined differently and treating other girls in ways their
mothers do not approve of for them is altogether unclear; additional research is
needed in this area. Nonetheless, black girls' resistance to a racial and gender devaluation finds expression in brassy and sassy behavior, whereas black males' responses
may be simply avoidance or aggressively violent behaviors. Fordham cautions that
black males' acceptance of subordination should not be interpreted as acquiescence.
She claims:

> Black parents who are deemed successful in rearing males display a nuanced understand-
> ing of when resistance as conformity or resistance as avoidance is appropriate. Not fully
> understanding these subtle differences can have devastating consequences. Indeed, in pa-
> triarchal societies, it appears to be the shame and degradation of humiliation that fuels the
> resistance of Black males—and perhaps all males. African American males are committed
> to resistance (as avoidance) to the norms and precepts which assign and consign them to
> a secondary status in America's gendered hierarchy and, in their perception, the negation
> or erasure of their claim to manhood. [More research is needed to gain insight into this
> very complex phenomena.] (p. 357)

In some respects, Fordham's explanation of black male resistance is ingeniously relevant. Her analyses, however, raise real concerns as to how black male resistance affects their intersubjective responses to black women. This subject is broached briefly
in the following section.

The GULTMC girls' group discussions about the gendered disciplinary practices that occurred in their families suggested that they were making every effort to
synthesize meanings related to their gender devaluation. While the GULTMC girls
could articulate some understanding of their mothers' expressions of tough love, the
girls' view of environmental risks as well as their own emotional and sexual vulnerabilities were simply different from those of their parents. Despite the fact that parents saw their daughters as being troublesome when it came to dating matters, the
girls tried to project identities valued by significant persons in their proximal environments. The GULTMC study girls wanted the new developmental changes they
were undergoing to be recognized and understood. Above all, they wanted their mothers to trust them to make decisions and become competent problem solvers.

It is likely that girls will best learn the emotional skills needed for companionable heterosexual relations from partnered committed adult relationships that they observe on a daily basis. Nonetheless, as indicated in the previous chapter, by late adolescence, when girls have gained romantic experiences of consequence and have experienced the ordeals of female-male relationships, girls come to appreciate the mothers' outlook about the nature of male-female relationships. The normative development of perspective taking that occurs in late-aged adolescent girls aids the development of intersubjective processes that influence dating and mate selection decisions.

When early aged adolescent girls make decisions of too early sexual involvement in dating relationships, they compromise the development of positive intersubjective processes of empathic intimacy. The positive intersubjective process of empathic caring (see Figure 3.1) includes the personal intactness that enables the individual to relate emphatically across a broad relational spectrum. Intergenerational familial vulnerabilities are likely to result when adolescent girls make poor mate choices. Mate choices that lead to painful emotional experiences can limit girls' development of healthy intersubjective processes that are needed to transmit to her offspring. Consider two 17-year-old pregnant PANSI girls, Terry and Tina. Both Terry and Tina had initiated committed dating partnerships early in adolescence, at age 13 years; however, sex was initiated at 16 years with the use of condoms, and eventually birth control pills, to prevent pregnancy. Both girls had unsuccessful experience with birth control pills; they recalled the pills having made them "sick" and terminated use. Neither of the young men with whom the girls were involved was aware that their partners were no longer using the pill. Emotionally, both girls felt that they were so negatively affected by the relationship with the expectant fathers that they saw themselves limited in their capacity to care for others in general. According to both respondents, the expectant fathers had abandoned them. When the respective young men were informed of the pregnancy, the relationships were terminated. Despite the fact that desertion by expectant fathers was atypical of the PANSI pregnant girls, the following responses reflect the emotional consequences of dating relationships that adversely affect girls' intersubjective development. Terry recounts:

> I do not feel right now I could care for someone. I've been hurt by the father of my baby. I've been hurt by him too much. I'm not sure that I would even want to care for anyone to tell you the truth. The pregnancy isn't going well, I feel sick all the time. And, when I think I have to really care for a baby—well, I just don't know how I'm going to do it. I never thought he just wouldn't care anymore—care about me or the baby. Sometimes I feel like I just want to hide and not be bothered with anyone. He knows the baby is his, but he act like it don't matter.

The young man with whom Terry had been involved denied that he was the father of her expectant baby. Terry's comments are particularly remarkable in recounting experiences of the emotional pain of romantic love as well as the uncertainty about her placement in her family. As an expectant mother, Terry's family sees her as an adult. Terry is unclear, however, about what the family expects of her in this ascribed role.

Tina was so pained by her relationship with her boyfriend that she thought she might harm her expectant infant:

> Thinking about caring right now is negative to me. I am hurt and scared of the feelings I have—I'm scared I might hurt my baby when it comes. My mother is good about talking with me about it. I've told her to watch me when the baby comes to make sure I don't hurt it. My boyfriend is the first person I loved and he ended up hurting me. I feel I can't get involved with anyone.

Tina felt that she was alone in her decision to carry the pregnancy to term. Tina's mother and maternal grandmother as well as the expectant baby's father wanted her to have an abortion. Tina's partner was an out-of-state college student who ended the relationship once Tina made the decision to carry the pregnancy to term. Did Terry and Tina desire pregnancy and motherhood? Clearly, both girls were saddened and depressed about their pregnancies. Both recalled entertaining fantasies about having a child when having sexual intercourse and both failed to discuss with their partners issues of contraception when they clearly had terminated use of the pill. Terry and Tina did not plan to become mothers. It could be that fantasizing about motherhood was the one way they could allow the pleasures of sexual intimacy. Both Terry's and Tina's experiences indicate the emotional cost and difficulties that result when girls are unprepared to manage decisions about sexual activity, romantic attachments, and contraceptive use. To adequately fulfill their maternal roles, Tina and Terry are likely to require considerable family support. Conjecturally, Terry was more likely not to receive the support that she would need, since significant family members had serious issues of drug misuse.

Indeed, the PANSI pregnant and nonpregnant girls diverged in decision making of dating and mate selection patterns. The mate selection patterns of the pregnant girls were such that they tended to be in a sustained relationship with expectant fathers. Where sustained partnered relationships existed, pregnant girls were especially concerned about the employability of expectant fathers. The nonpregnant girls had decided to engage in serial dating rather than being attached to one boy. Early romantic attachments and single-partner dating may place African American female adolescents at risk for premature childbearing. The nonpregnant girls expressed a greater desire to date males who had similar personality characteristics as themselves, whereas pregnant girls seemed less concerned about such issues. Such differences may account for the fact that pregnant girls were more concerned about parenting responsibilities. They were concerned about the ability of expectant fathers to contribute to the economic and emotional support of children.

Seventeen-year-old pregnant Margo decided that she would marry her 20-year-old mate, Carl. Carl, a college student and scholarship recipient, left school to return home to obtain employment and secure living arrangements for his new family. Margo took full responsibility for the decision to carry her pregnancy to term:

> This pregnancy was not a mistake; Carl and I knew what we were doing. We knew that we were taking chances by not using birth control. We have been together a long time, since when I was 15. When I got pregnant it was not the first time we had sex. Carl and I talked first about an abortion. I don't believe in abortion. We made a family, and we believed that we had to accept our responsibility for what we made happen.

"Love Yearnings": Dating and Mating Rituals

Ethnographers characterize dating among poor inner-city black adolescents as a ritualized game of trial and error wherein girls seek to test relationships to learn their desirability as love partners and boys seek to play-act the noncommittal role of "ladies man" or "player" (Anderson, 1990; Fordham, 1996). Obviously, remarkable differences exist about the aims of dating given these gendered-partnered roles. The "dating games" in which black teens are engaged as described by Anderson seemingly represent stereotyped gender roles. Anderson has contended, in particular, that girls are aware of the noncommittal attitude of males, but tend to view such attitudes as mere posturing, believing that they can change boys' outlook. Particularly, girls express mostly fantasized and sentimental longings about what they expect of other-sex relationships. Girls' romantic longings embody vague notions of wanting to be needed and loved by their partners, whereas boys' expectations of girls are focused on meeting their physical needs. Significantly, girls' beliefs about boys' relational aims and desires effect decision making in the selection of a dating partner.[3] All things considered, there is empirical evidence (Feiring, 1996) to suggest that the interpersonal experimentation and practices endemic to the dating rituals of poor black adolescents are similar to the dating customs of adolescents, regardless of ethnicity and class, since dating patterns are mostly influenced by socially constructed gender characteristics. Feiring contends that adolescent girls are more likely to consider interpersonal qualities important to romantic relationships, whereas adolescent boys consider physical attractiveness a significant feature in dating partners. Importantly, pubertal development affects girls' social maturity. In turn, social maturity has a significant impact on the unfolding of romantic interests among adolescent girls. Adolescent girls also show romantic interest in other-sex relationships earlier than boys do.

More particularly, racist societal practices significantly affect racial, ethnic, and gender role identity development. Additionally, as was noted at the beginning of this chapter, identity exploration typifies the adolescent period, including decision making about who to be. Poor black adolescents experience enormous hardship in the management of decision making relative to dating and mate selection, especially when one considers the normative emotional vulnerability of adolescent identity exploration, as well as vulnerabilities associated with the more complex issues of selfhood that black adolescents experience in a racist society and the psychosocial consequences of economic poverty. It can be argued that black adolescents' feelings of helplessness and powerlessness adversely affect romantic attachments. It may well be that black males are emotionally and sexually exploitative in romantic relations as a way to compensate for the diminished self-efficacy experienced in the larger society. Black males' socialization in patriarchal domination, within the black community, can frustrate the development of healthy intersubjective processes. At best, when adaptive intersubjectivity is repressed, the capacity for mutual empathic recognition is diminished and propensities for physical assertiveness and emotional dominance and subjugation are heightened (Benjamin, 1988).

Unquestionably, resilient girls can have successful social outcomes. However, to a large extent, decisions about dating and mate selection are an area where challenges will exist for the most resilient of black inner-city girls from adolescence throughout young adulthood. In inner-city communities, the marriageable pool for black females is affected by the extraordinarily high mortality and incarceration rates of black males (Gibbs, 1988). Thus, the numbers of black women far exceed those of black men during the marriageable years (Bureau of the Census, 1991). Developmentally, the issues of decision making, dating, and mate selection among black youth are vitally significant, but they also represent another study area largely neglected by researchers. Clearly, additional research is needed in this area. Reasons for the scholarly neglect of this genuinely complex topic are not altogether clear. It may well be related to the sensitiveness that characterizes gender relations among African Americans in general. Alice Walker (1983) writes poignantly about this issue:

> I will never forget my sense of horror and betrayal when one of the panelists said to me (and to the rest of the august body of black women gathered there): "The responsibility of the black woman is to support the black man; *whatever* he does." . . . It occurred to me that my neck could be at that minute under some man's heel, and this woman would stroll by and say, "Right on." . . . It was at the Radcliffe symposium that I saw that black women are more loyal to black men than they are to themselves, a dangerous state of affairs that has its logical end in self-destructive behavior. (pp. 317–318)

The point of Walker's narrative *In Search of Our Mother's Gardens* is the unrealistic expectation that black women have of themselves and of black men. Walker goes on to argue, in this womanish prose text, not only that black women are self-destructive when they demand or expect little or nothing of Black men in partnered relationships, but also that they demean black men. The case is made that black women can be overly idealistic about what they expect of themselves and of black men. Thus, the strength, resilience, and personal agency of black women can be in direct conflict with realistic self-interest in romantic relationships. Moreover, black females' sassy conduct, exhibited by bluntness and assertiveness, can be in direct conflict with black males' exercise of patriarchal domination. Black women can become emotionally overburdened in male-female relationships. Despite the care protective sensibility ethic endemic to African Americans, males are not necessarily equal contributors. Black women, like most women, assume the responsibility for the emphatic care and nurturance in other-partnered relationships. Importantly, Walker's sensitive observations raise the issue not only of gender, but also of class status. Walker's Radcliffe audience undoubtedly comprised women from the middle- to upper-class strata and middle-class aspirants. Certainly, middle-class women consider material advantages when selecting eligible marriageable mates. Moreover, middle-class women are emotionally invested in marital unions that will advance or maintain social status.

Likewise, poor black women have social mobility aspirations and expectations for both conventional marriage and nuclear family formations. However, poor black women differ from their middle-class counterparts in seeing themselves as obtaining little or no material gain from marital unions since both partners are equally poor. Thus, poor black women may not see legal marriage as a viable option (Jarrett, 1994). Evidently, poor black women are aware of the disparity between the pragmatic psychosocial adaptations that they are compelled to make, such as nonmarital childbearing and female-headed households, and the more conventional family formations they desire. Despite pragmatic attitudes about living poor, black women, like many women, also see themselves as emotionally and sexually vulnerable in whichever partnered arrangements they form. Sister Souljah (1994), a notable self-described New York ghetto woman and social activist, recalls her mother's anguished relationship with men:

> I confess that observing my mother's relationships with men made me decide that I would simply not be bothered with the pain of male-female relationships. I had never seen the involvement "pay off" or settle with a happy ending. There seemed to be short commercials of pleasure and long-running dramas of pain, tragedy, and confusion. So I tucked all of the emotional boy-girl stuff away in the corner of my existence and became extremely involved in the education of my mind; reading, writing, raising questions, and challenging thoughts. I also became extremely competitive, which can become an ugly and selfish trait. I felt I had to be the best in everything, whether it was an academic, athletic, creative, or artistic endeavor. I was also scarred by my New York experience. I had no belief in true friendship and would deny that it could exist. My father had taught me well. I guarded myself so well that I could cut off any person with whom I had been involved on any level if I thought that they had turned against me or hurt me in even the slightest way. (p. 35)

Souljah's narrative poignantly documents the psychological and social repercussions from poorly developed male-female partnered relationships that can beset resilient girls. Apparently Souljah, albeit emotionally injured, found refuge in competitive accomplishments at the cost of perhaps slowing down maturation in intersubjective processes. Her assertiveness is used in the service of competitive achievements. She failed to recognize her own experiences in the circumstances of other girls. Remarkably, most PANSI study girls differed from Souljah in that same-sex affiliations were a source of empathic support as they tried to deal with the challenges of other-sex relationships. Moreover, most girls learn the positive intersubjective processes that emphasize attachment, connection, and intimacy from heterosexual partnered relationships within the context of family and the kinship network, despite the absence of fathers in the household. Alice Walker (1983) eloquently comments on the companionable relationship between her parents and others in the community in which she was reared. Surprisingly, Walker is distrustful of early childhood remembrances of marital unions in rural Mississippi. Given the quality of contemporary male-female relationships, she questions whether her early recollections authentically represent the African American experience:

> The men in my immediate community seemed to love and appreciate their wives; and if the wife had more initiative and energy than the husband, this was not held against her. My father loved my mother's spunk and her inability to lie when asked a direct question. He was himself innately easygoing and disinclined to waste any part of life in argument, and with a mind that easily turned any question asked of him into a "story." This is what I remember; but surely this memory is too good to be entirely true. . . . While I was in college I became fascinated by the way women I knew remained loyal to men who had long since ceased being loyal to them, or even thought about being loyal to them. (p. 315)

Romantic Affiliations, Romantic Attachments

Typically, adolescence brings the first experience of romantic love. During this period decision making is critical, as it involves choices related to the capacity for emo-

tional and sexual intimacy. Eventually, a teen girl must make decisions about the selection of a dating partner. Typically, the term "dating" is employed as a sociological term to refer to the romantic attributions of courtship. Contrarily, the GULTMC
and PANSI study teens did not use the term "dating" to portray romantic involvement with boys. GULTMC and PANSI study girls used particular phrases to describe their romantic connections to boys. Descriptive expressions such as *dealing with*,
liking, going with, having sex with, and *being intimate with* constituted a range of idioms that defined romantic attachment, romantic interest, or sexual intimacy. Two
discrepant cases emerged in both subsamples of the PANSI study. Notably, the cases
seem pertinent to mate selection and decision making and, hence, are included here.
The discrepant cases differed from sample parameters of the field of study. There
was, within the pregnant sample, a 19-year-old married respondent living with her
21-year-old spouse, whereas within the nonpregnant sample, there was an 18-year-
old virgin teen. Unfortunately, the terms "marital status" and "virginal status" had
not been initially defined for the PANSI study. This rather glaring omission implied
that I held certain underlying assumptions about the study sample, namely, that a
pregnant teen would not be married and that birth control users would be sexually
active. The lesson drawn from the two PANSI respondents was the relative diversity
among poor resilient youth.

Developmentally the PANSI girls differed considerably from the GULTMC girls
in that the GULTMC girls were not independently and actively engaged in decision
making involving romantic issues, relational expectations of date selection, or parental
sanctions about dating. The GULTMC girls were simply trying to sort out attitudes
and behaviors that defined standards of conduct. At the same time, the GULTMC
girls seemed not quite ready developmentally to become involved in momentous decision making about sexual activity. However, early aged adolescent girls who engage
in guileful flirtations to attract older male adolescents are at a disadvantage emotionally and experientially in such relationships. This issue has received little attention in the literature, but it has enormous consequences given that many inner-city
adolescent girls are reared in nontraditional family formations where the involvement
of men may be peripheral or altogether absent. The brashness and sassiness of early-
aged adolescent inner-city girls seemed compromised in dating practices. Despite the
fact that the GULTMC girls were age appropriate in dating experimentation, they
also seemed at a loss about what to expect of male peers in general in social situations. Apparently, the girls' romantic attractions to male peers were, in part, a basis
for valuations of self-worth and self-definition. Perhaps the experience of a devalued
gender status may have been operative in relationships with male peers, especially
where affective responses were of a romantic nature. Or perhaps developmentally it
was more difficult for the girls to untangle or acknowledge their own sexual feelings
in a way that made sense to them. According to the girls' self-reports, many male
peers pursued multiple romantic relationships and rarely made a commitment to a
single girl. Although the study girls tended to develop assertive coping strategies, they
seemed most vulnerable in their relations with male peers, especially those with whom
they wanted romantic attachments. The girls seldom expected male peers to be accountable for their behaviors.

Additionally, self-esteem concerns were salient in the management of sexuality
and gender development among the GULTMC girls. While the GULTMC girls'

romantic interests and involvement with male peers tended, at times, to diminish an ethic of caring in female peer relations, it also stimulated them to clarify female attachments. Self-reports of the GULTMC girls suggested that most girls were virgins or not currently sexually active. Nevertheless, the girls seemed constantly preoccupied with real and imagined romantic affiliations. Most reports, however, indicated that personal self-esteem was often compromised in such affiliations, as girls saw themselves competing with each other for a boy's attention or interest. It was difficult to discern the context the GULTMC girls were using to make value judgments about norms of behavior for males. Decidedly, assertiveness is a useful skill in the management of hostile environments, yet the girls tended to assume more vulnerable postures when relating to male than to female peers.

The PANSI girls had resolved many of the developmental issues of early aged adolescence. Compared to the GULTMC girls, the PANSI girls evidenced greater personal complexity and differentiation and seemed more secure in resilient attributes of courage, integrity, ethnic pride, and a care protective sensibility, all of which indicated resolute personal agency.[4] Girls' decisions about male friendships correspond to the social challenges of high-risk social environments. The PANSI girls, in particular, were aware that many of their male peers were involved in nefarious activities. Rita, a 17-year-old pregnant teen, exemplifies both PANSI girls' awareness of their male peers' involvement in antisocial activities and the emotional nurturance derived from same-sex friendships:

> We have this little group. We dress alike, go to parties, spend the night at each others' houses. We consider ourselves godsisters; that's how close we are. We talk about school, because last year we acted up and didn't do well, but this year we said we're going to get ourselves together. We talk about who we gonna associate with because the people we used to associate with, they can turn on you. We talk about boys who are gonna try and make something of themselves. We try to decide whose gonna make it and who isn't. A lot of boys into gang banging. And gang banging don't get you nowhere. It didn't get my cousin anywhere. He got shot gang banging and this was some time ago and things are getting worse.

Interestingly, what was common to both pregnant and nonpregnant girls in the PANSI study was the importance of same-sex friendships, which offered opportunities for the maturation of intersubjective processes. In same-sex friendships, adolescents experience the growth of intersubjective processes, including empathic caring, acceptance, and trustworthiness, which are effortlessly transferred to other-sex relationships. Such was the case that nonpregnant girls had pregnant girlfriends or girlfriends who were mothers advising them about the pitfalls of romantic encounters. At the same time, however, GULTMC girls did not seemed troubled about boys' improper social behaviors, but appeared more interested in their own nascent romantic preferences in a competitive dating game with their female peers. Minimal anxiety or lack of distress about the improprieties of boys among the GULTMC girls may have been attributed to their younger age and less developed decision-making cognitive capacities. Certainly, the GULTMC girls were aware of neighborhood criminal behaviors, especially those related to illicit drug activities. Mostly, the GULTMC girls tended to discuss the behavior of boys and male-female relationships in more abstract terms. Generally, such discussions overlooked girls' personal involvement or male culpabil-

ity. The GULTMC girls' responses in the intervention group sessions suggested that
the girls were trying to create meanings from personal observations of adult male behavior in their environments.

The GULTMC girls initiated discussions related to self-esteem regulation in female male relationships:

JULIA: Like men put women down sometimes—but it goes both ways. What you
mostly see is in the men though. And they like, "I hope you don't think you all that,
you don't need to look good. I hope you don' think you look better than me. You
need to take that off, cause you look too stank." Or, whatever. Just puttin' a person
down. And that hurts. And, the girl think, since he the only one that find me attractive and he tell me other people won't—then I should just stay with him. That's what
girls think.
ELLA: Yep!
COLLEEN: If you have high self-esteem before you get with that person, and you
like, "I don't care what you say, I'll find somebody else if I have to look for one."
Then you just leave him alone. Then if you like, "Yo, don't nobody want me." And,
then you find this one person who wants you, and they start abusing you, then you
think they the only person in the world that care about you. Cause they keep telling
you, "Don't nobody want you." Or, they tell you what to wear so nobody would really want you for what you look like on the outside, cause that's mainly how they
judge you.

While the GULTMC girls were trying to figure out the meanings of their romantic interests in boys, the PANSI girls, in contrast, downright rejected certain
males, especially those who were involved in nefarious activities within the neighborhood. The PANSI girls seemed to be aware of their own relational needs and had
self-expectations for dating partners to have legitimate future goals. Phrases that typified PANSI girls' commentaries about boys were: "Too many boys deal with drugs
and gang banging"; "I don't want to be involved with a boy if he's a gang banger or
involved with drugs in any way"; "He's responsible"; "Some guys think they're grown
when they get a girl pregnant"; "I'm trying to decide whether I want to stay with him
or not"; "He has trouble keeping a job because I think he's immature"; "He's like a
person I admire, he's a caring and responsible person"; "Guys need to think about
the future and how they are going to make it." Significantly, these comments suggest that PANSI girls made unequivocal evaluative interpretations of the behavior of
young men to whom they were exposed in their environments. The PANSI late-aged
adolescent girls, despite the limited availability of black males, were motivated to make
calibrated decisions about the young men with whom they were either involved personally or knew only through neighborhood observations. Overall, the PANSI girls
did see themselves as "dealing with having sex" by engaging in decision-making activity. The girls did not view having sex as a momentous transitional behavior, but
perceived sexual activity as a normative occurrence. Studies show that middle- and
late-aged adolescents are more competent decision makers than their early aged counterparts, since they are more likely to anticipate future consequences (Keating, 1990).
On a more hopeful note, some PANSI girls were careful to look for resilient traits

in men they had selected for mates. The expectant father of 17-year-old Rita's un-born child was someone she thought not only would be a good father to her baby, but who had the wherewithal to earn a decent living:

> Well he works and he's got his education. He finished high school. He don't gang bang. When he gets off from work, he just goes in the house. He's not going to the places like the other boys who be drug dealing and gang banging, because he's not like that. His fu-ture is not gonna be dead and six feet under. He works at [at the public housing depart-ment]. He's gonna stay working. He's very responsible. I see him as good husband mate-rial, but marriage just isn't my thing right now. I have education to think of.

Clearly, Rita was committed to her relationship with her boyfriend, but before mar-riage, she wanted to complete her high school education. She was a high school senior.

"Dealing with Having Sex"

Contemporary adolescents engage in various sexual acts within distinct relationships, including casual dating and responsible committed relationships (Patten, 1981). Al-though investigators commonly use the term "sexual activity" to indicate sexual in-tercourse, the term denotes a wide range of adolescent sexual behaviors, including sexual intercourse. For instance, to avoid pregnancy, more and more adolescents en-gage in oral sex (Newcomer & Udry, 1985). A media report (Farmelant, 1997) showed that for more than 6 months, middle-class Black seventh- and eighth-grade teens rou-tinely engaged in oral sex (girls practiced fellatio) while a group of peers looked on. The behavior was stopped when one youngster told his parents. Adults were in a quandary as how to interpret such behavior. One parent considered the sexual prac-tices experimentation. At best, adolescents' motivation for sexual activity will differ from that of adults; still, adolescent sexual behaviors are as variable as those of adults (Brooks-Gunn & Furstenberg, 1989; Katchadourian, 1990).

An important challenge for adolescent girls is the initiation of sexual intercourse. Although sexual desire is associated with coitus, the literature is relatively meager about the development of sexual desire among female adolescents (Tolman, 1994). While there is a relationship between girls' sexual interest and their testosterone lev-els, girls' sexual behavior is also dependent on the meanings attributed to sexual readi-ness. Apparently, study findings support the commonly held notion that females and males attribute different meanings to sexual activity. Girls are more likely to decide to initiate sexual activity to meet relational needs of emotional intimacy rather than for physical reasons (Brooks-Gunn, 1989; Ensminger, 1990; Gibbs, 1996). Conjec-turally, the decision to engage in sexual activity can represent personal responsibility for sexual desires and sexual activity. Scholars consider early age sexual activity to be under 16 years. Empirical findings indicate that disadvantaged socioeconomic status is associated with both higher prevalence and early timing of sexual intercourse. Black adolescents are reported to initiate sexual intercourse 1–2 years earlier than both their white and Hispanic cohorts. Black males initiate sex at age 15, whereas black female adolescents are reported to initiate sexual intercourse at age 16.5 (Alan Guttmacher Institute, 1994). Moreover, there is evidence to suggest that black male adolescents may have their first sexual experiences with black females 5–10 years older than themselves (Jemmott & Jemmott, 1993).

Generally, studies have found that the correlation between peer influence and sexual activity is weak and inconclusive (Hayes, 1987). In regard to coitus and peer influence, researchers have typically suggested that permissive sexual norms account for the early sexual initiation of black youth, especially males (Furstenberg et al., 1987; Ku, Sonenstein, & Pleck, 1993). A case in point is the findings of Udry and Billy (1987), which claim that unlike their white counterparts, black adolescents did not develop friends whose sexual behaviors are similar to their own. The explanation for the finding, researchers hypothesize, is that the sexual permissiveness of blacks minimizes the moral significance of premarital sex and makes it inconsequential to the same-sex friendship process. Notwithstanding the importance of sexual norms, another explanation is that peer relations among blacks are both complex and subtle. For example, the GULTMC girls defined the friendship process on the basis of racial/ethnic reference group orientation as well as a sophisticated relational hierarchy to differentiate peer attachments. Accordingly, the GULTMC girls ranked peer relations as "hangers-on," "associates," and "friends." Apparently, parental rearing practices in some black families are such that youth are taught to make subtle distinctions in relational associations, especially during adolescence. As previously discussed, as a way of dealing with environmental risks, families teach children to differentiate between acceptance, association, and friendship both within and outside the family domain. Discriminating peer attachments are characteristic of youth in defended families and reflect efforts to maintain familial integrity and respectability, features of both kin-scriptions and community bridging. Possibly, the subtle gradations of black peer relationships are undetected by quantitative research, or the conceptual models used by researchers have little or no relevance to the social ecologies of black youth.

Notwithstanding, research findings of early sexual activity among black males suggest important implications to consider regarding ecological sexual risks to black girls. One consideration particularly is that black adolescent girls are likely to be exposed to male peers who are more sexually experienced than they are. Empirical studies show that black adolescent males initiate sexual intercourse at earlier ages (15 years) than their cohorts (Alan Guttmacher Institute, 1994; Furstenberg et al., 1987; Ku et al., 1993; Udry & Billy, 1987). Disparate gendered sexual experiences raises issues about dating and sexual harassment experiences of adolescent black girls. Simply put, what is the likelihood of black girls being unduly pressured to initiate sexual activity by older boys? Apparently, sexual harassment of black adolescent girls occurs in inner-city neighborhoods. The extent to which inner-city girls interpret the excessive flirting of black males as sexual harassment warrants additional study. The GULTMC girls, for example, reported a couple of instances of being sexually pressured by boys 3–5 years older than they are. The girls saw themselves as chiefly vulnerable in such circumstances. In the group discussions, girls sought help in becoming empowered to manage situations where they felt exposed and defenseless (Stevens, 1998a).

The PANSI girls reflected decisive judgments regarding sexual initiation, contraceptive use, and abortions. It should be recalled, however, that the PANSI pregnant and nonpregnant girls differed significantly on critical variables such as church attendance, social mobility aspirations, college attendance, mate selection, and care and empathy in relation to others, not just on the timing of initial sexual activity. As was previously noted, the PANSI pregnant and nonpregnant girls differed in situational, behavioral, and psychological-attitudinal variables. More than 50 percent of the PANSI girls reported that the decision to have sex for the first time was a mutual decision between them and their boyfriends. Thus, over one-half of the girls made conscious and deliberate decisions about having sex for the first time. The mean age for these decisions was 16 years old. Moreover, all the respondents used birth control at one time or another and were well aware of family planning services and birth control information. However, significant differences in abortion experiences did occur among the pregnant and nonpregnant girls. The pregnant girls were more likely to have had a spontaneous abortion, which might have been because of their young age, while the nonpregnant girls never had a spontaneous abortion. Nonpregnant girls were more likely to choose an elective abortion as a form of birth control, while pregnant girls were less likely to have had an elective abortion. In many regards, the PANSI girls were making momentous decisions about their bodies, their dating partners, and, above all, their future as women.

Presumably, the PANSI girls made pivotal decisions at middle adolescence, a period where fantasy life and self-absorption loses its appeal, sexual expression increases, and the identification with the parent of the same sex occurs. The abortion history of the pregnant girls suggests that they were inconsistent birth control users and could have become parents earlier, whereas the nonpregnant girls clearly chose not to become parents and effectively used birth control. Yet at the same time, the findings imply that both pregnant and nonpregnant girls exhibited a readiness to engage in sexual activity, as evidenced by their decision to do so. PANSI findings of the girls' decisions to have sex are consistent with previous research findings that suggest that adolescents do assume responsibility for their sexual behavior and its consequences (Patten, 1981). The theoretical explanation to account for these findings is espoused by psychodynamic psychiatry, which proposes that sexual activity constitutes a primary way of confirming existence and a sense of identity (Lichtenstein, 1977; Saari, 1986). More importantly, the PANSI pregnant girls engaged in very complex decision making as they had to decide whether to have an elective abortion, place their infants for adoption, or keep their babies.

Consider the situation of 19-year-old Deidra, who with help of an older sister decided that she had a responsibility to herself to carry her pregnancy to term and keep her baby:

> When I found out I was pregnant, it was my decision to have a baby or not to have a baby. I had talked it over with my sister, Eva. She told me that the family was against abortions, but it was my decision to make. She said that she would be there for whatever I decided. Even if I didn't have the baby, I still had responsibilities. I had to think about the responsibilities I had to take upon myself and not just looking out for me, but to look out for my child. Even if I didn't have the baby I had to be responsible for myself. I looked at my sister, Eva, knowing if she could do it, I could do it. Even though Eva is married, we're different in that way. She doesn't depend on her husband to bring home his check or not, because she can pay a mortgage on her own. Because she can live on her own salary. She doesn't need two salaries to make it.

Deidra, no less than her nonpregnant PANSI counterparts, was making consequential decisions about important transitional social concerns that girls considered problematic. Typical girls' concerns were whether to try drugs; whether to break up with a boyfriend, whether to stay in school, whether to go to college, and whether to have sex.

Developmentally, early age GULTMC girls seemed shy and reserved in discussions about romantic involvement, sexual commitments, and the consequences of sexual activity. Generally, the girls' diffidence was an attitudinal shift from their usual bold and sassy behavior, which suggested perhaps their inexperience in talking openly about sex. The girls found it easier to talk about flirting behaviors in vague and uncertain terms rather than to personalize experiences of sexual desire or of sexual activity:

LEAH: Flirting is just being nice to a guy. If you touch somebody, and you flirt with them, and you kiss them, that's flirting. And you go on top of them and stuff, that's flirting. A lot of girls just flirt 'cause they friends flirt.
EVA: Now, I'm talkin 'bout me, I don't care what other people do. I'm saying, if they're not my associate or something, or my friend, I don't care what they do—either way just because they do it, I'm not going to do it.

In the dating group session, the practitioner skillfully facilitated a discussion where the girls talked about their sexual desires and feelings more openly:

SW: Let me ask you this. Do you think you are ready to say no to a boy pressuring you for sex, if you won't want to talk about yourselves personally? Do you think girls your age are ready to have sex.[2]
DOREEN: Yeah.
LEAH: No. You know what I think. I don't think a lot of girls think about doing it, it just that it just happens.
SW: What about movies, what have you seen?
MURIEL: You know if you see a movie it makes you feel horny or something. You see the bodies moving up and down.
LELA: Yeah. I know what you mean about this horny thing. One day my mother caught me in bed and I was just moving the bed up and down. And you know what it was in my sleep and I was going like that in my bed. My mother told me I was sleep. You know one time I caught my cousin in bed with the teddy bear. She had the teddy stuck up in her. What is that called masturbation?

Clearly, early age adolescent girls developmentally are dealing are dealing with issues of managing sexual desires and desiring to learn how to mediate such desires in their interactions with boys. Yet many practitioners are reluctant to deal with issues of sexuality, sexual activity, or sensuality in work with adolescents since they have received little training in this area.

Without question, the adolescent developmental period is characterized by increased decision making whether to have sex or use drugs, which person to date, whether to achieve in school, or what peers to choose as friends. These represent examples of the varied arenas in which adolescents must make decisions (Byrne, 1997; Coles, 1997). GULTMC girls spoke adamantly about their desires to steer clear of negative peer influence; however, many adolescents are vulnerable to the influences of neighborhood streets where peers congregate and where one's best intentions are compromised. Besides the family, the neighborhood is the single most important context that will impact adolescent decision making and the transition to adulthood. The neighborhood environment represents both ecology of jeopardy and a resource of strength. Obviously, where individuals assemble, intersubjective processes will transpire to mediate neighborhood context. The social ecology of the neighborhood locale will be discussed in more detail in the next chapter.

Conclusions

Obviously, decision making can entail consequential outcomes. Moreover, adolescents are consistently required to make repeated decisions involving comparable situations, such as whether to use drugs or to engage in coitus. Decisions then must be constantly repeated within the same occurrences until one's self-image has coalesced around certain behavioral decisions among peers. For example, the adolescent girl constructs an identity derived, in part, from decisions about her social behaviors, such as using drugs, dating older males, engaging in coitus, or the converse of these behaviors. At the same time, however, the intersubjective processes of mutual recognition, assertion, and empathic caring guide an adolescent girl's decision-making processes. Decidedly, adolescents normally seek adventure and engage in high-risk behaviors. Notwithstanding a seeming paradox, I theorize, from clinical observation, that some adolescents practice risky behaviors as a way to feel empowered and self-actualized. Adolescent high-risk behaviors are often manifest in thrill-seeking actions and are indulged in precisely because of the unpredictability of their consequences. Often, for early adolescents, the future is distant and the present is pregnant with meaning for creating happenings instantaneously. For many adolescents, self-efficacy is gained from taking immediate action in the here and now. Motivationally, adolescents differ in their decisions to engage in risky or antisocial behaviors. Motivational differences in the engagement of risky behaviors often relate to decision making involving peers. When adolescents practice highly risky behaviors, perhaps they seek to be recognized by peers as trend-setters, whereas those who avoid thrill seeking are fearful of peer harassment and badgering and, because of their timidity and apprehensions, wish to escape peer scrutiny altogether. Despite the dichotomous generalization I propose here of *thrill seekers* and *stimulant avoiders*, adolescents generally negotiate their adolescent trajectory at variant levels of maturation and can have healthy, developed outcomes.

Without question, poor black inner-city adolescents are confronted daily with hazardous environmental conditions that in recent years have been manifested in the ravaging effects of drug use and drug trafficking in the communities in which they live. Yet many resilient youth learn from the devastating environmental circumstances to which they are exposed. Resilient youth make decisions to avoid the self-destructive lifestyle that drug misuse engenders. To be sure, given the many social problems indigenous to inner-city neighborhoods, adolescents in these communities reasonably confront very complicated social ecologies where decisions concerning daily hassles determine life or death. The fact that the decisions that adolescent girls make in socially at-risk environments involve life-threatening circumstances speaks to the resilient coping efforts that are needed to survive such conditions. There is some empirical evidence to support the clinical observation that inner-city black males engaged in criminal behaviors introduce their female partners to deviant behaviors, such as drug use and drug trafficking (Sterk, 1999). Many such romantic liaisons are initiated during the adolescent years before socially deviant careers have become solidified. For instance, an adolescent girl may be influenced by her boyfriend in her decision to carry a gun, sell drugs, engage in gang warfare, or steal. Folkman, Chesney, McKusick, Ironson, Johnson, and Coates (1991) argue that adolescents generally make highly complex appraisals of their environments to inform decision making and to enhance coping efforts. I have explained elsewhere (Stevens, 1997b) how resilient adolescent girls respond to negative social appraisals, within the social environment, by acute discernment of hostile social situations without attributing unwarranted self-blame. This particular quality I identified as attributional style (Valliant, 1993). In such circumstances, black adolescents distinguish the personal and social responsibility for the good and the bad events that befall them. In short, black adolescents, I propose, must learn to differentiate personal inadequacies and social or societal deficiencies. In the use of the term "attributional style," I suggest a learned capacity of existential social being where one is finely attuned to the environment by utilizing enhanced cognitive and self-relatedness skills. As an attributional style, the resilient black adolescent girl learns to develop a mode of being that is sassy, bold, and courageous. However, many such qualities are compromised for some black girls when confronted with romantic feelings.

In sum, several considerations about the PANSI girls are noteworthy. For the PANSI girls, decision making was a critical descriptive psychological variable that reflected deliberations about perceived important situational events. Findings indicated that both the pregnant and the nonpregnant girls were similar in their perceptions about the world around them and in self-evaluations about how they were coping with personal situations that required critical decision making. As such, the two groups were alike in accepting responsibility for making a decision as well as perceiving that they had made the best possible decision about a significant life event. Consequently, both groups believed in the efficacy of their decision making. The PANSI girls were able to evaluate the meaning of events in their lives. They were able to acknowledge personal competencies in the management of these events. Decisions and commitment go hand in hand. Expectedly, both the GULTMC and the PANSI girls will discover and confirm their identities as they mature and move toward adulthood by way of their commitment to decisions that are made in daily living.

Notes

1. This situation was graphically illustrated to me at a very personal level. My two daughters approached the adolescent period in markedly different ways. The eldest daughter en-

thusiastically approached adolescence. She shared that she could hardly wait to make her own decisions, whereas the younger daughter experienced a sense of trepidation in the face of the numerous choices available to an adolescent girl.

2. Children in Need of Services is a more recent translation of this acronym.

3. Anderson's text, in particular, describes a bleak picture of dating rituals among poor urban youth, wherein emotional and sexual exploitation by males is commonplace and sexual activity leads to premature parenthood. He observes that black males prey upon black females. Certainly, both the GULTMC and PANSI girls were aware of males who commonly practiced seduction and betrayal in romantic liaisons. While it was too early to determine how the GULTMC girls would manage romantic attachments while meeting age-related developmental tasks, clearly the PANSI girls made decisions about mate selection, avoiding males who were perceived as exploitative.

4. In Figure 3.1, I identify adaptive and maladaptive attributes within the intersubjective triad of empathy, recognition, and assertion. The positive or adaptive attributes of self-relatedness may also be seen as resilient traits. In 3.3 the domains of experience throughout the life span are identified. I conjecture that the domains of experiences represent a developmental spiral of these processes and attributes, which suggests that personal growth within a person-process-context model is ever-evolving. While the GULTMC girls were perhaps developmentally appropriate, it is likely that they too would mature along the developmental spiral. Nonetheless, since the person-process-context equation model is interdependent, changes in either component can alter development dramatically.

Opportunity Mobility and Adulthood Preparation

Because Americans have always expected to make their own fortunes,
rather than inherit them, the issue of identity is inevitably associated with
how you expect to make your living.

(Hine, 1999, p. 293)

A grownup woman has her own place, her own job,
and complete responsibilities for self.

(PANSI respondent)

Introduction

Social and economic opportunities contribute significantly to the actualization of adulthood status. A grown-up status is both achieved and ascribed. Adulthood status is achieved inasmuch as it is culturally defined and ascribed insofar as it is biologically determined. *Who is an adult?* In American society, lucrative employment is intrinsic to the social identity of an adult (Hine, 1999). A paramount quest of youth in the transition to adulthood is to obtain economic self-sufficiency. Seemingly, a college education is held up to American youth as the most fitting route to adulthood success. Such is the case that American colleges and universities provide structured environments for adolescent identity exploration, where an end goal is preparation to enter the labor economy in order to become financially independent of parental support. One can well argue that in contemporary culture, institutions of higher learning facilitate adolescents' rite of passage to adulthood. Concomitantly, the extended pursuit of higher education prolongs the adolescent period. A protracted adolescence phase of economic dependence is only possible when parental financial support is provided. Possibly, the lengthened economic dependence of American adolescents is a social indicator of the country's economic vitality. Privileged middle- and upper-class youth matriculate, in significant numbers, to institutions of higher learning before taking on the adulthood role. It is not my intent to suggest here that low-income or poor adolescents do not attend college; many do.[1] Universities function as opportunity venues to enhance social mobility, mate selection, and the opportunity to mature as well as to secure social status. The societal expectation is that entry into the labor market occurs once college is completed, approximately between the ages of 22 and 25. Thus this age range may well figure in contemporary culture as the normative age benchmark for adulthood. More importantly, completion of college at age 22–25 signals the social termination of adolescence. Yet the protracted adolescence period needed for the completion of college should not be required for all young people to be incorporated in society as useful adults. A 4- to 7-year postsecondary education benchmark may be incongruous for 18-year-olds who do not plan to attend college. A sizeable segment of the adolescent population must meet the social maturity demands of employment, marriage, and independent living when high school is completed.

Given present-day social mores, the expectation that a college education is needed to compete successfully in today's economy places poor youth at great disadvantage when entering adulthood since most are not likely to attend college. Additionally, most poor youth are not likely to receive even postsecondary training to become mid-level skilled entrants into the labor economy. Even when African Americans attend college, they are the least likely to attend elitist schools or to benefit from the social status networks indigenous to privileged colleges and universities.[2] *What are the opportunity pathways society provides for adolescents' transition to adulthood?* One wonders if American society has narrowly defined socially sanctioned opportunity pathways to achieve adulthood status. Restricted trajectories for adulthood preparation say much about society's commitment to youth. Unfortunately, a high school education does not prepare young people to assume adulthood roles. Grubb (1989) has compellingly argued:

> The loose connection between schooling and work at the lower levels of the educational system generates several problems. Most obviously, the meaning of a high school education has become unclear, at least to many students (i.e. poor and minorities). They universally acknowledge that they are in school to gain access to decent employment, but—except for those who are bound for the better colleges—the cognitive content of the high school will not be rewarded by employers, is largely irrelevant to most jobs they are likely to get, and is much less important than skills learned on the job. For these students, the vocational promise of the high school is at best confusing, and at worst completely empty. (p. 21)

High schools that are considered "good schools" are those that are well positioned to prepare students to enter college. Seemingly, alternate pathways to adulthood are enormously important, particularly when a college education is a privilege, not a civil or universal right. Realistically, all of America's youth, and certainly for valid reasons, will not attend college. Undoubtedly, many reasons for college nonattendance will include intellectual competence, interest, or financial means. Social and economic opportunities must advance and support the preparation for an adult status in order for young people to participate fully as productive citizens in American society. Unskilled youth are more likely to experience the stigma of age when entering the labor market, as they are unfavorably compared to their college-trained cohorts. It could be argued that the labor market itself is not equipped to incorporate 17- to 22-year-old youth. Clearly, social inequity results from both limited and blocked opportunity pathways. The point to be made here is that in contemporary culture, college matriculation signifies the sanctioned rite of passage to adulthood. It seems noteworthy to reiterate what has already been highlighted in earlier chapters of this text: For some inner-city adolescents, a response to restricted opportunity venues has been the participation in underground economies, the most common of which is drug trafficking. Or as I have argued elsewhere, some adolescent females realize a social identity as an adult by becoming parents (Stevens, 1994).

Scholars have noted particular events that signify a transition to an adult social identity, including exit from school, entry into the labor market, economic self-sufficiency, marriage, parenthood, and the establishment of a new household (Marini, 1984). Scholars disagree, however, about the timing of these events. Conceptual differences about the appropriate sequencing of transitional events have mostly to do with the way scholars define the social norms that govern their occurrence. When social norms are viewed as universal standards, the timing of age sequencing events are rigidly fixed. On the other hand, social norms are defined, in part, by the reality of daily living, as explicated by Cancian (1975) and discussed previously. Social norms defined in this way are less objectified and the chronological timing of transitional occurrences less rigidly defined. During the life cycle, the timing of significant transformative events, such as birth, work, and adulthood preparation, can be particularized within families to ensure their generational survival (Stack & Burton, 1993). This specific point was highlighted in the explication of Stack and Burton's concept of *kinscripts* in Chapter 4.

A significant transitional marker for adulthood is entry into the labor economy. A societal expectation is that young adults will be equipped with technical skills and job readiness, necessary ingredients for employability. The destructive effects of joblessness among African Americans in inner cities have been well documented by Wilson (1996). Accordingly, Wilson notes that low-skill employment is declining in society and that inner-city youth lack the necessary skills to be employed in higher-skill jobs. Moreover, the communities in which poor youth live lack economic opportunities to upgrade job skills. Poorly educated to participate in an upscale economy that demands highly skilled labor, African American youth find the transition to adulthood problematic and distressing. There is empirical evidence to suggest that once African American youth complete high school, the achievement of an adult social identity is fraught with difficulties. Evidently, African Americans experience extreme psychosocial vulnerability both in the late adolescent and the early adulthood years. Even when youth remain free of trouble during their early adolescent years, they are more likely to engage in drug misuse and other antisocial behaviors later on in early adulthood (Wallace, 1999). The ill effects of racialist structural strain discussed in Chapter 4 underscore the consequences of limited macrostructure opportunities, one of which was restricted social mobility. Given the narrow range of opportunities for the actualization of adulthood status, inner-city African American youth learn to create meaningful adult identities within a macrosystem of persistent poverty and limited opportunity pathways.

I ask the question: How is resilience among adolescent girls and their families manifested when structural opportunities are blocked? I propose that the moral agency of liberated resistance displayed in girl's sassy behavior or agential functioning is a quality of strength and resilience, which makes it possible to overcome restricted opportunities. This notion has been well articulated by Richard Williams, father of tennis champions Venus and Serena. The Williamses reared their daughters in Compton, California, a poor and low-income black community. Mr. Williams eloquently articulates the importance of a historical perspective of an ethnic collective struggle. The strength and resiliency of Venus and Serena, according to Mr. Williams, is rooted in the collective struggle of African Americans. The following statement, in part, was Mr. Williams's comments to media the day Venus won the Wimbledon Grand Slam:

Once you learn your history, you don't have to go and move out of the neighborhood you're in. We ain't walking a line. We are the line. We are the history. That's why you're talking to me and everyone else is right now. Because when people see the history, they want to know, "What's going on?" When we first came up, they said "They're cocky; you can't talk to them. They're crazy. Something's wrong." They didn't know whether we was a bulldog, a hound dog or what—but they knew it was something. But as they kept talking to us, they learned that we knew our history; we don't need to walk no line. Anytime a man walks a line, that means he needs something to follow. We ain't following nothing. Now, if you want follow behind us, great. You'll learn how to get to the top of the mountain. (Rhoden, 2000, p. 5)

The Williams sisters' behavior, as seen by others and as described by their father, exhibits sassiness. I interpret the Williams sisters' sassy behavior from the viewpoints set forth in Chapter 5, which considered sassy behavior as a representation of liberated resistance that embodied a resolute racial, ethnic, and gender identity characterized by the moral agency of collective struggle. Plainly, the sisters have incorporated the father's teaching. After wining the championship, Venus commented:

This was meant to be, I worked hard all my life. I had a lot of sacrifices, I had a lot of injuries and I had a lot of losses, too. But I didn't let that get to me. I kept working hard and I kept believing, even at some points when I didn't have a reason to because I played so badly sometimes. (Rhoden, 2000, p. 5)

The chapter makes limited use of narrative illustrations from the GULTMC study. This is mainly because of the ages of the GULTMC girls. Mostly, the GULTMC study data presented in this chapter serve to illustrate the girls' perceptions and observations of adulthood behaviors in their neighborhoods. More importantly, given the developmental patterns of the GULTMC girls, the study data provide insight into the girls' understanding of adulthood preparation and social mobility opportunities as they operate in the environmental context of their lives. On the other hand, the PANSI girls reported particular attributes of adulthood status actualized in them and in peers known to them. Additionally, the PANSI girls report their self-expectations for social advancement and how such expectations are influenced by opportunity structures. The data from both the GULTMC and PANSI studies are used to elaborate and explore adolescent girls' self-expectancies for access to opportunity pathways and to realize the transition to an adult identity. Additionally, the chapter examines the processes involved in securing community social resources for protection and social uplift and explores the difference between real and fantasized opportunity pathways. An explication of social resources as opportunity filters and their importance for social mobility is also introduced. For purposes of the focus of this chapter, it is important to recall that the PANSI findings supported the study hypotheses.[3] Specifically, findings suggested that there were significant differences between the PANSI subsamples relative to situational, behavioral, and psychological-attitudinal variables. These differences were reflected in social mobility goals and in the establishment of linkages beyond the immediacy of the family, reflected in the engagement of church, community, work, and educational environments, which tended to offer support for the development of social mobility goals.

Additionally, it is important to recall the meanings of the domains since they are the subjects of this particular chapter. Adulthood preparation refers to awareness of the self-expectancies of character traits within the social environment of family, school, and peers. Such character attributes are perceived as effective for coping and necessary in becoming a functioning adult. Opportunity mobility literally means opportunity access. In this regard, it refers to self-expectancies for social mobility as well as engaged activities of social status advancement where there is awareness that such activities are designed "to improve one's lot in life." The self-actualization of social mobility goals includes socially sanctioned activities that open pathways to enhance upward mobility, such as jobs, school, and social development clubs. Two key ideas are inherent in the meanings of the two developmental domain terms. First, the notion of opportunity mobility signifies those particular opportunities, including economic and social, that are required for an individual to realize social class transition or social class stability or anchorage. Second, the term "adulthood preparation" embodies the idea that developmentally adolescence is a pivotal rite of passage.

Adulthood Readiness and Adulthood Status Negotiation

Adolescent preparation and transitional adulthood status are topics that are relatively nonexistent in the adolescent literature (Santrock, 1998). This state of affairs is not altogether clear. It might well be because the area of developmental transitions is a newly emergent one (Schulenberg, Maggs, & Hurrelmann, 1997) or because heretofore most adolescent developmental research was narrow in its problem focus. Increasingly, adolescent research deals less with the storm and stresses of the period. There is reason to believe that "adolescence is regarded less as a stage than a number of circumstances in which youth find themselves and within which options and gratification are uniquely restricted" (Frydenberg, 1997, p. 7). However, even related representative topics of vocations, careers, and employment are limited in the literature. Without question, vocations and the like are pertinent to adolescent adulthood preparation, especially from a standpoint of intersubjective recognition. Adulthood status is a key construct that undergirds the explication of the adulthood preparation and opportunity mobility developmental domains. Concretely, adulthood status represents certain reality assumptions about what adult social roles exist and what actions and attributes validate an adult identity.

I define an adulthood status as *an acquired status that infers the right and obligation to participate in the citizenry and the right to secure goods and services for the care of self and others*. Adulthood rights and obligations can be actualized through authentic work consonant with human dignity that directly or indirectly promotes the communal good. Concomitantly with these rights and obligations is the right to influence others so that the legitimacy of the claim to such a right is recognized. The achievement of this status is considered problematic by those conferring the status as well as by those on whom the status is conferred. The attribution of adulthood means that a distinctive qualitative transformation in the sexual and social development of the individual has occurred.

Apparently, early aged inner-city low-income adolescent girls demonstrate fewer concerns about adulthood preparation than their older PANSI counterparts. The differences among the two cohorts may be attributed to adolescent maturational needs. The GULTMC girls considered an adulthood status related to behaviors that they knew were clearly prohibitive because of their young age and parental restrictions. Perhaps the girls were titillated by the alluring activities in their immediate surroundings and wished to grow up quickly. A research assistant's field notes are illustrative of this point:

> At times the girls seemed to be in a big rush to grow up in a way that seemed, at times, almost desperate or frantic. Some of the girls described situations in which their parents seemed to be exerting excessive amounts of control, but more often it seemed that the girls wanted to do things that were a bit much for their age, such as staying out until 2 a.m. Some had circumstances which greatly limited their freedom, such as having to babysit or having to come home at an early hour, which I would imagine also exacerbated their desire to grow up quickly.

The girls' seemingly frantic and desperate manner reflected in the field notes could be considered a developmental attribution. Commonly, developmentalists describes early aged adolescents as typically exhibiting a kind of spirited restlessness as the need for self-differentiation within the context of family occurs. Such is the case that oftentimes adolescents seek to imitate adult behaviors simply to experience connection to the world of adulthood. Additionally, the wish to engage in certain behaviors is plainly fanciful vocalization. Nonetheless, an additional reason for the GULTMC girls' energized maturational development is that they were quite uncertain about future goals beyond high school. The girls, at times, were anxiety ridden about entering high school, especially when rumors about ominous events at local high schools peaked. This usually happened when reports from former graduates were circulated about the difficulties of class work, unfriendly teachers, vicious bullying girls, and, on occasion, actual gang killings. Most girls articulated a desire to attend college, but such wishes seemed largely capricious since, by and large, the girls were either not earning good grades or not adjusting to the middle-school regime. Still, they would articulate futuristic goals and a wish to do things differently than they observed daily in their neighborhoods. The girls' inconsistent behaviors may well have been related to their developmental age, which is characterized by increased self-absorption and introspection. Developed social cognitive monitoring and perspective taking, as discussed in the previous chapter on decision making, are not likely to take place until middle-age adolescence. The follow-up study findings showed that by the high school sophomore year the GULTMC girls' academic performance had improved considerably and overall school adjustment was better, as evidenced by fewer absence and tardy reports. The girls were earning average and above-average semester grades.

The transition to adulthood and the assumption of an adult social identity can be problematic. In such circumstances, the new social identity and the status change must be negotiated among those individuals directly affected by the transformation. The predicament of the transition to adulthood is strikingly evident in the comments of 17-year-old Tina, a PANSI study respondent:

> My family says I'm no longer a kid—to them the pregnancy means being a grownup. But, I don't feel like a grownup. They expect me to be a grownup, but I don't know exactly if I know what that is.

In a family, the granting of an adulthood status is negotiated by way of inter-subjective relational processes. Accordingly, when a transformative attribution has been asserted, mutual recognition of the status must be acknowledged. The transition to adulthood status for Tina is complicated insofar as her change in status is as-cribed because of her maternal status; she is an expectant mother. In Tina's family, pregnancy and motherhood indicated a transformative transition to adulthood. An ascribed status, such as pregnancy, can force adulthood negotiation irrespective of the preparedness for a change in social roles. Apparently, overwhelmed by the change in social status, Tina seems unsure about what is expected of her. Tina's status must still be negotiated within the family context to have real meaning for her and family mem-bers. Changed social statuses within families are negotiated between individual sub-jects. The negotiation occurs in a social interaction whereby one individual engages another to have a perceived change recognized. Family members perceive Tina's so-cial persona as transformed; hence her identity status within the family undergoes change. Tina's parenthood alters the relational status of other family members as well within the kinship network. Kinship status changes occur related to the birth of a newborn. Obviously, Tina's mother now becomes a grandmother. Generally, adult-hood status negotiations are carried out within a situation that has been self-evalu-ated as problematic (Horowitz, 1984). The change in status attribution is more eas-ily facilitated if the negotiation is carried out with empathic understanding. It is noteworthy that most of the pregnant PANSI study girls did not appear to experi-ence the dilemma of status change as poignantly as Tina did. Most pregnant girls were not in such a quandary. Most experienced a greater readiness for a transforma-tion of status. In situations where an alteration in one's social status change is antic-ipated, the negotiation process is less complicated and mutual recognition occurs with some spontaneity.

Additionally, adulthood status negotiations take place in other social contexts, in-cluding among peers, in neighborhoods, and in religious, social, and economic insti-tutions. Particularly, the adulthood preparation domain suggests that the adolescent is socialized into an adult role and commits to transitional behaviors in readiness for functioning in that role. In the PANSI study, perceptions of the importance of cer-tain transitional behaviors (sexual activity, alcoholic consumption, driving a car, and voting) were examined. The self-reports of both nonpregnant and pregnant girls sug-gested that negligible importance was attributed to sexual activity, alcoholic con-sumption, and driving a car as milestones en route to adulthood. Yet the pregnant and nonpregnant girls differed in attitudinal perceptions of voting as a transitional behavior toward adulthood. The nonpregnant girls were more likely to perceive the significance of voting as a transitional behavior, whereas the pregnant girls were less likely to perceive voting as an important transitional behavior. Moreover, PANSI nonpregnant girls were more likely to view voting as having some direct benefit in their lives. Typically, the nonpregnant girls believed that exercising one's right to vote was a way to bring about changes in their communities. Nineteen-year-old Aleisha explains:

> I'm not sure [voting] will really help, but in a way I believe it will in the long run. Well, when I hear the grownups in my family talk, they believe it will. I'm a registered voter,

like them. It's a way to participate in your community and neighborhood and maybe change things. It's so many bad things going on 'round here that really need changing. Drugs and people gettin' killed and all. Some of the kids I grew up with are dead now. Sometimes it kinda gets to you. My mother talks to me about being responsible for my own actions. Being involved by voting is an opportunity to change things.

PANSI study girls were asked specifically who encouraged and prepared them to be a grown-up and what the person said to encourage and prepare them. Interestingly, the PANSI girls saw their mothers as the most important person preparing them to assume adulthood social roles. Most girls' mothers provided direct and terse instructional guides for adult living. Although the PANSI girls identified other women in their immediate environments as esteemed role models, it was the mother who was always named as the most important person who encouraged and prepared them to be a grown-up. According to the girls' reports, it seemed that parental guidance and supervision, albeit rigorous, were not punitive and harsh. The girls easily recollected the exemplary instructional prescriptions for adult living given to them by their mothers. Generally, the four reports that follow are representative of PANSI cohorts. The responses include only those of the nonpregnant girls because, behaviorally, they appeared to be making every effort to live up to their mothers' counsel:

My mother tells me about how to look for jobs. She tells me about how to conduct myself in job interviews. Right now I'm interested in getting my own apartment and she is helping me with that. I'd like trying be out on my own—maybe have a roommate.

She says be the best person you can be and it's important to treat people as you want to be treated. She's had a hard life, but she's come out OK. She's told me that as you go through life, sometimes self-sacrifice is needed. I think everything she tells me about trying to make it is important, but what I carry around most is that she says, "Stand up for what you believe in and don't be easily discouraged."

Well, I can talk to her about things I want to know. All the time she is telling me don't be afraid to try to go out and do things. She encouraged me to go back to school. I know that she will stand by my side and be there for me. I can always come to her if I don't know anyone else to talk to.

She explains that I must do things on my own. It's important to get a good job and not get married and have children too early. She advises me to make my own decisions and to be as strong-minded as I can and learn to please myself and not try and please everyone else without pleasing myself also. I try and help her manage her money. I believe we are like friends. Most of all she encourages me to get an education.

Certainly, these comments could be seen as suggestive of the girls' understanding of their mothers' influence in their lives. Moreover, the girls' comments inadvertently reflect the strengths of their mothers. The mothers' lives were such that they faced constant economic hardship and had experienced tragic personal circumstances, including domestic abuse and the murder or incarceration of a child. Similarly, from a contextual viewpoint, there is one caveat that should be noted: These troublesome experiences affected families and, therefore, the girls themselves. Still, the mothers' advice suggests that they were trying to instill independence, courage, and moral steadfastness, all traits typical of a "smart and sassy" social identity. Moreover, all of the girls' homesteads were in communities where drug misuse and its sequelae had seriously transformed neighborhoods from places of communal caring to locales of corruption and demoralization. The girls' mothers were survivors. Without question most mothers were able to give their daughters hope and optimism for the future.

While both anecdotal accounts and empirical studies recount the harsh discipline exercised by the black parents, the other picture is that black mothers exhibit faith, trust, and confidence in their children's future. Above all, the girls generally saw their mothers as desiring their success and wanting them to have a better life than they had for themselves. Moreover, girls saw themselves modeling behaviors for adult functioning observed in women they admired and esteemed as role models within their immediate surroundings. Consequently, the PANSI study girls could well articulate what they thought was expected of them as adults. At late adolescence, the PANSI girls demonstrated specific behaviors and attitudes that reflected their perceptions of adult traits. Character attributes the PANSI study girls perceived as effective in becoming a functioning adult included (1) gaining independence socially and financially to become a grown-up in one's right, (2) a beginning awareness of self-responsibility for reproductive choices, (3) assuming responsibility for one's actions, and (4) developing a sense of respect for self and others. Moreover, these behaviors were seen as sound and effective coping strategies. Albeit problematic, the negotiation of adulthood is a process of intersubjective recognition by which the adolescent asserts an identity in which she seeks to be mirrored as an empowered, capable, and responsible person.

Social Investment and Opportunity Mobility

Importantly, the socialization of the adult role occurs at the microcontextual level of the family and the immediate environment. Equally important, it also occurs at the macrostructure institutional level, where economic or business structures are located. In the socialization of a work role, for instance, the individual engages in an intersubjective process with other adults to undertake the responsibilities, obligations, and duties endemic to an occupational role. Notably, a demand for productivity occurs in both school and work institutions; however, the rewards and punishments for output in the two settings differ considerably. Consequently, work orientations in school environments may not be transferable to actual occupational settings. For one thing, a paycheck can be a great incentive for productivity and may be more potent than the motivation to earn good grades. Monetary remuneration in the workplace has instantaneous value regardless of the amount earned; even workers who are underpaid are likely to respond positively to a paycheck. Earning good grades perhaps is based on self-regulatory competitive needs. In any event, students may not perceive good grades as an immediate advantage or reward. High grades offer promise, indicating potential and future rewards, such as admission to college (Hansen & Johnson, 1989).

Accordingly, it could be argued that academic achievement and part-time employment are indicators of resiliency among youth. Overall, the PANSI girls demonstrated resiliency in their motivation to remain in school, as they were less likely to be high school dropouts. The PANSI girls were attending high school, high school graduates, or attending college. Specifically, the nonpregnant girls were more likely to have postsecondary educational experiences. The educational perseverance of the PANSI girls was in marked contrast to other inhabitants of the targeted study area. Census data indicated that well over 50 percent of community residents ages 15–34 were high school dropouts. Similarly, the GULTMC study girls, at the 3-year follow-up, had remained in school and were likely to have part-time employment. Moreover, the PANSI nonpregnant girls were likely to hold part-time jobs while attending school. Interestingly, the PANSI subsamples differed in that the pregnant girls were less likely to have mothers that had post–high school educational achievement, while the nonpregnant girls were more likely to have mothers who had post–high school educational achievement. There were no differences between the pregnant and nonpregnant girls relative to their fathers' educational attainments.

These demographic data strengthen the idea that the actualized educational aspirations of parents (mothers in this particular instance) may have had some bearing on the social mobility goals of their offspring. The comments of 18-year-old Willistean, a nonpregnant PANSI, are exemplary. Willistean, a high school senior and a part-time cashier at a local drug store, had plans to attend college. She resided in public housing and was the youngest of three siblings. Her mother was a high school graduate who when employed worked at midlevel skilled jobs. Willistean's father was killed when she was 8 years old. Willistean believed that she had many older adults in her life that provided her with the guidance and the hope needed to succeed in life. She seemed especially proud of an elder sister who was a hairdresser and who was, according to Willistean, "a businesswoman who owned her own beauty shop." However, Willistean credited her mother as being the most influential person in her learning about becoming an adult. Clearly, the significance of the intersubjective relationship of recognition and empathic connection is apparent in this resilient teen's reflections:

> My whole family is active in the church. So I learn a lot about being a grownup from lots of different people. But, it's my mother who really guides me. She talks about different things that may be obstacles, but not to let that get you down. She tells me to be strong, to keep my goals and to carry myself in a way that people respect me. She also tells me I have to be responsible for my own actions. My mother wants me to succeed in life and she's there for me 100%. She tells me so often that she is proud of me.

Given the educational achievements and employability of the nonpregnant girls, social mobility goals may have been perceived as attainable. Evidently, the nonpregnant girls had greater social investment in societal structures since they were actually involved in social institutions where social mobility goals could be realized. Additionally, college attendance and part-time employment provide greater exposure to those macrostructures, which, in turn, offer adolescents varied contexts for self-expression. Conceivably, limited exposure to social contexts limit opportunities for social mobility, whereas greater exposure maximizes opportunities. Conclusively, the nonpregnant girls had noteworthy experiences outside the perimeters of the family and neighborhood peers. The nonpregnant girls differed remarkably from the pregnant girls in the breadth of their relational experiences, having established well-meaning adult relationships in various social contexts.

These sets of observations highlight the significance of Jarrett's (1995) concept of *community bridging* outlined in Chapter 5. Accordingly, Jarrett has identified those families who exercise social mobility stratagems as *defended families*. I contend that, from a strength perspective, an equally important descriptor of the resilient socially mobile PANSI families is that of *socially invested families*. Engagement in social mobility stratagems are valuable insofar as they enable poor black girls to legitimatize their claims and rights to participate in the citizenry.

Adolescents who participate systematically in the life of institutional organizations learn valuable lessons about how adults cope. Most learning in such circumstances occurs indirectly as adolescents struggle to make coherent sense of the ways in which adults function. However, adolescents will need the direct guidance and direction of adults to sort out many social experiences. For instance, in an earlier chapter of this text, it was discussed how the GULTMC girls struggled to arrive at some kind of meaningful understanding about teachers' negative responses to their learning needs. Unfortunately, many of the GULTMC girls were not positively involved in community-sponsored youth activities. Ordinarily, the girls understood "community institutions" to mean social service agencies (e.g., child welfare and the juvenile justice system), which represented for them not support or pleasure but intimidation and interference. By and large, the study girls' efforts to synthesize coherent meanings about themselves as Americans or even to see themselves as having a legitimate stake in mainstream society were made all the more difficult by their limited view of societal institutions. The girls' persistent efforts at meaning-making synthesis in this regard went largely unnoticed by parents and teachers.

Adolescents require the assistance of caring adults to sort out the meanings of complex social situations to offset the development of pessimistic and hostile attitudes about future possibilities and opportunities. The point to be made here is that individual rights and duties as well as competitive and cooperative modes of adult interaction can be learned in structured and systematic learning situations designed specifically for the education of adolescents. Certainly, this type of instructional learning situation occurs formally in school settings, but it also takes places in churches and community organizations.[4] Because of the importance of social status enhancement to the adulthood preparation and opportunity mobility domains, two of the social mobility stratagems are expressly pertinent and are restated here: a supportive adult network and strategic alliances with mobility-enhancing institutions and organizations. The PANSI nonpregnant study girls specifically reported involvement in both church- and community-sponsored youth programs designed to build and refine the social and leadership skills of participants. Importantly, such programs introduced participants to larger, more diverse communities of youth and adults through national conferences and citywide, national, or international summer camplike experiences. Chiefly, the value of such programs is that they contribute, in the broadest sense, to the social and cultural socialization of youth. The socialization experiences offered advance intersubjectivity in that they enable youth to become less privatized and more universally empathic, qualities that make for competent citizenship. The specific program components were threefold: (1) They provide exposure to groups of various social classes, races, and ethnicities; (2) they offer simulated learning activities that teach healthy adulthood behaviors and practices; and (3) they afford distinct travel experiences to culturally diverse regions. The merit of the activities I have described here is that they serve as opportunity filters in that adventuresome experiences function to refine youth socialization for eventual adulthood membership and the future assertion of a grown-up status. Commonly, middle- and upper-class adolescents engage in these types of activities. Finally, underlying adolescents' engagement in these activities is the intersubjective nexus to supportive adult mentors who provide the recognition and empathic understanding that adolescents need to grow and develop.

Conclusions

Adulthood preparation and opportunity mobility are developmental domains that are inextricably related. Clearly, the intersubjective dynamics that occurred among the poor black families of the PANSI study, specifically between the girls and mothers, was such that adolescent girls were counseled about social norms for adult survival. Within the context of family, the girls began the process of negotiating an adult social identity. The PANSI girls resided in extremely vulnerable neighborhoods characterized by various drug-related social problems. The nonpregnant PANSI girls, in particular, restricted neighborhood relations and were involved with individual macrocontexts that extended beyond the community. Seemingly, some adolescents, with the help of well-meaning and caring adults, are able to shun the temptations of antisocial or illegal activities that occur in neighbor streets. Certainly, it is an indication of strength when adolescents are able to do so. The GULTMC study girls were not yet at the age where they seriously reflected on adulthood status. At the posttest 3-year follow-up, most of the girls had matured and had made sound adjustments to high school. None of the girls reported a pregnancy. All of the GULTMC girls expected to graduate from high school, and some of them considered attending college.

The person-process-context model infers that there is an intersubjective nexus to macrostructures where formally sanctioned recognition occurs. I have also proposed that metaphorically the person-process-context model is analogous to the jazz art form wherein intersubjective processes are improvisational. When the improvisational analogy is applied to families, it becomes apparent that social norms are composed freely and spontaneously as individuals live out their lives. In this way, families take the lessons learned from daily experiences to make up the rules and standards that guide and influence their lives. On the other hand, macroinstitutions are characterized by established rules of social conduct. Obviously, the "contexting" (Hall's concept) experiences of family life and formal institutions are strikingly different, yet adolescents need both experiences to become competent and humane adults. In the negotiation of an adult social identity, girls benefit from the spontaneity of family life as well as from respectful traditions of organizational life. The PANSI mothers' rectitude about life's hardships seemed to have given some of their daughters the sense of moral agency needed to seek opportunities to realize their social mobility goals. Within the context of family, adolescents require opportunity passages to macrostructures that provide the socialization experiences for full membership in the adult social world. Simply put, poor adolescents must have experiences that allow entry into the intersubjective spaces of macrostructures to learn the rights and duties of community citizenship. Crossley (1996) persuasively argues that "the formal rights of citizenship can be interpreted as an institutional embodiment of an intersubjective relationship of recognition, which is in turn the outcome of an intersubjective [negotiated] struggle" (p. 155). The adolescent's capacity to perceive opportunity mobility implies social investment in futuristic goals and the belief that opportunity pathways exist in wider macrocontexts. Individuals have the capacity to lead healthy lives, but to do so they also require recognition, equity, and opportunity. Problem-solving competencies alone are not enough to manipulate environmental effects.

Notes

1. However, college education for less privileged adolescents is more likely to be subsidized with federal monetary loans. Seemingly, temporal financial aid has created an indentured middle class, since it takes years to repay student loans.

2. See Lewis and Walker (1995). Lewis, an African American, discusses white male privilege in the old-boys' network operative in elitist universities, colleges, and the corporate business world. The book describes how Lewis created a billion-dollar corporate business.

3. Study hypotheses were delineated in the Prologue.

4. I do not mean to suggest here the kind of boot camp experiences that have grown in popularity for troubled poor inner-city youth in recent years. Rather, I am suggesting more benign experiences than the simulated rigorous military training common to the boot camps. Adolescents can benefit greatly from simulated adult experiences, such as a United Nations Security Council meeting, court trials, committee meetings, board meetings, work situations, and the like. Additionally, there are special rallies that could engage the interests of youth—apparently spiritual rallies have been especially successful among certain religious denominations.

3

CLINICAL IMPLICATIONS

8 A Social Work Practice Model: Core Principles of Intervention

The most effective interventions will likely be derived from more precise understandings of environment-development relations.
(Hauser & Bowlds, 1990, p. 412).

If you have a place to stand in the world, you can bear its pain.
(Vaillant, 1993, p. 87)

Introduction

McMahon and Allen-Meares (1992) contend that social work practitioners have limited success in helping minority clients. Moreover, these scholars forcefully argue that social workers have been reluctant to embark on a course of social action in the macrocontext and that minority populations may not be a priority concern of social work. This predicament in social work practice, according to McMahon and Allen-Meares, is because the lives of minority clients are understood, by practitioners, *acontextually*. McMahon and Allen-Meares' assertion highlights both a professional concern and a paradox, since a core knowledge claim of the profession is to understand individual functioning within the context of the social environment. Accordingly, the person-process-context model directly addresses the issue of context in clients' lives and, therefore, serves as a useful theoretical framework for social work practice. The model is necessarily theoretical, but it accommodates the person-in-environment configuration construct central to social work theory and practice. The significance of the person-process-context model is the inclusion and specificity of environmental factors precluded in other practice models. More importantly, the person-process-context model explicates the transactional interplay of person and intersubjectivity and its influence on social context. Accordingly, from a contextual perspective, the environment constitutes dynamic effects rather than a mosaic of objective, inanimate, external constraints. On this account, the twin therapeutic components, assessment and intervention, are reflective of the intersubjective processes themselves.

In this chapter, a social work practice model identified as the collaborative intervention context model (CICM) is introduced. While the model makes use of basic social work practice knowledge, theoretically it is grounded in the person-process-context paradigm presented in Chapter 3. The intervention strategies of the model differ from traditional strategies of environmental modification and manipulation, as the CICM involves the dynamism of ecological and intersubjective processes. Empirical data from the GULTMC and PANSI studies are used to generate hypotheses about specific clinical intervention approaches in working with at-risk black adolescent females. Additionally, study findings are used to identify developmental dilemmas that occur among at-risk adolescent girls and for which the CICM therapeutic methods are believed to be useful. Finally, a family-related clinical prevention program is introduced to target at-risk preadolescent girls and their families. Obviously, the conceptualization of the CICM is influenced by study findings from the empirically tested intervention program of the GULTMC study. However, since the CICM is grounded in the person-process-context model, theoretical considerations of human development within a life course perspective (Neugarten, 1968; Neugarten & Hagestad, 1985; Neugarten, Moore, & Loine, 1973), the nested contexts theory of Bronfenbrenner (1979), and an intersubjectivity perspective (Atwood & Stolorow, 1984; Crossley, 1996; Stern, 1985; Stolorow & Atwood, 1992) are also considered.

The Collaborative Intervention Context Model (CICM)

The person-process-context formulation is germane to the actual relational therapeutic encounter. Importantly, the intersubjectivity of individual self-assertion, mutual recognition, and empathic caring permeates all interpersonal relationships. Certainly, the elements of intersubjectivity are critical to the collaborative therapeutic working relationship with adolescents. In essence, individual self-assertion, mutual recognition, and empathic caring are the very elements of a clinical relationship. In the CICM clinical work is seen as a therapeutic encounter. *The therapeutic encounter is an intersubjective experience involving two or more persons engaged in ameliorative interventions, of a psychological and social nature, directed toward the change of the person, her situation, or context.* Intersubjectivity, as previously noted, involves three key elements: mutual recognition, assertion, and empathic caring. An argument can be made that these particular intersubjective elements are reflective of the ingredients of the therapeutic encounter and are inextricably bound in the therapeutic process. Given the significance that these elements have to that process, a brief explanation of the meaning of these terms relative to therapeutic work is needed. "Recognition" is a reflexiveness that includes the others' confirming response, and how one finds the self in that response. The others' response may be represented by the intimate relational other or the more "generalized other" of society, as represented by varied units of social structures.[1] "Individual assertion" is the affirmation of a coherent self that possesses personal agency and acts on decisions made in concrete situations. Individual assertion is a symbolic declarative statement of "I am." Individual assertion is manifest in social contexts or adolescents' various social worlds. "Empathic caring," or "empathy," is an imaginative process that involves mutual recognition of the other (i.e., I can perceive that the other is like myself) characterized by an attitude of care and understanding. Empathy involves imagination and perspective taking and, thus, allows an individual to imagine self in the context of other.

The CICM practice techniques are based upon areas of knowledge related to (1) human functioning, (2) the social context in which human activity takes place, and (3) change processes. The practitioner's knowledge base is employed in the service of reflective theorizing to support clinical interventions. In working with troubled adolescent girls, the critical issue that confronts the practitioner is the management of age-related developmental challenges. The seven developmental domains and the social contexts in which adolescents function reflect the basic knowledge areas of adolescent psychosocial functioning within a life course trajectory. Of considerable importance in work with minority adolescents is a consideration of the adolescents' eventual conversion to adulthood status and the contextual processes that facilitate that transformation. In clinical work, practitioners normally engage in the reflective study of client needs and how they can best be met (Schon, 1996). Reflective inquiry leads practitioners to deliberate about the needs of clients as foreground and background issues. In this regard, adulthood preparation is seen as the ultimate contextual background issue that structures therapeutic work with minority youth, including interventions with groups, families, or individuals. As I have argued previously in this text, the trajectory of adolescence is firmly rooted in the social contextual dimension of society precisely because of the passage to adulthood. To ignore this aspect of contextual grounding is to court failure in work with at-risk youth, especially minority adolescents.

At-risk minority youth ordinarily despair of becoming productive grown-ups who contribute to society. These youth see opportunity mobility as limited or nonexistent. As many at-risk youth believe that they have no claims to opportunities to participate fully in American society, they are more likely to become disengaged from social institutions. At the same time, these same youth do demonstrate a hardiness and courageous resistance to the contextual negativity that surrounds many of their lives. Clearly, the GULTMC girls, despite their obvious school adjustment problems, were asserting such claims in their expectation that the school environment should be more responsive to their needs. But the real issue for the clinician to consider is how to enable troubled youth to sustain individual assertion in the face of failed or negative institutional responses. The phrase "troubled youth" is used here to refer to those youth engaged in antisocial behaviors as identified by human service organizations, such as mental health agencies, child welfare agencies, and juvenile courts. The term is used to refer to youth engaged in mildly serious antisocial activity who are perhaps at risk for developing delinquent careers. These youth are likely to exhibit such behaviors as poor academic achievement, combative and bullying behaviors, early coitus, and experimental substance use. Additionally, such youth are likely to live in neighborhoods with high levels of crime, drug trafficking, and gangs. The CICM considers that prevention and early intervention strategies are likely to benefit at-risk and early delinquent career youth to ease the adolescent developmental course.

The value of the at-risk construct is evident when it is employed for identifying certain groups for prevention and early intervention strategies or programs. I consider a strengths perspective, which accents the salutogenic aspects of psychosocial functioning, including hardiness, courage, and social supports as integral to the CICM. While the needs of both seriously disturbed youth and those who are well established in delinquent careers require sound intervention, the CICM does not specifically address the needs of these particular youth. Notwithstanding, there is a sound argument to be made for the fact that even at-risk youth have begun to relinquish or certainly question social claims to the social citizenship. When youth experience this kind of despair they relinquish what Crossley (1996) calls the "fabric of social becoming"; the fabric alluded to here is intersubjectivity. The real nature of clinical work with at-risk troubled youth is the restoration of the intersubjectivity of social life so that the individual is reconnected to social institutions and kinship networks. A sign of sound mental health is individual self-assertion, but if that assertion is not recognized and responded to emphatically then the individual is likely to experience attitudinal and behavioral disengagement from social institutions and alienation from the private self.

Accordingly, consider the empirical evidence by Fordham and Ogbu (1986) that suggests that the school failure of many black adolescents is due to their reluctance to achieve academically for fear of being labeled as "acting white" by peers. From a clinical perspective, the real issue of this empirical observation is: *How is it that black students label achievement or success as "acting white"?* Perhaps a translation of this attitude is that success for a black person in America is for whites only. Nonetheless, the "acting white" phenomena, coupled with the empirical observation cited earlier in which the GULTMC girls experienced teachers' low expectations for school performance, speaks to the negativity of minority adolescents' commitment to an ethnic or racial role formation and to feelings of helplessness and powerlessness in denigrating situations. Altogether, these empirical observations highlight three developmental domains in which clinical work is primarily focused: (1) racial, ethnic, and gender role commitment; (2) care protective sensibility; and (3) decision making. A clinical focus in these domains is not meant to minimize therapeutic engagement of the other developmental domains. Assisting adolescents in the management of developmental issues in these domains is more directly related to well-being and health-related correlates, including self-esteem, relational connectedness, self-efficacy, and a coherent racial or ethnic identity. Essentially, the perspective proposed is that the role of the practitioner is based on the idea that development occurs within a context of intersubjectivity. The intersubjectivity of the therapeutic relationship is such that the adolescent and therapist collaborate not only to effect change, but also to make sense out of disordered contexts or environmental situations. Simply put, the practitioner and adolescent collaborate in the therapeutic encounter.

Unfortunately, most practitioners are so overwhelmed by the immediate problems young people present to them and the administrative demands of the agencies in which they deliver service that the impact of structural strain, generated by disordered social contexts, on adolescents' lives is largely ignored in clinical work. Practitioners in human service organizations, including child welfare agencies, juvenile courts, and mental health agencies, rarely include, in clinical assessments, outcome evaluations of the various organizational programs that are designed to aid youth in their trajectory to adult status. More importantly, human service organizations seldom conduct evaluation studies of youth programs to determine their effectiveness. The most compelling contextual issue that practitioners face in therapeutic work with minority youth is the manner in which macrostructure actually engages adolescents for adulthood preparation and how adolescents respond to that engagement. The questions practitioners must ask are: To what extent did agency program services advance the maturational goals of this particular adolescent? Were agency services adequate to assist the adolescent in the eventual transition to adulthood? Will the particular intervention advance adolescents' development? The position is taken that adulthood preparation issues are a part of the practitioner's reflective theorizing regardless of the adolescent's age inasmuch as the end stage of puberty is an adult status.

Moreover, the adolescent's strategies for coping with essential issues involve systems of intersubjectivity, including microsystems, macrosystems, and exosystems. Her intersubjective coping provides insight into the manifest strengths and weaknesses of adolescents in the management of developmental issues. "What most adolescents may lack in their development is "regular times for structured talking or communication (Bloom, 1985) in life-affirming relationships with trustworthy persons, other than parents, who invite them to explore their uncertainties about new experiences, and encourage them to deal with the sources of their insecurity" (Fry, 1998, p. 99). In this regard, a therapeutic encounter can actually facilitate identity exploration, a specific developmental task of adolescence. The CICM involves certain principles that direct the therapeutic encounter process to effect change in the participant's contextual situation. The therapeutic principles in the discussion that follows are principles of sound clinical work unique to most therapies.

Principles of the Therapeutic Encounter

The principles of the CICM therapeutic encounter are grounded in foundational tenets of psychotherapeutic work. Greenspan (1997) argues that there are basic dynamic, relational, and behavioral procedural processes common to most therapies which promote emotional growth at the same time that they direct and organize the therapeutic effort. Greenspan has summarized rudimentary therapeutic practices: (1) developing a relationship that communicates warmth, sincerity, authenticity, and acceptance; (2) empathizing with the client's difficulties, joys, satisfactions, and wishes; (3) enabling the client to fully relate her concerns, problems, strengths, relational subtleties, and the full range of affective responses; (4) helping the client recognize patterns in relationships, feelings, and difficulties; (5) enhancing the client's capacities for elaborating intentions, wishes, feelings, and fears; (6) increasing self-awareness of feelings, intentions, and interactive patterns that are not obvious to the client; (7) helping the client identify contradictory desires and wishes; (8) using visual imagery to guide and direct changes in behavior (as in cognitive and behavioral therapies); (9) parsing complex behavioral patterns into smaller learnable and manageable steps; (10) creating conditions for behavioral change (as in reinforcement, punishment, and reward of appropriate behaviors); (11) increasing tolerance for anxiety through systematic exposure to anxiety-provoking situations as desensitization procedures; and (12) assisting the client through support and guidance to regulate and organize attention and mood. Accordingly, these fundamental procedural processes are considered "tried and true" practices and infer developmental considerations and emotional and cognitive growth.

These practices make developmental sense, but they seem to be only inadvertently grounded in the processes that promote human development. Importantly, the practitioner has the responsibility to utilize therapeutic processes to promote maturational growth and development in a deliberate and conscious fashion. To realize this therapeutic aim, a sound developmental framework must undergird the practitioner's therapeutic interventions. Using foundational therapeutic interventions, such as those postulated by Greenspan, I suggest that the therapeutic process for adolescence be based on the developmental tasks and domains with which adolescents must cope—the developmental domains delineated and discussed in this text. The *person* of the adolescent comprises her abilities, inclinations, temperament, age, and physical characteristics, all ontogenetic factors considered significant to the developmental trajectory. Moreover, I address the therapeutic encounter within the framework of intersubjective processes, including a view of the world of inner experience as primarily contextual and embedded with other contextual worlds in a continual flow of reciprocal mutual influence of recognition, assertion, and empathy (Orange, Atwood, & Stolorow, 1997). I have selected to use the term "participant" rather than "client" or "consumer" to indicate the collaborative efforts of involved parties in the therapeutic process.

The first principle in the CICM is that the natural strengths, needs, and interests of participant(s) (family, parents, and adolescent) are empathetically recognized and engaged, by the practitioner, for collaboration or partnership in the therapeutic encounter.[2] The engagement of clients in the therapeutic process is the most critical clinical work that the practitioner will carry out. The engagement of the participant for therapeutic work occurs irrespective of the particular intervention modality. Foremost, the practitioner, when possible, must legitimately contract with the family to become involved with the adolescent. The practitioner must secure the parents' consent to engage the adolescent for therapeutic work. In the contracted work with parents, the practitioner arranges follow-up or check-in sessions with parents. The purpose of these periodic meetings is to collaborate with the parents to assess the adolescent's therapeutic progress and to acquire parental input significant to the therapeutic process. The intersubjective engagement of the practitioner and adolescent is characterized by four stages. The first stage is the co-creation of a safe and authentic intersubjective contexts so that the actual therapeutic work can take place. In this initial stage, the practitioner orients the adolescent and parents to the helping process by outlining the role expectations of participants. For example, confidentiality is a sacrosanct value in therapeutic work, but there are critical limitations in working with adolescents. The practitioner must spell out the exact restrictions to confidentiality in the therapeutic work. Commonly, confidentiality limitations are meant to safeguard the adolescent's health and well-being. Information or material shared in the therapeutic encounter that compromises the protection or well-being of the adolescent must be shared with parents or legal guardians. The practitioner may engage in role-rehearsal or role-playing so that the helping process is experienced as an occurrence of concrete reality. In particular, insofar as the GULTMC study was essentially an intervention process, the girls had to be sufficiently engaged to consent to participate in the research intervention process. As well, face-to-face meetings with some of the parents took place to involve them in agreeing to their daughters' taking part in the study (Stevens, 1999).

Importantly, in addition to the delineation of participants' roles, the practitioner communicates that change is possible. In the second stage, the practitioner becomes an active facilitator and collaborator by empathetically attuning to the adolescent's need to be heard. This empathic attunement enables the adolescent girl to openly share her story with participants. Meaningful communication with a caring adult in a structured setting is a context for meeting the adolescent's developmental inter-subjective needs of self-assertion, recognition, and empathy. This implies that the practitioner recognizes self-assertion through storytelling. The adolescent experiences the therapist's empathy—meaning that the client's sense of self-care is evoked, by the empathic therapeutic response, as the sharing of the personal narrative unfolds. The third stage involves the evaluation or appraisal of the adolescent's needs, natural strengths, and interests that has been brought to light by the client's narrative. A working assessment is co-constructed as part of the evaluation process. Finally, the fourth stage is a ratification of the working assessment whereby the congruence of the meaning of the participant's narrative is achieved by way of a shared reality. Thus, congruence of meaning makes possible a well-defined contractual agreement for ad-vancing the therapeutic work. Nevertheless, practice experience indicates that par-ents of at-risk adolescents can be reluctant collaborators in the therapeutic process. This means, however, that the practitioner is called upon to allay parental anxieties about the process and to instill hope and a sense of empowerment that situations can improve and that the practitioner can be an ally in "making things better."

In the GULTMC study engagement sessions, the girls were encouraged to re-port back to parents about what took place in the meetings and to share parental feed-back in subsequent sessions. In sum, this first principle of the CICM was used in con-ducting the GULTMC study. The GULTMC girls participated in several group sessions that had as their focus the steps outlined here (Stevens, 1999). The follow-ing is excerpted from the second engagement session with the recruited sample GULTMC girls:

JOHNETTA: Last week you said that we didn't have to be in this group if we didn't want to.
SW: Yeah, that's right it's your decision to make. But, as we discussed last week, we believe that the group would be of benefit to you, and that you have something to contribute and we would learn from you as well.
BELLA: She said all that last week. To me it's a matter of making up your mind—what you wanna do. You know Bella, we've already talked about this, among our-selves anyway. What we really wanna know though, will we get chance to say what we really want to say, about what we think and how we feel and all.

Moreover, the adolescent in particular needs the reassurance that the intervention process will recognize her needs and strengths. Apparently, what adolescent girls are concerned about in any therapeutic contract is the honesty and sincerity of the prac-titioner and the degree to which they will be able to share a sense of the persons that they believe themselves to be. Moreover, the practitioner must also engage the client who is nonvoluntary in a way that honors and respects decision making. The invol-untary adolescent client, for example, can decide whether only to go through the mo-tions of entering into the therapeutic process or to become authentically involved as a participant.

The second principle in the CICM involves the recognition, identification, and interpretation of particular developmental areas in the participant's life that give rise to profoundly intense struggles, challenges, or difficulties. Personal difficulties are identified in the working assessment and become the focus of the therapeutic encounter. The practitioner and participant, in a committed alliance, consistently search for comprehensibility, manageability, and meaningfulness (Korotkov, 1998) in the experiences shared in the therapeutic encounter, including experiences intrinsic to the alliance itself. Importantly, the practitioner and participant try to reach consensus about what is being understood, how the therapeutic material is handled, and creating meaning out of confused and disorganized experiences. Traditionally, particular issues inherent in the subject-to-subject therapeutic context have been perceived as transference and countertransference issues. The phrase "experiences intrinsic to the alliance" is meant to suggest a description of consciously experienced aspects of the therapeutic context that occur in the "here and now" rather than in the earliest experiences of the past. The practitioner bears witness to the intensely personal struggles, challenges, or difficulties in living shared by the participant through "sustained empathic inquiry" (Stolorow & Atwood, 1992). Selectively, personal difficulties and challenges are framed and reframed developmentally throughout the therapeutic process. The practitioner supports the participant's developing skill in the interpretation of developmental issues underlying personal difficulties. In the case of adolescence, the formulation of personal difficulties in the light of maturational issues is a way to acknowledge the developmental area in which the participant's troubles are situated. As well, the therapeutic work renders a concise conceptualization of challenges and difficulties in which the participant is currently engaged and trying to manage without the help of the practitioner. Equally important, attention to the developmental domains provides, for the practitioner, focus and structure in the therapeutic process. The developmental domains explicated in this text are, indeed appropriate for this kind of therapeutic acknowledgment. Individual troubles understood in this way enhance the participant's perception of life's difficulties as having both special and prosaic dimensions.

As previously, noted the Social Skills Curriculum in the GULTMC study involved sessional therapeutic games that were thematically related to developmental issues typically confronted by adolescents during puberty. In the case of GULTMC study, the sessional themes prompted the participants to introduce material that was developmentally salient. Given the temporal constraint of the group sessions, developmentally thematic sessions serve to advance the therapeutic process. Moreover, the introduction of developmental thematic sessions enabled the GULTMC girls to discuss sensitive issues with a caring adult that normally would be difficult at early adolescence. Excerpted from a group session where the theme was dating, the following discourse transpired:

JULIA: She's saying that guys can be your friends.
NANETTE: Yeah! See, that's why a lota girls want to fight you because you get cool with a guy they wanna go with, and then they like, "She think she all that." And, then it gets back to you and all hell breaks out.
SW: So there's alot of fighting about guys.
ELONDA: Yep!
TONELL: Yep! I'm more comfortable with guys anyway than I am with girls. Girls, all they do is talk about other girls, "Let's go beat up so and so."

SW: This goes on here in the Middle School.

MURIEL: Yep! Now, it's happening right now.

ELLA: See, cause to me, you know guys be about people, they don't be like, "I don't think such and such like you." Or, "You should do this to such and such, and I think he really like you now." They don't do the things girls do.

ZORELLE: Hey! You remember when we were talking last week about this same subject, about going with somebody and about how boys wanted to have sex and all. Well, then we were saying guys were just "real dogs".

SW: I wonder if Layla is now trying to sort out what relationships with boys really mean to her. Some boys Layla sees as possible romantic dates and other boys as simply friends. You like boys for just friends, someone who is your ace—someone in your corner, but not for romance.

TERISA: I'd have to say that is why I choose a boy for a friend.

ELONDA: The reason why I choose a boy for a friend is because, you're not gonna get in a lota trouble with boys, like you would a girl. Girls most of the time in the street. They give themselves to [*meaning having indiscriminate sex*] to anybody.

Although the sessional theme was that of dating, the girls were forthright in sharing related issues. The practitioner, in this simple illustration, sustained empathic inquiry and gave recognition to the fact that girls have complex relationships with males. Having varied contextual worlds, from which participants' experiences are shared, as in group sessions, engenders opportunities for adolescent girls to arrive at meaning synthesis regarding their experiences. From an intersubjective perspective, all clinical work occurs in the contextual field formed by and involving the interplay of varied subjective worlds (Orange, Atwood, & Stolorow).

The operationalization of the second CICM principle is to acknowledge working intersubjectively to create meaning construction and meaning synthesis. The identification of underlying developmental areas is equally important in individual clinical work with each age-graded developmental stage during the adolescent period. An example of the salience of the developmental issues that commonly transpire in individual clinical work is found in the individual case of Nickie, a case in which I consulted in a community mental health agency. The Nickie vignette is presented to make up for the lack of a therapeutic intervention process with a late-age adolescent. However, the multiple developmental domains of dating, mate selection, decision-making and care protective sensibility seems apparent in this case illustration:

Nickie, a 17-year-old Black female, was brought to counseling by her mother who felt she no longer could supervise her daughter without becoming violently angered. On one occasion mother and daughter had physically fought. Nickie was an only child. The 37-year-old mother, a low-income woman with middle-class aspirations, was a single parent who was employed as a hotel maid. The mother complained that 17-year-old Nickie was dating, without permission, a young man who was 7-years older. The young man, Malcolm, was unemployed and single, but had fathered two children at ages 16 and 17 years old. Nickie had no prior experiences in dating. Nickie never knew her father. Apparently, the mother had never married and had kept the identity of the father a well-kept secret. Nickie had started keeping late hours beyond curfew and on two occasions was truant from school. The mother believed that Nickie was sexually active, but was not using contraceptives.

Nickie, a high school senior, was an academic achiever and wanted to attend college. Nickie was unhappy about her current relationship with her mother and wanted things to be better between them. Nickie felt that her mother was overreacting and that she had reasonable explanations for her recent transgressions. Nickie felt hurt because her mother would not listen to her. Nickie was fond of Malcolm and thought that he was mature and bright, but had "tough breaks in life".

As previously noted, the emphasis on the developmental domains makes it possible for the practitioner to focus on health and well being rather than pathological concerns. In the case of adolescents, a salubrious emphasis in the therapy context is less threatening and, consequently, facilitates affective attunement with the practitioner. Since there are interrelated developmental domains involved in this particular case, as the practitioner, I must decide which domain carries the most "emphatic salience" for the participant. Additionally, when working intersubjectively, the practitioner must consider which is the most salient of the triadic elements: assertion, recognition, or empathy. In the participant's narrative, the saliency of any one of the three is where pain, discomfort, or anxiety is most intensely experienced. The degree of intense affectivity in any of these elements is an indicator for the practitioner to determine where the work should begin. It should be noted that areas of affective saliency would vary throughout the therapeutic encounter. As the practitioner engages in ongoing assessment, she must evaluate when a shift in intersubjective and developmental saliency has occurred in the participant's narrative. In Nickie's case the starting point for the engaged work was in the developmental domain of protective care sensibility and the intersubjective element of empathy, two areas of affectivity that were personally meaningful. Nickie needed acknowledgment and recognition that she cared for her relationship with both her mother and with Malcolm. Focus in these areas is initiated in the engagement phase, leading to the therapeutic alliance, and becomes the focus of the therapeutic work.

The third principle in the CICM involves the practitioner's efforts to maximize personal agency and self-efficacy by consistent analysis of social, contextual, or relational inequities that intersect the participant's daily life. Here the practitioner helps the participant mobilize efforts to develop an "attributional style." Recall that in the discussion of the racial, ethnic, and gender role commitment domain that "attributional style," a conceptual phrase coined by Vaillant (1993), meant the manner in which individuals regard responsibility for the good and bad events that take place in life. I modified the concept to connote a sense of agency in self-assertion, which includes the ability to discriminately appraise one's social context for effective self-efficacy. In the alteration of the concept, I considered the problem of structural strain and the issue of racist and discriminatory practices. Undeniably, the individual cannot be held responsible for such macrocontextual problems and issues, but in the face of such circumstances, self-efficacy and personal agency can be diminished. Accordingly, the problem for blacks in racially oppressed situations is far more complex than self-esteem regulation. The individual's core self, in such circumstances, has undergone assault and injury. Still, a girl's personal actions can have serious repercussions for which she must assume responsibility. Without question, the practitioner must hold an adolescent girl accountable for her behavior while making every effort to sustain empathic attunement concomitant with macrosocial analysis and critique. The following field notes exemplify this principle:

> One of the most striking observations that I made were the girls' sense of societal aware-
> ness. The girls are aware of the different forms of racism. Zorelle provided an example of
> a teacher's patronizing attitude. Clarice and Terisa talked about her teachers talking down
> to them at school and feeling very frustrated and angry. The girls spoke of watching the
> televised O.J. Simpson verdict at school. Muriel said that the day that it was televised,
> teachers locked them in their rooms to prevent the students from leaving. She thought it
> was because the teachers believed that the students could not control themselves and would
> riot. Caretha brought up the subject that White people try and constantly undermine Black
> people. She went on to blame white people for supplying neighborhood groceries with
> the unhealthy foods that Black people eat. She blamed black people for not asking ques-
> tions and not becoming aware of what is going on. We [this session was conducted by two
> social work interns] tried to get the discussion to focus on what they could do and how
> they could respond to such situations when they were feeling especially frustrated and an-
> gry. They began to speak about trying to eat healthier. They wondered that maybe lock-
> ing the door on the O.J. televised verdict was an attempt to try and insure [sic] safety and
> protection, but maybe not the best possible way. [The session with the girls was incredi-
> ble. I left feeling really good about what I was doing with them. One of the major rea-
> sons I felt so positive about this session was because I felt that we made a great deal of
> progress with the girls—we had really established rapport and empathy with them. I be-
> lieve that they were really feeling comfortable with us. During the session, Zorelle said,
> "I really like you guys."]

Thus, the third principle calls attention to situations of structural strain and conditions of social oppression and circumstances of relational victimization. I have included relational victimization to account for situations in which persons experience
oppression within intimate intersubjective relations, such as domestic violence and
abuse. The concept of empowerment is anathema to most therapy disciplines, but has
gained credibility in social work because of the profession's value base and commitment to social justice. From a social work practice perspective, the third principle is
directly associated with an empowerment approach in clinical work. Gutierrez (1990,
1994), in particular, has contributed significantly to the understanding of this concept relative to women of color. She contends that power-enhancing intervention
strategies involve the critique of social inequities that help women of color diminish
or eliminate personal feelings of guilt or self-blame experienced in socially oppressed
situations. I have discussed elsewhere the empowerment perspective in working with
the strengths of black adolescent females (Stevens, 1998a). Thus, an indispensably
important component of clinical work within this perspective is reiterated: The practitioner helps the participant to become consciously aware of the personal strategies
normally used to counter feelings of helplessness and powerlessness in socially de-
valuing situations. The development of self-awareness in deprecating circumstances
is to enable the participant to evaluate whether the tactics used maximize a sense of
agency and whether they are detrimental in the achievement of self-efficacy. Chiefly,
the third principle addresses the issue of recognition within a macrostructure or ex-
osystem context. The developmental domain that seems inextricably related to the

intersubjective element recognition and macrostructure context is that of racial, ethnic, and gender role commitment. Benjamin (1990) has provided a suitable clarifica-
tion of the processes of mutual recognition:

> The other must be recognized as another subject in order for the self to fully experience
> his or her subjectivity in the other's presence. This means, first, that we have a need for
> recognition and second, that we have a capacity to recognize others in return—mutual
> recognition. But recognition is a capacity of individual development that is unevenly re-
> alized [*since there always tension between two incompatible human needs, the need for acknowl-*
> *edgment and validation by another and the need to be left alone, independent of the other's de-*
> *manding gaze.*]. (p. 35, Italics mine)

This terse explanation of recognition points the way for a discussion of the function of recognition in clinical practice. Recognition as it relates to the therapeutic
process—a macrosocial hierarchy of power and privilege; its correlate, oppression;
and the developmental domains, specifically racial, ethnic, and gender role commitment, role model formulation, opportunity mobility, and adulthood preparation—
seems especially relevant. In her exegesis, Benjamin has elaborated on the substantive premise of recognition in that an individual subject must acknowledge she no
longer reigns supreme, but must deal with the difficulty in recognizing the equiva-
lency of self and other in the centrality of experiences. Simply put, all individual subjects are situated in the center of experience equally. Plainly, the collaborative therapeutic relationship that is proposed in the CICM model finds support in the fashion
in which recognition has been defined. Moreover, recognition may serve as an intervention technique in which the practitioner demonstrates acceptance of the participant as an equivalent center of experience when the practitioner adopts the situated stance of insider in the collaborative work and acknowledges and validates the
participant as an expert witness to her shared narrative. These clinical implications
are, indeed, rudimentary, but the subject of culturally sensitive practices in clinical
work where ethnocultural differences exist, however, warrants brief elaboration.

Social workers have selected to use varied forms of cultural pluralism to expand
the profession's knowledge base and to make more relevant intervention strategies.
Pluralism, while it implies the incorporation, appreciation, and genuine acceptance
of differences within a given society, also suggests the existence of structural barriers
to minority group societal participation. Here, too, the specific application of the
model in social work has involved a victim-powerless differential in the psychosocial
assessment of the client's functioning that has not served clients well. Clinical researchers have argued that class, race, and culture are critical factors operative in a
client's use of psychotherapeutic services. Dropout and discontinuance rates are often attributed to class, race, and ethnic variables, as clinicians are most empathetic
with clients who are most like them. Consequently, clients of color have not bene-
fited by and large from traditional psychotherapeutic clinical intervention models
(Atkinson, Morten, & Sue, 1993; Overall & Aronson, 1966; Tsui & Schultz, 1955).
Along these same lines, Sue and Sue (1990) claim that meanings endemic to traditional Eurocentric psychotherapeutic counseling services are biased and can be dia-
metrically opposed to the values of minority groups of color. Accordingly, Western
counseling places emphasis on such features as (1) cause and effect approaches, (2) a

linear concept of time, (3) the pursuit of long-range goals, (4) a communication pattern of openness and intimacy from client to counselor, and the (5) ambiguous and unstructured approach to problem solving. Nonetheless, these features may not be universally applicable to all ethnic and cultural groups. While Sue's conservative argument regarding the universal applicability of these therapeutic features has credibility, his contention must be viewed in the light of developmental or maturational issues. Certainly, adolescence by definition in Western societies infers future orientation, the pursuit of long-range goals, and effective psychosocial proficiencies, including problem-solving, decision-making, and communication skills. Nonetheless, scholars stress, as a response to these clinical deficiencies in Western therapies, that effective intervention with people of color should empower individuals and communities (Gutierrez, 1990, 1994). Developmentally, empowerment for adolescents infers a sense of psychosocial mastery and accomplishment. Practitioners should develop sensitivity and awareness about cultural and racial biases (Comas-Diaz & Jacobsen, 1987, 1991). Moreover, emphasis has been placed on the notion of the dual consciousness of African Americans and the complexity of identity formation in the bicultural adaptation to society (Stevens, 1997a).

Additionally, scholars argue for a theoretical understanding of the cultural differences of subordinate groups by recognizing their existing adaptive strengths (Saleeby, 1997; Stevens, 1998a). Other scholars (Chau, 1991; DeHoyos, DeHoyos, & Anderson, 1986; Wilson, 1987, 1996) have identified cultural and social dislocation as more creditable conceptual frameworks for the understanding of societal placement of minorities. These authors believe that the persistence of social problems faced by minorities is basically a structural one. Accordingly, less emphasis is placed on personal behavior as a factor in contributing to social inequities. Moreover, this perspective acknowledges a multicultural view while recognizing the blocking of opportunity structures and the need for a compromised solution in the accommodation to the dominant structure. Intervention strategies within this perspective focus on the enhancement of opportunity structures and client investment in social mobility behaviors and discourage perceiving the client as victim. Additionally, the model stresses that survival adaptive actions are not pathologized but are valued for their manifestation of competence and resiliency (Stevens, 1997b).

In the GULTMC study, the intervention curricula was designed specifically to address matters of culture and ethnicity relative to identity exploration, which invariably raised concerns among the girls about their experiences of racial denigration and social devaluation. Inevitably black and other marginalized adolescents experience situations where the recognition of full subjectivity by the other is denied. Intersubjectively, the denial of recognition can occur wherever subjects are engaged with one another, among peers, family, and the like. Essentially, adolescents' usage of the slang "dissed" and "dissing" refers to this denial of recognition and their concerns about being treated with disrespect. Notwithstanding, the point of the third principle is the elaboration of the helplessness and powerlessness adolescents experience in the face of social devaluation. Adolescents respond in such situations by disavowing the subjectivity of the other. The disavowal of the subjectivity of the other can become an embodiment of the adolescent's social identity. When the adolescent's repudiation of the other becomes an accepted part of self-identity, then repudiation

of the other is often accompanied by hostile, apathetic, or even enraged affective behaviors. As previously discussed, these behaviors can be more extreme than the sassy
behaviors exhibited by the GULTMC girls. Frequently, in working with inner-city
adolescents, the practitioner is initially confronted with disinterest and hostility in the
adolescent participant. One way the practitioner can respond is to intervene in ways
that acknowledge that the adolescent has experienced circumstances where her full
subjectivity has been disregarded or repudiated. As noted earlier, the most challenging contextual problem in work with minority youth is that macrostructure may actually engage adolescents in ways that disclaim preparation for adulthood.

Seen in this light, it is understandable how adolescents of color may become disengaged from social institutions. Tellingly, one of the most impressive finding of the
GULTMC study is the difficulties the girls experienced in the school setting, the
most significant of which was bold and sassy confrontations with school personnel.
This empirical evidence offers significant clinical insight into black adolescents' psychosocial adjustment in the school context. It is the school context that is tremen-
dously important for adolescent adulthood preparation. Nevertheless, the experiences
of the GULTMC girls happen too often among minority adolescents. What occurrences of this nature depict is institutional disengagement. I define institutional disengagement as a compensatory defense against institutions, such as schools, that reg-
ulates feelings of helplessness and powerlessness in one's encounter with perceived
or actual racialist practices. Institutional disengagement has its roots in fear and distrust, but can occur among both minority adults and youth. It is perhaps more injurious in the young, since psychologically a young person may be less equipped to cope
with the structural strain of racist macrostructure. Moreover, among adolescents, institutional disengagement can constitute attitudinal and behavioral responses, including contempt, bullying, or mendacity, that are adopted as one's social identity,
especially if a racial, ethnic, and gender role commitment has not become resolute.
In adults, who have developed a more socially adaptive persona, institutional disengagement is likely to be transitory and situational, especially if issues involving racial
and ethnic role commitment have been successfully dealt with in the past.

More importantly, working with the third principle requires the practitioner to
move beyond culturally sensitive or culturally competent practice. While the practitioner interprets and clarifies situations of social or racial injustice, the practitioner
must also become a cultural critic of American social-cultural values in general, independent of any particular ethnic group. The practitioner must be able to critique
and discern cultural values to assist the adolescent in adulthood preparation. The
practitioner becomes a cultural critic of what may be revered in American popular
culture, including material acquisitiveness, pleasure seeking, excessive competition,
celebrity worship, unbridled ambition, and subject (person) as marketable commod-
ity. There are many social-cultural ways in which our society denies the recognition
of one's full subjectivity in the form of its popular culture. This is extremely important and sensitive clinical work, as many American social values must be disentangled
from race and ethnicity since at some level all ethnic groups participate in the cultural forms of American society. Moreover, the practitioner may be wedded to popular cultural values in ways that she is unaware of. Last, the practitioner must be able
to critique American social values without cynicism. This critique is necessary if the
practitioner is to avoid being seduced by the moral cynicism of the adolescent client.

The fourth principle of the CICM involves the efforts of the practitioner to strengthen the participant's sense of hope and hardiness to realize present and future personal goals. There are two primary techniques of working with minority adolescents that instill hope. First, the practitioner makes use of social and environmental circumstances to help the adolescent in the self-creation of personal meaning and wisdom to began deliberations about what it means to be an adult. Second, the practitioner makes use of techniques that include visual imagery that enables the adolescent to become more future oriented. Equally important is that the practitioner serves as a role model with which the adolescent can identify. The developmental domain is that of role model formulation and adulthood preparation. Appropriate areas to discuss are self-disclosure and style of working. It is important that the therapist communicate genuineness and caring. Adolescents are clearly aware when they are being manipulated, so it is important that the therapist not assume a false identity, as the adolescent participant would easily recognize it. The following methods or interventions are suggested to actualize the fourth principle:

1. Make use of role models that are in geographical proximity and are older individuals.
2. Make use of community bridging techniques that advance the social mobility of adolescents.
3. Encourage parents to discuss the goals of their children and how they can best achieve them.
4. Encourage parents of adolescents to become actively involved in their communities through institutional activities in schools, churches, and the like.
5. Enlist the help of parents to sort how they themselves can participate in the future of their children.

The clinical activity occurring in all previous principles comes to bear in the fourth particular principle. The fourth principle also involves termination of services, which suggests that while the actual services have been terminated, the work that has occurred between participant and practitioner is now part of the participant's and practitioner's life experience. The affective attunement that occurred cannot be terminated. In essence, the relational connection between the two cannot be terminated. Many of the clinical activities required to reach inner-city adolescents will take practitioners out the office into the communities of the adolescents they serve. Once practitioners access the communities in which clients reside, they are able to identify the strengths of the communities in which their participants live in order to make available, in a new way, strengthened community resources to client-participants.

Conclusions

I have set out to identify a practice model of clinical intervention that will be effective with adolescents, especially marginalized youth who reside in inner-city communities. My main thesis is that this model must be developmentally and contextually based. I believe that this thesis would support most theoretical-based therapeutic interventions, including psychodynamic, cognitive, behavioral, and experiential. The four principles identified are by no means exhaustive and perhaps only demonstrate just some of the guidelines for involving marginalized youth empathically. Social workers intervene when disequilibrium occurs between person and the situation and when personal and social resources indispensable for coping are depleted. The person, aware that present coping efforts are unsuccessful, subsequently seeks professional intervention. Frequently, social workers are involved in situations where individuals have not sought help voluntarily. Particular situations generate social concerns that cause responsible observers to bring these concerns to the attention of social workers. Commonly, in such instances, the observer has surmised that an individual is without resources to manage extreme person-situation imbalances. The examples of child abuse, domestic violence, adolescents in need of supervision, and homelessness readily come to mind to illustrate this point. Recognizing that change, conflict, and suffering are endemic to human life and that individuals develop naturally the strengths to cope with the ever-changing conditions of life, social workers will continue to be challenged by the social problems of society and the sufferings of the poor. Notwithstanding, the profession must find new ways to respond to new and ever-changing challenges.

Notes

1. The "generalized other" is Mead's (1934) term for the construction of society and the law in the individual's reflexive consciousness. The term is meant to be a dynamic concept. Crossley (1996) has compellingly argued that the "generalized other" must now include new technologies and media, such as the Internet, videos, and the like. I would add that the "generalized other" includes Bronfenbrenner's "nested contexts."

2. Family here implies parents or any significant family member or extended kin *in loco parentis*.

EPILOGUE

*[M]any people's sense of worth, the value they place on the image
of the self, is directly related to the number of situations in which
they are in control, which means that many people have a problem
with their self-image, because they are in control of so little.*

(Hall, 1977, p. 6)

In this text, I have endeavored to argue that many poor inner-city minority adolescents successfully manage developmental issues and embark on educational career paths to advance their social and economic statuses (Stevens, 1993). I have maintained that development and context are essential elements that must be considered if the vicissitudes of the lives of poor inner-city black female adolescents are to be fully understood. Traditionally, to interpret adaptation and conflict in human development, social scientists have emphasized the importance of the interrelationship between personal attributes and environmental circumstances. At present, the emphasis on the interrelatedness of the individual and environment finds support in an at-risk explanatory model that suggests that some youth are in jeopardy for poor life outcomes because of individual characteristics and the social contexts in which they live. Likewise, the model proposes that despite environmental jeopardy, some youth are resilient and protected by social assets, such as friendships and membership in formal and informal organizations. Although whether resiliency is innate or learned is unclear, resilient capacities are thought to be multidimensional and flexible. Nonetheless, I have proposed that resilient individuals demonstrate hardiness, a focused commitment to follow events through, and a strong sense of self-efficacy. Additionally, social support resources that serve as shock absorbers (Barbarin, 1993; Demos, 1989; Garmezy, 1991; Jessor, 1993; Mastin, Best, & Garmezy, 1990; Rutter, 1987) may protect resilient individuals from some adversities. Paradoxically, resilient black female adolescents portrayed in this text engaged in motivated choices of resistance based on a discriminate understanding of their social context. Marginalized individuals have the capacity to sustain self-relatedness and maintain self-integrity while adopting a posture of resistance and liberation. Sawicki (1997) clarifies this point:

> The scientist understands how realization redounds recursively onto the causal factors that conditioned it, and may very well alter them. The "mechanisms" of resistance and liberation turn out not be casual mechanisms at all; rather, they are motivated choices that have been constrained by material conditions without being determined by them. (p. 263)

Further, I proposed that the at-risk model suggests an interactive relationship between person and social context. It was also argued that this epidemiological model failed to consider mediating processes that also take place. To this end, I suggested that the at-risk model should be expanded to include the capacity for self-relatedness or intersubjectivity (Spencer, 1995). The capacity to seek recognition and engage others indicates that the individual is an active agent in the social environment (Stern, 1985). I set forth a new inclusive model, identified as person-process-context. Further, I proposed that the principal capacities in self-relatedness are assertion and recognition, both of which contribute to self-efficacy (Benjamin, 1988; Bronfenbrenner, 1979; Spencer, 1995). I argued that self-relatedness provides a standpoint from which to examine adolescents' self-development. It is uniquely relevant to focus on self-relatedness in studying the maturational development of minority adolescents. Female adolescents of color must synthesize varied and complex experiences, some of which are negative gender and race self-assessments (Stevens, 1997a). Thus female adolescents of color must learn to negotiate hostile environments while developing personal and cultural integrity. I contended that the concepts of risk, self-relatedness, and strengths be incorporated within a person-process-context model. The person-process-context model was thought to provide a useful conceptual framework to explicate developmental struggles of black adolescent females.

The concept of intersubjectivity, which included empathy, assertion, and recognition, was central to my argument for the person-process-context model. Intersubjectivity, considered as a nexus, was viewed from both psychological-individual and social-political levels. Fundamentally, a society, in order to ensure its survival as a sociopolitical entity, engages its young in three primary cultural processes. First, society undertakes the moral and social training of the young in order that they may be eventually incorporated into the cultural life of the adult citizenry. In particular, this acculturation takes place within a sanctioned macrostructure, such as schools, churches, economic corporations, political and social structures, and military institutions. Second, society sanctions various opportunity pathways so that the citizenry can realize material and spiritual accomplishments. Third, society provides access to opportunity pathways so that the moral, social, and economic success of the citizenry is likely. It can be argued that when the three cultural processes operate at optimal levels, the transition of youth to adulthood is less problematic. Normatively, during puberty, the adolescent reevaluates society's basic social and moral values to arrive at meaning synthesis as way to prepare for adult status. I argued that adolescents engage in the vital developmental process of meaning synthesis, to revitalize social and moral values for the eventual adoption and ownership that is necessary to participate and invest fully in the citizenry. Inasmuch as individuals function in varied contexts, meaning synthesis may constitute the various intersubjective experiences in which the adolescent is engaged. Bronfenbrenner's theory of nested contexts was used to support these observations, as the socialization of the individual is seen as occurring in concentric circles of bidirectional embedded contexts.

In Chapter 7, I made an effort to address what was needed to bring poor black adolescents to participatory citizenship and adulthood. I addressed the difficulties that poor black youth experience in accessing opportunity pathways. In my struggle for coherency in this chapter, I believe that I was consciously aware of many socioeconomic issues that remain unapprised in our society. I was especially aware of the fact of the incarceration of millions of black males, and increasingly black females, many of which are involved in the drug culture of the streets. In American society, the cultural processes outlined previously do exist in varying degrees. However, in contemporary culture, the socialization of the young for citizenship has become disparate and ambiguous, making a successful transition to adulthood all the more difficult and problematic, especially for poor minority adolescents of color. Seemingly, material and nonmaterial social values have increasingly become unbalanced. The decade of the 1980s, for instance, saw the ascendance of financial gain by any means necessary as an esteemed value—individualistic greed was considered respectable. Individualistic material gains at any cost are not esteemed values for youth to emulate. Yet youth normally desire economic success. They wish to be productive, responsible, and principled adults—creating culture as valued and respectful citizens.

Individuals experience a variety of social experiences quite early in life. Influenced by divergent and multiple contexts in which they are involved, individuals are affected by the norms that govern diverse contexts. Most norms for adulthood functioning differ remarkably from those for children. I presented the theory of sociologist Cancian regarding social identity and norms. I theorized that the development of social norms could be seen as flexibly responsive to social conditions. According to Cancian, social behaviors are governed by certain reality assumptions that constitute meaning-making actions that are represented by shared meanings and perceptions about the possible in everyday life (*norms*). Norms that direct behaviors give rise to communal validated social identities. I used the Cancian postulate to reason that all social actions are relational and occur within a mutual and reciprocal transactional context mediated by intersubjective processes. Essentially, intersubjective processes mediate reality assumptions on both a communal and an individual level. Moreover, this argument finds support in the person-process-context model that is fundamental to the text. Additionally, the Cancian postulate of social actions as contextually situated speaks to the person-process-context model as a jazz metaphor. In jazz individual musicians' refined attunement to the group context brings about improvisational harmonic responses that are communally validated. As in jazz, I suggest that this improvisational style of relating occurs in daily life.

In Chapter 8, I introduced a model of intervention to address the complex needs of adolescents. The model, a collaborative one, is grounded in foundational practice principles that include empowerment and strengths perspectives. Foremost, however, I used the model to take into account the adolescent developmental domains that were explicated in the text. I reasoned that for clinical intervention to be successful with adolescents, the practitioner must not be only be aware of specific adolescent developmental challenges, but must also see developmental maturation as a desirable therapeutic goal—that is, the practitioner promotes or augments adolescent psychosocial growth in the helping process. In this regard the application of developmental domains in the clinical work provides the practitioner with the conceptual tools and framework to assess an adolescent's trajectory and to evaluate in what area intervention needs to take place. Moreover, I proposed that the conceptual framework and model of intervention outlined in this text are sufficiently abstract to accommodate an understanding of not just black female adolescents, but adolescents' journey in general and the clinical assessments and interventions needed to work with this very special developmental age group. Throughout the text, I offered specific case illustrations that I thought would guide student learning for critical thinking in application of the proposed intervention model. In some respects, the collaborative intervention context model (CICM) is just a different way to conceptualize common social work practices that include an integrated situational, environmental, or con-textual perspective that embodies self-relatedness.

An argument can be made that for American youth the middle-class attribute of postsecondary education is, perhaps, the most eventful culturally sanctioned rite of passage to adulthood. Consequently, the adolescent developmental period has been extended to age 22–25, the age at which college graduates are expected to enter the labor market. Seemingly, the legitimization of the college degree as the port of en-try for adulthood and the means of social mobility indicate both the expansion and rigidity of class in American culture. The prolongation of adolescence has enormous social consequences. It is unlikely that all youth will ever attend college. Moreover, many youth obtain postsecondary education at enormous financial costs, incurring expenditures that extend far into the adult years. An argument can be made that the educational debt young people accrue creates an indentured middle class. Also, un-fortunately, with the dismantling of affirmative action programs, vital opportunity pathways for minority youth will be blocked. Thus, black youth face enormous chal-lenges for adulthood preparation. Certainly, when individuals enter the world of adulthood as competent persons, there is an expectation that they will possess the moral strength and courage to nurture the next generation. In postmodern society, adolescents will require multiple culturally sanctioned and esteemed pathways to adulthood. Advisedly, society fails its youth when there is only one opportunity path-way to social well-being.

Enormous chronohistorical systemic (see Figure 3.2) changes affect the societal context in which adolescents must develop and become adults. Overall, contempo-rary adolescents grow up facing extraordinary challenges, which perhaps G. Stanley Hall, who originated scientific theories of adolescence, could not imagine. Paradox-ically, one of the most pivotal challenges for contemporary adolescents is learning to manage reproductive maturity in an era of sexual permissiveness and HIV/AIDS new to this society. As inheritors of profound sociocultural transformations, today's youth are unlike any other in American history. Radically altered by liberal sexual mores, progressive technological-electronic inventions, pervasive media consumerism, and evolutionary biomolecular discoveries, American society is forever changed. While social disruptions may well differ in type, intensity, and duration, it can be argued that adolescents who come of age during periods of extreme societal upheavals are highly susceptible to risk behaviors. This is due, in large part, to the parallel occur-rences of maturational changes the adolescent undergoes and the transitional cultural transformations that transpire. For example, significant media coverage in the West concerning the cultural disintegration of Soviet communism documents the despair and hopelessness many Russian youth experience (Wines, 2000). Apparently, without societal supports to achieve basic living necessities, the loss of aspirations among some of Russia's young people have given way to serious problems of drug addiction and HIV/AIDS.

Unfortunately, the impact of sociocultural disruptions on adolescent development is rarely subject to either scholarly analyses or empirical investigation (Noack & Kracke, 1997). Assuredly, cultural transformations affect the social context of ado-lescent decision making. I postulate that the social effects of disorder and disruption associated with the crack pandemic in inner-city neighborhoods are analogous to the seismic societal upheavals that occur in war-ravaged cities (Wines, 2000) or in communities that suffer from natural disasters crises, such as hurricanes, earthquakes, and tornadoes. The PANSI study was conducted at the peak of the crack drug outbreak, whereas the GULTMC research took place when the epidemic began to settle (Adler, 1993; Ratner, 1993). However, as the crack epidemic abated, in poor inner-city communities, drug trafficking escalated to warring battles among sellers coupled with "drive by shootings." Both the GULTMC and the PANSI study girls were aware of the personal and communal devastation brought on by drug trafficking and drug misuse in their communities. It can be argued that drug trafficking in black communities has undermined traditional communal values. Thus, social work intervention with minority adolescents will warrant nontraditional approaches that utilize activities including the visual and performing arts and sports (Delgado, 2000). In essence, such focus on nontraditional approaches is a focus on strengthening the contextual development of communities.

The fact that a moral cynicism increasingly has permeated both the American populace and the academy also seems to imply that a skepticism of life itself seems commonplace. Not surprisingly, it has been argued that religious faith in the lives of blacks in poor inner cities if not absent altogether has been significantly diminished (Anderson, 1990; West, 1993). The augury is that African American poor inner-city communities are enclaves of hopelessness and desolation. Poor inner-city black youth are seen as amoral. The nihilism of these communities is due in part, it is claimed, to the flight of the black middle class, the intensification of materialism and hedonism, and a crisis in black leadership. The loss of a middle-class constituency represents the loss of role models, businesses, and moral leadership. As such, inner-city communities have become crime- and drug-ridden wastelands of unemployment and violence. Many black churches sustain residence in these communities, and middle-class congregations return only for religious services. No longer participants in communal life, church members become community visitors. Seemingly, the role of the church is analogous to that of a negligent absentee slum landlord. When poor black ghetto communities are seen as morally, socially, and economically bankrupt, we inadvertently infer that blacks are not only victims, but lack human resources. Still, despite this rather despairing portraiture of the faithlessness of poor black inner-city communities, the PANSI study girls, in particular, saw the value of religious values and church membership and perceived themselves as individuals embodied with spiritual values even when church membership was lacking.

Finally, race has been a fundamental dilemma of American life. I attempted to demonstrate how contemporary black female adolescents, regardless of class status, struggle developmentally with the issues of race and gender. This issue, while addressed specifically in Chapter 4, was interwoven throughout the text. The public demonizes racially marginalized groups, which may also suggest a societal spiritual aridity. Banality impedes the formulation of relevant and pragmatic social welfare policies that actually benefit the poor. In any analysis of epidemiological populations, contextual meanings must be examined and clarified. Particularly, ethnocultural (Afro-American) meanings must be examined in light of dominant or mainstream (Euro-American) cultural meanings. For instance, one can conjecture that spiritual sterility is likely to occur in societies where materialism, consumerism, and individualism are regarded as consummate values. As much as these values constitute the American cultural ethos, they are commonly esteemed by all its citizenry. However, behavioral manifestations of such values may differ among social classes and ethnic groups. Poor ethnic minorities, for example, can experience spiritual impotence due to a lack of material commodities. On the other hand, moneyed classes experience spiritual desolation as a consequence of material excess. For example, research suggests that poor youth are more likely to traffic in drugs for economic gain, while middle- and upper-class youth have considerable discretionary income to purchase drugs. It can be argued that materialistic and consumerist values can have negative outcomes for both the poor and upper classes.

Ethnographers Williams and Kornblum (1985, 1994) have poignantly argued that the lure of street activities in poor inner-city communities can have disastrous effects even among the most resilient and achieving youths, especially early aged adolescents. The authors contend that early aged adolescents, mostly males, are likely to form the most fearless segment of the illegal economy of poor communities. Conceivably, early aged adolescents are used by older adolescents to undergird the illegal economy of poor inner-city neighborhoods, as early aged adolescents are great risk takers since they have less experience in the ways of the streets. Unquestionably, neighborhoods can be hazardous and represent social risks, but they also can be resources. Unquestionably, poor inner-city black youth are vulnerable to the enticements of the streets. The decisions they make to deal with the street economy of drugs and its accoutrements are, indeed, consequential to their future development. The social placement of black males in an illegal street economy has enormous consequences for girls when one considers the ritual game of dating and male availability. Still, for most youth, I would argue that the soul of the community constitutes what occurs on its streets from a perspective of strength. Neighborhood streets are also where community institutions are located, such as the church, grocery stores, and community organizations. Understandably the communal connection for adolescents is the street life of a neighborhood. For youth, neighborhood streets are not the alien localities that adults perceive them to be since the community's blocks and pathways represent physical spaces of playful activities of the adolescent's earlier latency years. Adolescents' communal connection to the physical spaces of neighborhoods is unappreciated by parents, mainly because parents and their offspring occupy diverse physical and social spaces. Parents primarily view neighborhood streets from a perspective of physical and psychological threat. Both the GULTMC and the PANSI girls made discriminating analysis of the hazardous conditions of their environments. The resilience of these girls spoke to the fact that they made every effort to avoid nefarious community activities.

Finally, the power-victim model, in the light of current thinking about resiliency and competence, is the least attractive explanatory model to understand the adaptation of blacks in American society. Generally, I believe it is difficult for many black people to view themselves as authentic Americans given their pariah social status due to race. An internalized view of the self as victim can render a sense of profound hopelessness that undermines moral strength and values. It seems sound to argue that the social problems experienced by African Americans are constitutive of American life, not separate and apart from American life. It seems likely that the social problems manifest in the life of African Americans may be symptomatic and may represent early warning signs of serious deficits in the quality of American life in general, which will eventually affect other segments of the American populace. It is reasonable to contend that social structure and personal behavior are inextricably related, as both are features of the culture of a given society. I have tried to propose such a relationship between persons and social structures in the person-process-context model. In so doing, I employed social context in the person-process-context model to include sociocultural factors in all their intersectional complexity. I have attempted to offer a more cogently complex theoretical framework for the traditional person-situation configuration framework of social work practice. I have argued elsewhere that despite social work's historical "emphasis on the influence of environmental factors, the dynamic intersection of environment and personality has not been fully explicated within the foundation of social work knowledge" (Stevens, 1997b, p. 460). On this point, Saari (1991) has incorporated current thinking about human cultures in her newly developed psychodynamic constructivist model of social work practice. Current theoretical understandings about culture state that culture is not represented by objective structures but is, in fact, those shared meanings of a people that are reflected in personal behavior and social institutions. Saari places culture within the context of meaning that eliminates the schism between the person and social configuration. She notes that this unnatural schism has made for specious arguments between micro and macro theorists in social work practice. This argument may not be as false as is first apparent. The profession recognizes that the problems of minority populations are impacted considerably by systematic and endemic racism. What is of critical import, for clinical practice, is the identification of the meanings within the context of oppression and how the oppressor as well as the oppressed mediates these meanings. In so doing the clinician may enable the client to transcend some features of racial or sexual oppression.

Glossary

Adolescence A consequential transitional developmental period within the life course that occurs between childhood and adulthood and is marked by vital biological, cognitive, and socioemotional changes. Age-related developmental markers that include early, middle, and late maturational stages as well as experiential domains differentiate the period.

Adulthood preparation A developmental domain that represents an awareness of the need for the development of particular character traits that will promote the successful transition to adulthood. This self-awareness is developed from one's immediate surroundings where adulthood behaviors are learned. Self-awareness concomitant with adult support leads to the engagement in prosocial activities where adulthood attributions, such as civic duty and responsibility, economic independence, and the care and protection of others, can be learned and acquired.

Agency The conscious experience of the self as an engaged, coherent, and competent individual in contextual transactions.

Care protective sensibility A developmental domain that characterizes a sense of care and protection in relation to self and others; an individual's developed capacity to recognize self-relatedness in others and to be empathic.

Collaborative intervention context model (CICM) A developmentally and contextually based model of practice that focuses on the transactional interplay of person(s) and processes of intersubjectivity, including empathy, assertion, and recognition, located in personal, interpersonal, and social structural contextual domains.

Community-bridging Strategies poor families use to promote the social mobility of offspring. These strategies represent an awareness of structural resources and limitations, including those of family and community.

Contexting The analytical processing of information in a given cultural or social situation. It represents the capacity to think in complex ways about things conditioned by cultural or social perspectives. Contexting enables individuals to build and develop complexity in their thoughts and behavior.

Contextualized development A hypothesis of human development that suggests that the maturational life span is context dependent, representing reciprocal and transactional processes of engagement within multifarious domains, such as family, neighborhood, peer group, school, and church. It also infers that decisive developmental challenges be systemically met and modulated by transactional relationships occurring at pivotal periods and in critical domains throughout the life course.

Culture The shared meanings of a people that are reflected in personal behavior and social institutions.

Dating/mate selection A developmental domain that refers to the development of evaluation standards about the behavior of male peers or males in general based on observations or experience. In making such evaluations, a new understanding and acceptance of self as a sexual being who has the capacity for reproduction is developed. The capacity for emotional and sexual intimacy is enhanced while maintaining a core sense of self-differentiation and self-coherence.

Decision making A developmental domain that suggests the development of problem-solving strategies, made possible by the effective use of new capacities in cognition and carried out in the proximal ecological spheres of family, peers, and school. These problem-solving strategies and coping skills are developed from dealing with issues in living and the anticipation of future goals.

Developmental domains Seven experiential spheres that characterize the adolescent maturational period. The seven domains—racial, ethnic, and sex gender role commitment; role model formulation; care protective sensibility; decision making; dating/mate selection; opportunity mobility; and adulthood preparation—are context dependent and are distinguished by developmental challenges, tasks, and psychosocial demands common to each.

Domains of experience Context-dependent self-experiences initiated in infancy that are formulated and reformulated throughout the life span. Self-experiences include domains characterized as emergent, core, subjective, and narrative. An emergent self uniquely occurs at critical developmental junctures within the life span, such as adolescence.

Identity complexity The conscious experience of the self as coherent, versatile, creative, and differentiated.

Intersubjective responses The qualities of empathy, assertion, and recognition. These qualities are reflexive in that they are mirrored and validated in and through others. Empathy is the capacity for the appreciation of another and the context of that individual's experiences. Assertion and recognition are companion capacities that suggest a reflexive mode of interaction where the self is asserted in the presentation to others or in a social identity. Assertion states "I am." Recognition affirms and validates the self that is asserted by another who responds, "Yes you are." Empathy, assertion, and recognition are qualities that can be either adaptive or maladaptive.

Intersubjectivity The domain of consciousness/unconsciousness and perception by which the individual self is linked to others and to the self-related elements (empathy, assertion, and recognition) of contextual experiences. Intersubjectivity occurs at the personal and structural levels of experience.

Kin-scriptions Those mundane practices, including critical life events, familial relationships, and work roles, that embody specific cultural norms and established patterns that are used over time to ensure a family's generational survival. For minority families subject to historical discrimination many kin-scriptions have developed over time in response to the structural strain brought about by racist practices.

Meaning-making processes Processes that involve cognitive and emotional capacities and social practices the individual uses to make coherent moral and social sense of the world around her and her place in that social world.

Meaning synthesis An evolved and integrated worldview derived from disparate moral and social values and perspectives about the society in which one seeks adulthood.

Moral career A transformational experience that serves as a turning point defined by integrity and rightness during the life span developmental course. Such an experience brings about a new identity or social persona. The identity transformation has a sense of rightness and integrity about it; hence the designation of the term "moral." The concept of moral career is used to theorize about sassiness in the development of adolescent black girls.

Morality A developed sense of right and wrong about one's actions and the actions of others.

Motivated acts of meaning Adaptive behaviors or social actions guided by intentional empathic affect in the recognition of another's contextual experiences. Essentially, motivated acts of meaning are behaviors or social actions guided by intentional empathic affect in the recognition of another's contextual experiences.

Natural helping networks The social supports and assets determined by the needs of the group in which the boundary maintenance of those social resources is flexible.

Negotiation The navigation of a particular course of action in the social context in which the individual finds the self situated or located. Negotiation implies that interaction is dialectical and that meanings are socially constructed and created.

Nested contexts Successive multileveled and bidirectional systemic ecological domains of biopsychosocial-historical influences that affect individual development.

Norm-modeling actions Social actions or behaviors that occur within social contexts that the individual projects to have a social identity validated by others.

Opportunity mobility A developmental domain characterized by self-expectancies for social mobility where there is awareness that such activities are designed "to improve one's lot in life." The companion to this self-expectancy must be the availability of socially sanctioned activities that open pathways to enhance upward mobility, such as jobs, school, and social development clubs.

Person-process-context model An explanatory model of transactional psychosocial developmental functioning within social ecologies. The process component of the model infers intersubjective elements of empathy, assertion, and recognition through which individual, group, family, and structural actions and operations are carried out. The model also takes into account the spontaneity of daily life, suggesting that the jazz musical idiom of improvisational responses is a likely metaphor for the model.

Perspective taking The capacity for empathic understanding that allows the individual to view a situation from the standpoint or the point of view of another.

Protective factors Those dynamic aspects of living usually located in social contexts or ecologies that interact with stress to moderate or buffer hazardous situations that ordinarily would produce negative outcomes.

Racial, ethnic, and sex gender role commitment A developmental domain that represents normative behaviors for males and females and embodies the assertion and acceptance of a gender role situated in a particular social identity.

Reflective inquiry and reflective theorizing The investigations and deliberations in which practitioners engage to better understand the complexities of people's psychosocial development and their social needs.

Resilience Personal hardiness or the self-righting tendencies that naturally occur in individuals. Resilience infers adaptive strategies learned from experience that makes possible achieving a good outcome from misfortune as well as steering clear of avoidable dangerous or hazardous situations. Resilience can also be evolutionary, evolving over time to become highly developed by stress or adversity.

Risk Exposure to anyone or anything that represents danger or injury. Risk models are either cumulative, additive, or interactive. Additive and cumulative risk are used interchangeably, as both infer that stress, danger, or hazard can be summative over either short or long periods or occur in parallel circumstances. Cumulative risk is more commonly used and specifically indicates continuous exposure to jeopardy over time. Individuals or families are at greater risk for adverse effects when stress or perilous events occur in equivalent situations in a certain period. Generally, such stresses in environmental situations persist over generations. Interactive risk is a more dynamic way of understanding risk in social environments. It suggests that persons interact with risk circumstances in ways that may increase or lessen jeopardy or hazardous situations.

Role model formulation A developmental domain characterized by evaluations about highly regarded behaviors and nonvalued behaviors as personified by persons within both proximal and distal nested contexts. The adolescent begins to self-construct meaningful behaviors and values and revises the idealized images of parents and other role models formed during earlier developmental periods.

Sassy-sassiness Willful forthrightness in demeanor that expresses a spirited behavioral expressive style of boldness, independence, and courage, which black adolescent girls learn early to deal with everyday hassles. Sassiness can become a form of healthy social resistance that embodies the moral integrity needed to deal with daily confrontations of social and racial inequities and indignities. During adolescence sassy behavior often emerges as an expressive function of identity exploration.

Self-efficacy The ability to exercise mastery and competence in one's social environment to achieve desirable social goals.

Smart African American vernacular used to suggest an individual of high intelligence or possessing highly developed intellectual capacities. It incorporates the idiom of mother wit, which implies a judicious pragmatic outlook.

Social capital The cumulative patterning of resources or assets of a particular ethnic group over an extended or fixed period of time where the boundary maintenance of those assets or resources are time-honored and inflexible.

Social ecology A perspective of the social environment that views human beings as living in a constant reciprocal relationship with their contextual surroundings; also refers to various ecologies and is used interchangeably with social ecologies or social contexts, such as family, neighborhood, and social institutions. From this perspective problems arise at the various contextual levels when intersubjective responses are unstable, unbalanced, or inconsistent.

Social identity The cultural anchorage of the self that is socially constructed and self-owned. It refers to a social self that comprises multifarious social roles while bearing individual distinctiveness as a coherent and differentiated self.

Social norms Socially constructed meanings embodied in rules, standards, and assumptions about the behavior or social actions of individuals, families, and groups that are group created. Social norms embody reality assumptions and ranking and membership norms. Reality assumptions are social actions represented by shared meanings and perceptions by a social or cultural group about the possible in everyday life. Ranking norms are social actions that represent the standard of conduct in a given community, which is used to evaluate the praxis of everyday life. Membership norms comprise both reality assumptions and ranking norms and are the evaluative standards for including or accepting a person in a given group or community.

Social supports Social resources or assets that promote social structural opportunities.

Social stigma The negativistic and injurious social attribution of shame, disgrace, or inferiority to a social status, such as ethnicity, race, sexual orientation, gender, or age, that engenders contempt, scorn, hatred, intimidation, or terrorization from others.

Strengths perspective A view of human development that perceives personal attributes, abilities, talents, and resources as natural endowments as well as those gained from lived experiences that enhance self-empowerment tendencies. A strengths perspective is a lens through which to view the therapeutic helping process.

Structural strain When social structural or historical factors constrict social opportunities or when legitimate access to social status is denied or blocked.

Therapeutic encounter The basic practice work of the collaborative intervention context model (CICM). The therapeutic encounter is characterized by an intersubjective experience involving two or more persons engaged in ameliorative interventions, of a psychological and social nature, directed toward the change of that person, her situation, or context. The principles of the therapeutic encounter are the foundational viewpoint of the CICM that undergirds its specific intervention strategies.

References

Adler, P. (1993). *Wheeling and dealing: An ethnography of an upper-level drug dealing and smuggling community* (2nd ed.). New York: Columbia University Press.

Alan Guttmacher Institute. (1994). *Sex and America's teenagers*. New York: Author.

Albertson, C. (1972). *Bessie*. New York: Stein & Day.

Als, H. (1997, October 20, 27). The new negro. *The New Yorker*, pp. 144–169.

Anderman, J. (2000, January 23). Lolitas with a beat: Behind the gloss that preteen girls love are the sexy lyrics that older men write. *Boston Sunday Globe*, pp. D1, D2.

Anderson, E. (1990). *Streetwise: Race, class, and change in an urban community*. Chicago: University of Chicago Press.

Angelou, M. (1994). *Phenomenal woman: Four poems celebrating women*. New York: Random House.

Apter, T. (1990). *Altered loves: Mothers and daughters during adolescence*. New York: Fawcett Columbine.

Aschenbrenner, J. (1973). Child development strengths in black families. *Journal of Comparative Family Studies, 4*, 257–268.

Aschenbrenner, J. (1983). *Lifelines*. Prospect Heights, IL: Waveland Press.

Atkinson, D. R., Morten, G., & Sue, D. W. (1993). *Counseling American minorities: A cross cultural perspective* (4th ed.). Madison, WI: Brown & Benchmark.

Atwood, G., & Stolorow, R. D. (1984). *Structures of subjectivity: Explorations in psychoanalytic phenomenology*. Hillside, NJ: Analytic Press.

Barbarin, O. A. (1993). Coping and resilience: Exploring the inner lives of African American children. *Journal of Black Psychology, 19*(4), 478–492.

Barnes, J. A. (1954). Class and committees in a Norwegian island parish. *Human Relations, 7*, 39–58.

Beaucar, K. O. (1999, July). Project emphasizes strengths of youth. *NASW News*, p. 11.

Becker, E. (1964). *The revolution in psychiatry*. New York: Free Press of Glencoe.

Becker, H. (1963). *Outsiders*. New York: Free Press.

Belenky, M. F., McVicker, C. B., Goldberger, N. R., & Tarule, J. M. (1986). *Women's ways of knowing: The development of self, voice, and mind*. New York: Basic Books.

Benjamin, J. (1988). *Bonds of love*. New York: Pantheon Books.

Benjamin, J. (1990). An outline of intersubjectivity: The development of recognition. *Psychoanalytic Psychology, 7*(Suppl.), 33–46.

Benjamin, J. (1995). *Like subjects, love objects*. New Haven, CT: Yale University Press.

Berger, P. & Luckman T. (1967). *The social construction of reality*. New York: Anchor Books.

Biggs, M. A. (1998). *Puerto Rican ethnic identity: Contextual determinants and psychosocial outcomes*. Unpublished doctoral dissertation, Boston University, Boston, MA.

Billingsley, A. (1968). *Black families in white America*. Englewood Cliffs, NJ: Prentice Hall.

Billingsley, A. (1992). *Climbing Jacob's ladder*. New York: Simon & Schuster.

Bloom, B. (1985). *Developing talent in young people*. New York: Ballantine.

Blos, P. (1962). *On adolescence, a psychoanalytic interpretation*. New York. Free Press of Glencoe.

Blos, P. (1967). The second individuation process of adolescence. *Psychoanalytic Study of the Child*, 22, 161–186.

Boykin, A. W. (1983). The academic performance of Afro-American children. In J. T. Spence (Ed.), *Achievement and achievement motives* (pp. 321–362). San Francisco: W. H. Freeman & Company.

Boykin, A. W. (1986). The triple quandary and the schooling of Afro-American children. In U. Neisser (Ed.), *The school achievement of minority children* (pp. 57–75). Hillsdale, NJ: L. Erlbaum Associates.

Boykin, W. A. (1994). Harvesting talent and culture. In Robert J. Rossi (Ed.), *Schools and students at risk: Context and framework for positive change* (pp. 116–138). New York: Teachers College, Columbia University.

Boykin, W. A., and Ellison, C. M. (1995). The multiple ecologies of black youth socialization: An Afrographic analysis. In Ronald L. Taylor (Ed.), *African- American youth: Their social and economic status in the United States* (pp. 93–128). Westport, CT: Praeger Press.

Brewster, K. L. (1994). Race differences in sexual activity among adolescent women: The role of neighborhood characteristics. *American Sociological Review*, 59(June), 408–424.

Brewster, K. L., Billy, J. O. G., and Grady, W. R. (1993). Social context and adolescent behavior: The impact of community on the transition to sexual activity. *Social Forces*, 71(3), 713–740.

Bronfenbrenner, U. (1979). *The ecology of human development*. Cambridge, MA: Harvard University Press.

Brooks-Gunn, J., & Furstenberg, F. (1989). Adolescent sexual behavior. *American Psychologist*, 44(2), 249–257.

Brooks-Gunn, J., and Reiter, E. O. (1990). The role of pubertal process. In S. S. Feldman and G. R. Elliott (Eds.), *At the threshold* (pp.16–53). Cambridge, MA: Harvard University Press.

Brown, J. A., S. J. (1998). *To stand on the rock*. Maryknoll, NY: Orbis.

Bruner, J. (1990). *Acts of meaning*. Cambridge, MA: Harvard University Press.

Bruner, J. (1996). *The creature culture of education*. Cambridge, MA: Harvard University Press.

Brunswick, A. F. (1999). Structural strain: An ecological paradigm for studying African American drug abuse. In M. R. De La Rosa, B. Segal, & R. Lopez (Eds.), *Drugs and society* (pp. 5–19). Place: Publisher.

Buber, M. (1970). *I and thou. A new translation*. With prologue and notes by Walter Kaufman. New York: Scribner.

Bureau of the Census. (1991). *The black population in the United States: March 1990 and 1989*. (Current Population Reports, series P-20, no. 448). Washington, DC: U.S. Government Printing Office.

Burt, M.R. (1998). *Building supportive communities for at-risk adolescents: It takes more than service*. Washington, DC: American Psychological Association.

Burton, L. M., & Bengston, V. L. (YEAR?) Black grandmothers: Issues of timing and meaning in roles. In V. L. Bengston & J. Robertson (Eds.), *Grandparenthood: Research and policy perspectives* (pp. 61–77). Beverly Hills, CA: Sage.

Byrne, J.P. (1997). *The nature and development of decision making*. Mahwah, NJ: Erlbaum.

Cancian, F. M. (1975). *What are norms?* New York: Cambridge University Press.

Cannon, K. (1996). *Katie's cannon*. New York: Continuum Press.

Chapelle, T. (1998). Slaves of fashion: Black culture sells. *Emerge, 9* (3), 42–49.

Chau, K. L. (1991). Social work with ethnic minorities: Practice issues and potentials. *Journal of Multicultural Social Work, 1*, 23–29.

Chestang, L. W. (1972a). *Character development in a hostile environment* (Occasional Paper no. 3 [series], 1–12). Chicago: University Press.

Chestang, L. W. (1972b). The dilemma of biracial environment. *Social Work, 17*, 100–105.

Chodorow, N.J. (1989). *Feminism and psychoanalytic theory*. New Haven, CT: Yale University Press.

Clifton, L. (1987). *Good woman: Poems and a memoir 1969–1980*. Brockport, NY: BOA Editions, Ltd.

Coleman, J. S. (1974). *Youth transition to adulthood*. Report of the Panel on Youth of the President's Science Advisory Committee. Chicago: University of Chicago Press.

Coleman, J. S. (1988). Social capital in the creation of human capital. *American Journal of Sociology, 94* (Suppl.), 95–120.

Coleman, J. S. (1988b). The creation and destruction of social capital: Implications for the law. *Journal of Law, Ethics, and Public Policy, 3*, 375–404.

Coles, R. (1967). *Children of crisis*. Boston: Little, Brown.

Coles, R. (1986). *The moral life of children*. Boston: Atlantic Monthly Press.

Coles, R. (1997). *The moral intelligence of children*. New York: Random House.

Collins, P. H. (1990). *Black feminist thought*. Boston: Unwin Hyman, Inc.

Comas-Diaz, L., & Jacobsen, F. M. (1987). Ethnocultural identification in psychotherapy. *Psychiatry, 50*, 232–241.

Comas-Diaz, L., & Jacobsen, F. M. (1991). Ethnocultural transference and countertransference in the therapeutic dyad. *American Journal of Orthopsychiatry, 61*, 392–402.

Cone, J. H. (1972). *The spirituals and the blues*. Maryknoll, NY: Orbis Books.

Cone, J. H. (1991). *Martin & Malcolm & america: A dream or a nightmare*. Maryknoll, NY: Orbis Books.

Cross, W. (1971). The Negro to black conversion experiences. *Black World, 20*, 13–27.

Cross, W. E., Jr. (1991). *Shades of black: Diversity in African-American identity*. Philadelphia: Temple University Press.

Crossley, N. (1996). *Intersubjectivity: The fabric of social becoming*. London: Sage Publications.

Crouch, S. (1995). *The all American skin game, or the decoy of race: The long and short of it, 1990–1994*. New York: Pantheon Books.

Cruse, H. (1967). *The crisis of the Negro intellectual*. New York: William Morrow & Co.

Dancer, D. C. (1998). *Honey hush, an anthology of African American women's humor*. New York: W. W. Norton & Company.

De Anda, D. (1984). Bicultural socialization: Factors affecting the minority experience. *Social Work, 29*, 101–107.

De Hoyos, G., De Hoyos, A., & Anderson, C. B. (1986). Sociocultural dislocation: Beyond the dual perspective. *Social Work, 31,* 61–67.

Delgado, M. (2000). *New arenas for community social work practice with urban youth.* New York: Columbia University Press.

Demos, E. V. (1989). Resiliency in infancy. In T. Dugan & R. Coles (Eds.), *The child in our times: Studies in the development of resiliency* (pp. 3–22). New York: Brunner-Mazel.

Devore, W., & Schlesinger, E. G. (1991). *Ethnic-sensitive social work practice* (4th ed) Boston: Allyn & Bacon.

Devore, W., & Schlesinger, E. G. (1996). *Ethnic-sensitive social work practice.* (4th ed.) Boston: Allyn & Bacon.

Dill, B. T. (1990). The dialectics of black womanhood. In M. R. Malson, E. Mudimbe-Boyi, J. F. O'Barr, & M. Wyer (Eds.), *Black women in America: Social science perspectives* (pp. 65–78). Chicago: University of Chicago Press.

Dryfoos, J. G. (1990). *Adolescents at risk: Prevalence and prevention.* New York: Oxford University Press.

Dubas, J. S., & Petersen, A. C. (1993). Female pubertal development. In M. Sugar (Ed.), *Female adolescent development* (2nd ed., pp. 3–26). New York: Brunner Mazel Publishers.

DuBois, W. E. B. (1903). *The souls of black folk* (pp. 247–260). New York: Signet.

Dubow, E. F., & Luster, T. (1990). Adjustment of children born to teenage mothers: The contribution of risk and protective factors. *Child Development, 63,* 542–557.

Dyer, G. (1996). *But beautiful.* New York: North Point Press, Farrar, Straus & Giroux.

Eames, E., & Goode, J. G. (1977). *Anthropology of the city: An introduction to urban anthropology.* Englewood Cliffs, NJ: Prentice-Hall.

Elliott, G. R., and Feldman, S. S. (1990). Capturing the adolescence experience. In S. S. Feldman & G. R. Elliott (Eds.), *At the threshold* (pp. 1–14). Cambridge, MA: Harvard University Press.

Ellison, R. (1964). *Blues people in shadow and act.* New York: Random House.

Ensminger, M. E. (1990). Sexual activity and problem behaviors among black, urban adolescents. *Child Development, 61,* 2032–2046.

Erikson, E. (1964). *Childhood and society* (2nd ed.). New York: Norton.

Erikson, E. (1968). *Identity youth and crises.* New York: W.W. Norton & Company, Inc.

Erikson, E. (1969). *Identity and the life cycle.* New York: International Universities Press, Inc.

Farmelant, S. (1997, July 2–5). Head of the class. *The Improper Bostonian,* pp. 34–35.

Feagin, J. R., and Sikes, M. P. (1994). *Living with racism.* Boston: Beacon Press.

Feiring, C. (1996). Concepts of romance in 15-year-old adolescents. *Journal of Research on Adolescents, 6*(2), 181–200.

Flanagan, W. G. (1999). *Urban sociology: Images and structure* (4th ed.). Boston: Allyn and Bacon.

Folb, E. A. (1980). *Runnin' down some lines: The language and culture of black teenagers.* Cambridge, MA: Harvard University Press.

Folkman, S., Chesney, M., McKusick, L., Ironson, G., Johnson, D., & Coates, T. J. (1991). Translating coping theory into an intervention. In J. Eckenrode (Ed.), *The social context of coping* (pp. 239–260). New York: Plenum Publishing.

Ford, D. Y. (1994). Nurturing resilience in gifted black youth. *Roper Review, 17*(2), 80–85.

Fordham, S. (1996). *Blacked out: Dilemmas of race, identity, and success at Capital High.* Chicago: University of Chicago Press.

Fordham, S., & Ogbu, J. U. (1986). Black students' school success: Coping with the "burden of 'acting white.'" *Urban Review, 18*(3), 176–206.

Fox, S. (1989). *Blood and power: Organized crime in twentieth-century America.* New York: William Morrow and Company.

Frankenberg, R. (1993). *White women, race matters: The social construction of whiteness.* Minneapolis: University of Minnesota Press.

Frankl, V. (1985). *Man's search for meaning.* New York: Washington Square Press.

Franklin, D. L. (1997). *Ensuring inequality: The structural transformation of the African American family.* New York: Oxford University Press.

Frazier, E.F. (1957). *Black bourgeoisie.* Glencoe, IL: The Free Press.

Freud, A. (1958). Adolescence. *The Psychoanalytic Study of the Child, 13,* 255–278.

Fry, P. S. (1998). The development of personal meaning and wisdom in adolescence: A reexamination of moderating and consolidating factors and influences. In P. T. P. Wong & P. S. Frey (Eds.), *The human quest for meaning* (pp. 91–110). Mahwah, NJ: Lawrence Erblaum Associates, Publishers.

Frydenberg, E. (1997). *Adolescent coping.* London: Routledge.

Fukuyama, F. (1995). *The end of order.* London: The Social Market Foundation.

Fullilove, M. T., Golden, E., Fullilove, R. E., Lennon, R., Porterfield, D., and Schwarcz, S. (1993). Crack cocaine use and high-risk behaviors among sexually active black adolescents. *Journal of Adolescent Health, 14*: 295–300.

Furstenberg, F. F., Brooks-Gunn, J., and Chase-Lansdale, L. (1989). Teenaged pregnancy and childbearing. *American Psychologist, 44,* 313–320.

Furstenberg, F. F., Jr., Morgan, S. P., Moore, K. A., and Peterson, J. L. (1987). Race differences in the timing of adolescent intercourse. *American Sociologist Review, 52*(August), 511–518.

Gage, N. (1971). *The Mafia is an equal opportunity employer.* New York: McGraw-Hill.

Gang girl: The transformation of Isis Sapp-Grant. (1998, August). *Essence,* pp. 74, 128–133.

Gargilo, J., Attie, I., Brooks-Gunn, J., & Warren, M. P. (1987). Girls' dating behavior as a function of social context and maturation. *Developmental Psychology, 23,* 730–737.

Garmezy, N. (1991). Resilience and vulnerability to adverse developmental outcomes associated with poverty. *American Behavioral Scientist,* 34(4), 416–430.

Garmezy, N. (1993). Children in poverty: Resilience despite risk. *Psychiatry, 56,* February, 127–136.

Gates, H. L., Jr. (1988). *The signifying monkey.* New York: Oxford University Press.

Germaine, C., & Gitterman, A. (1980). *The life model of social work practice.* New York: Columbia University Press.

Gibbs, J. T. (1986). Psychosocial correlates of sexual attitudes and behaviors in urban early adolescent females: Implicattions for intervention. *Journal of Social Work and Human Sexuality, 5,* 81–97.

Gibbs, J. T. (1988). Young black males in america: Endangered, embittered, and embattled. In J. T. Gibbs (Ed.), *Young, black, and male in america: An endangered species*. New York: Auburn House.

Gibbs, J. T. (1990). Mental health issues of black adolescents: Implications for policy and research. In A. R. Sheffman & L. E. Danes (Eds.), Ethical issues in adolescence (pp. 21–52). Newbury Park, CA: Sager.

Gibbs, J. T. (1996). Health compromising behaviors in urban early adolescent females: Ethnic and socioeconomic variations. In B. J. R. Leadbeater & N. Way (Eds.), *Urban girls* (pp. 309–327). New York: New York University Press.

Giddings, P. (1984). *When and where I enter*. New York: William Morrow & Company, Inc.

Gilligan, C., Ward, J. V., & Taylor, J. M. (1988). *Mapping the moral domain: A contribution of women's thinking to psychological theory and education*. Cambridge, MA: Harvard University Press.

Gladwell, M. (1998, August 17). Do parents matter? *The New Yorker*, 54–64.

Goffman, E. (1961). *Asylums*. Chicago: Aldine Press.

Goffman, E. (1963). *Stigma*. Englewood Cliffs, NJ: Prentice-Hall.

Goffman, E. (1973). *The presentation of self in everyday life*. Woodstock, NY: The Overlook Press.

Goffman, I. (1976). *Interaction ritual*. Chicago: Aldine Press.

Goodwin, M. H. G. (1990). *He-said-she-said: Talk as social organization among black children*. Bloomington: Indiana University Press.

Gordon, S. (2000). *Flannery O'Connor: The obedient imagination*. Athens: University of Georgia.

Gourse, L. (1993). *Sassy: The life of Sarah Vaughan*. New York: C. Scribner's Sons.

Graff, H. J. (1995). Conflicting paths growing up in America. Cambridge, MA: Harvard University Press.

Greenspan, S. I. (1997). *Developmentally based psychotherapy*. Madison, WI: International Universities Press, Inc.

Grewal, G. (1998). *Circles of sorrow, lines of struggle: The novels of Toni Morrison*. Baton Rouge: Louisana State University Press.

Grier, W. H., & Cobbs, P. M. (1968). *Black rage*. New York: Basic Books.

Grossman, F. K., et al. (1992). Risk and resilience in adolescents. *Adolescence*, 21(5), 529–550.

Grubb, W. N. (1989). Preparing youth for work: The dilemmas of education and training programs. In D. Stern & D. Eichorn (Eds.), *Adolescence and work: Influences of social structure, labor markets, and culture* (pp. 13–45). Hillside, NJ: Lawrence Erlbaum Associates.

Gutierrez, L. M. (1990). Working with women of color: An empowerment perspective. *Social Work*, 35, 149–154.

Gutierrez, L. M. (1994, September). Beyond coping: An empowerment perspective on stressful life events. *Journal of Sociology and Social Welfare*, 21(3): 201–219.

Hacker, A. (1992). *Two nations*. New York: Charles Schribner & Sons.

Haggerty, R. J., Sherrod, L. R., Garmezy, N., & Rutter, M. (Eds.). (1994). Resilience and development: Contributions from the study of children who overcame adversity. *Development and Psychopathology*, 2, 445–444.

Halberstam, D. (1998). *The children*. New York: Random House.

Hall, E. T. (1969). *The hidden dimension*. Garden City, NY: Doubleday Anchor Books.

Hall, E. T. (1971). *Beyond culture*. Garden City, NY: Doubleday Anchor Books.

Hall, G. S. (1904). *Adolescence: Its psychology and its relations to physiology, anthropology, sociology, sex, crime, religion, and education*. New York: D. Appleton and Company.

Hamilton, C. V. (1972). *The black preacher in America*. New York: Morrow.

Hansen, D. A., Johnson, V. A. (1989). Classroom lesson strategies and orientations toward work. In D. Stern & D. Eichorn (Eds.), *Adolescence and work: Influences of social structure, labor markets, and culture* (pp. 75–99). Hillside, NJ: Lawrence Erlbaum Associates.

Harris, J. R. (1998). *The nurture assumption: Why children turn out the way they do*. New York: Free Press.

Harter, S. (1990). Self and identity development. In S. S. Feldman & G. R. Elliott (Eds.), *At the threshold: The developing adolescent* (pp. 352–387). Cambridge, MA: Harvard University Press.

Hauser, S. T., & Bowlds, K. (1990). Stress, coping, and adaptation. In S. S. Feldman & G. R. Elliott (Eds.), *At the threshold* (pp. 388–413). Cambridge, MA: Harvard University Press.

Hayes, D. (Ed.) (1987). *Risking the future: Adolescent sexuality, pregnancy, and childbearing, Volume 1*. Washington, DC: National Academy Press.

Hays, W., & Mindel, C. (1973). Extended kinship relations in black and white families. *Journal of Marriage and the Family, 35*, 51–57.

Heckhausen, J. (1999). *Developmental regulation in adulthood*. Cambridge, England: Cambridge University Press.

Henley, J. (1995, Spring). Comparative research on adolescent childbearing: Understanding race differences. *African American Research Perspectives, 2*(1), 70–81.

Hill, R. B. (1972). *The strengths of black families*. New York: Emerson Hall Publishers, Inc.

Hill, R. B. (1997). *The strengths of African American families: Twenty-five years later*. Washington, DC: R & B Publishers.

Hine, D.C., & Thompson, K. (1998). *The history of black women in America*. New York: Broadway Books.

Hine, T. (1999). *The rise and fall of the American teenager*. New York: Avon Books.

Horowitz, R. (1984, Spring). Passion submission and motherhood: The negotiation of identity by unmarried inner city Chicanos. *The Sociological Quarterly, 22*, 241–252.

Ignatiev, N. (1995). *How the Irish became white*. New York: Routledge.

Japan's youth finds black culture is in. (1998, May 31). *Boston Sunday Globe*, p. A19.

Jarrett, R. L. (1994). Living poor: Family life among single parent African American women. *Social Problems, 41*, 30–39.

Jarrett, R. L. (1995). Growing up poor: The family experience of socially mobile youth in low-income African American neighborhoods. *Journal of Adolescent Research, 10*(1), 111–134.

Jemmott, J. B., III, and Jemmott, L. S. (1993). Alcohol and drug use during sexual activity, predicting the HIV-risk-related behaviors of inner-city black male adolescents. *Journal of Adolescent Research, 8*(1), 41–47.

Jessop, D. J. (1981). Family relationships as viewed by parents and adolescents: A specification. *Journal of Marriage and the Family, 43*, 95–106.

Jessor, R. (1993). Successful adolescent development among youth in high-risk settings. *American Psychologist, 48*(2), 117–126.

Jessor, S. L., & Jessor, R. (1975). Transition from virginity to non-virginity among youth: A social-psychological study over time. *Developmental Psychology, 11*(4), 473–484.

Jewell, K. S. (1987). The changing character of black families: The effects of differential social and economic gains. *Journal of Social and Behavioral Sciences, 33*, 143–154.

Johnson, M. (1997, September). Face to face: Oprah Winfrey. *Life*, pp. 44–61.

Kagan, J. (1992). Risk behavior in adolescence: A psychosocial framework for understanding and action. In D. E. Rogers & E. Ginsberg (Eds.), *Adolescents at risk* (pp. 8–18). Boulder, CO: Westview.

Kaplan, H. B. (1996). Toward an understanding of resilience: A critical review of definitions and models. In M. D. Glantz, J. Johnson, & L.

Katchadourian, H. (1990). Sexuality. In S. S. Feldman & G. R. Elliott (Eds.), *At the threshold: The developing adolescent* (pp. 330–351). Cambridge, MA: Harvard University Press.

Keating, D. P. (1990). Adolescent thinking. In S. S. Feldman & G. R. Elliott (Eds.), *At the threshold: The developing adolescent* (pp. 54–89). Cambridge, MA: Harvard University Press.

Keith, J. B., McCreary, C., Collins, K., Smith, C. P., & Bernstein, I. (1991). Sexual activity and contraceptive use among low-income urban black adolescent females. *Adolescence 26*(104), 769–785.

Keniston, K. (1965). *The uncommitted: Alienated youth in American society*. New York: Harcourt, Brace, & World, Inc.

Kilty, K. M., & Meenaghan, T. M. (1995). Social work and the convergence of politics and science. *Social Work, 40*, 445–454.

Kolvin, I., Miller, F. J. W., Fleeting, M., & Kolvin, P. (1988). Risk and protective factors for offending with particular reference to deprivation. In M. Rutter (Ed.), *Studies of psychosocial risk: The power of longitudinal data* (pp. 77–95). Cambridge, England: Cambridge University Press.

Korotkov, D. (1998). The sense of coherence: Making sense out of chaos. In P. T. P. Wong & P. S. Frey (Eds.), *The human quest for meaning* (pp. 51–70). Mahwah, NJ: Lawrence Erlbaum.

Ku, L., Sonenstein, F. L., & Pleck, J. H. (1993). Factors influencing first intercourse for teenage men. *Public Health Reports, 108*(6), 680–694.

Ladner, J. (1972). *Tomorrow's tomorrow: The black woman*. Garden City, NY: Doubleday.

Langer, L. M. (1996). Modeling adolescent health behavior: The preadult health decision-making model. In C. B. McCoy, L. R. Metsch, & J. A. Inciardi (Eds.), *Interviewing with drug-involved youth* (pp. 45–78). Thousands Oaks, CA: Sage.

Larson, R. W. (1983). Adolescents' daily experience with family and friends: Contrasting opportunity systems. *Journal of Marriage and the Family, 45*, 739–750.

Lawrence-Lightfoot, S. (1994). *I've known rivers: Lives of loss and liberation*. Reading, MA: Addison-Wesley.

Lowe, J. (1994). *Jump at the sun: Zora Neal Hurston's Cosmic Comedy*. Urbana: University of Illinois Press.

Lerner, R. M., Ostrom, C. W., and Freel, M. A. (1997). Preventing health- compromising behaviors among youth and promoting their positive development: A developmental contextual perspective. In J. Schulenberg, J. L. Maggs, & K. Hurrelmann (Eds.), *Health risks and developmental transitions during adolescence* (pp. 498–521). New York: Cambridge University Press.

Lewis, C. G. (1981). How adolescents approach decisions: Changes over grades seven to twelve and policy implications. *Child Development, 52*, 538 554.

Lewis, E. A., & Suarez, Z. E. (1995). Helping networks. In *Encyclopedia of social work* (19th ed., pp. 1765–1772). Washington, DC: NASW Press.

Lewis, E. A., & Walker, B. S. (1995). *"Why should white guys have all the fun?" How Reginald Lewis created a billion-dollar business empire.* New York: Wiley.

Lichtenstein, H. (1977). *The dilemna of human identity.* New York: Jason Aronson.

Lifton, R. J. (1970). *History and human survival.* New York: Random House.

Long, J. F. V., & Valliant, G. E. (1989). Escape from the underclass. In T. F. Dugan & R. Coles (Eds.), *The child of our times: Studies in the development of resiliency* (pp. 200–213). New York: Brunner/Mazel.

Lourdeaux, L. (1990). *Italian and Irish filmmakers in America.* Philadelphia: Temple University Press.

Loury, G., et. al. (1972). *Ethnic enterprise in America.* Berkeley: University of Californa Press.

Madhubuti, H. (1990). *Black men: obsolete, single, dangerous?* Chicago: Third World Press.

Magnusson, D., Stattin, H., & Allen, V. (1985). Biological maturation and social development: A longitudinal study of some adjustment processes from mid-adolescence to adulthood. *Journal of Youth and Adolescence, 14*(4), 267–283.

Marini, M. M. (1984). Age and sequencing norms in the transition to adulthood. *Social Forces, 63*(1), 229–244.

Masten, A. S., Best, K. M., & Garmezy, N. (1990). Resilience and development: Contributions from the study of children who overcome adversity. *Development and Psychopathology, 2*(4), 425–444.

McAdoo, H. P. (1988). The study of ethnic minority families: Implications for practitioners and policymakers. *Family Relations, 37,* 265–267.

McAdoo, H. P. (Ed.) (1993). *Family ethnicity: Strength in diversity.* Newbury Park, CA: Sage.

McAdoo, H. P. (1997). *Black families* (3rd ed.). Thousand Oaks, CA: Sage Publications.

McCall, G. J. (1966). *Identities and interaction.* New York: Free Press.

McClain, L. (1986). The middle-class black's burden. In C. Page (Ed.), *A foot in each world* (pp. 12–14). Evanston, IL: Northwestern University Press.

McCord, J. (1990). Problem behaviors. In S. Feldman & G. R. Elliott (Eds.), *At the Threshold* (pp. 431–456). Cambridge, MA: Harvard University Press.

McLaughlin, M. W. (1993). Embedded identities: Enabling balance in urban contexts. In M. W. McLaughlin & S. B. Heath (Eds.), *Identity & inner-city youth* (pp. 36–68). New York: Teachers College, Columbia University.

McMahon, A., & Allen-Meares, P. (1992). Is social work racist? A content analysis of recent literature. *Social Work, 37*(6), 533–539.

Mead, G. H. (1934). *Mind, self, and society.* Chicago: University of Chicago Press.

Mirkin, M. P. (1994). Female adolescence revisited: Understanding girls in their social contexts. In M. P. Mirkin, *Women in context: Toward a feminist reconstruction of psychotherapy* (pp. 77–95). New York: Guilford Press.

Mithaug, D. E. (1996). *Equal opportunity theory.* Thousands Oaks, CA: Sage Publications.

Merton, R. K. (1957). *Social theory and social structure.* Glencoe, IL: Free Press.

Morrison, T. (1970). *The bluest eye.* New York. Holt, Rhinehart and Winston.

Morrison, T. (1973). *Sula.* New York: Alfred A. Knopf.

Morrison, T. (1998). *Paradise*. New York: A. A. Knopf.

Murray, A. (1970). *The omni-Americans*. New York: Outerbridge & Dienstfrey.

Murray, A. (1978). *Stomping the blues*. London: Quartet Books.

Murray, A. (1996). *The blue devils of nada*. New York: Pantheon.

Myers, H. F. (1989). Urban stress and mental health of Afro-American youth: An epidemiologic and conceptual update. In R. L. Jones (Ed.), *Black adolescents* (pp. 123–152). Berkeley, CA: Cobbs & Henry.

Neugarten, B. (1968). *Adult personality: Toward a psychology of the life cycle*. Chicago: University of Chicago Press.

Neugarten, B., & Hagestad, G. O. (1985). Age and the life course. In R. Binstack & E. Shans (Eds.), *Handbook of aging and the social sciences*. (pp. 35–55). New York: Van Nastrand Reinbald.

Neugarten, B., Moore, J., & Loine, J. (1973). Age norms, age constraints, and a direct socialization. *American Journal of Sociology, 70*, 710–717.

Newcomer, S. F., & Udry, J. R. (1985). Oral sex and the adolescent population. *Archives of Sexual Behavior, 14*, 41–56.

Newman, B., & Newman, P. (1987). *Development through life, a psychosocial approach*. Chicago: The Dorsey Press.

Nicholson, S. (1994). *Ella Fitzgerald: A biography of the first lady of jazz*. New York: Charles Scribner & Sons

Noack, P., & Kracke, B. (1997). Social change and adolescent well-being: Healthy country, healthy teens. In J. Schulenberg, J. L. Maggs, & K. Hurrelmann (Eds.), *Health risks and developmental transitions during adolescence* (pp. 54–84). New York: Cambridge University Press.

Nobles, W. W. (1973). Psychological research and the black self-concept: A critical review. *Journal of Social Issues, 29*, 11–31.

Nobles, W. W., et al. (1976). *A formulative and empirical study of black families* (DHEW Publication OCD-90–C-255). Washington, DC: U.S. Government Printing Office.

Norton, D. (1978). The dual perspective. In D. Norton (Ed.), *The dual perspective: Inclusion of ethnic minority content in social work curriculum*. (pp. 1–19). New York: Council on Social Work Education.

Nouwen, H. (1972). *The wounded healer*. Garden City, New York: Doubleday.

Offer, D., Ostrov, E., Howard, K. I., & Atkinson, R. (1988). *The teenage world: Adolescents' self-image in ten countries*. New York: Plenum.

Ogbu, J. (1978). *Minority education and caste*. New York: Academic Press.

Orange, D. M., Atwood, G. E., & Stolorow, R. D. (1997). *Working intersubjectively: Contextualism in psychoanalytic practice*. Hillsdale, NJ: The Analytic Press.

Overall, B., & Aronson, H. (1966). Expectations of psychotherapy in patients of lower socioeconomic class. *American Journal of Orthopsychiatry, 33*, 421–430.

Page, R. M., Allen, O., Moore, L., Hewitt, C. (1993). Co-occurrence of substance use and loneliness as a risk factor for adolescent hopelessness. *Journal of School Health, 63*(2), 104–108.

Palombo, J. (1985). *An outline of adolescent development*. Paper presented at the Tenth Annual Self Psychology Conference, Chicago, IL.

Palombo, J. (1988). Adolescent development: A view from self psychology. *Child and Adolescent Social Work Journal, 5*, 171–186.

Palombo, J. (1990). *The cohesive self, the nuclear self, and development in late adolescence*. Chicago: University of Chicago Press.

Partners in the engine room of rap. (1999, August 1). *New York Times*, pp. 27–28).

Patten, Marie. (1981). Self concept and self-esteem: Factors in adolescent pregnancy. *Adolescence*, *XVI*(64), 765–778.

Pearlin, L. I. (1991). The study of coping: An overview of problems and directions. In J. Eckenrode (Ed.), *The social context of coping* (pp. 261–276). New York: Plenum Press.

Peebles-Wilkins, W., & Koerin, B. (1992). Moral goodness and black women: Late nineteenth century community caregivers. In P. N. Reid & P. R. Popple (Eds.), *The moral purposes of social work* (pp. 155–169). Chicago: Nelson-Hall.

Pile, S. (1996). *The body and the city: Psychoanalysis, space, and subjectivity*. New York: Routledge.

Pinderhughes, E. B. (1979). Teaching empathy in cross-cultural social work. *Social Work*, 24, 312–316.

Pipher, M. (1994). *Reviving Ophelia*. New York: Ballatine Books.

Pollard, W. L. (1997, March). *The other social work root: Lessons from the past*. Carl A. Scott Memorial Lecture presented at the Council on Social Work Education Annual Program Meeting, city, state.

Powers, S., Stuart, H., & Kliner, L. A. (1989). Adolescent mental health. *American Psychologist*, *44*(2), 200–208.

A question of style vs. intention. (1996, November 5). *Boston Globe*.

Rains, P. M. (1971). *Becoming an unwed mother*. Chicago: Aldine.

Rainwater, L. (1970). *Behind ghetto walls: Black families in a federal slum*. Hawthorne, NY: Aldine.

Ratner, M. (Ed.). (1993). *Crack pipe as pimp: An ethnographic investigation of sex-for-crack-exchanges*. New York: Lexington Books.

Rhoden, W. C. (July 9, 2000). A victory that was much more. The New York Times, Sports Sunday, Section 8, p. 5.

Rhodes, J. E., Gingiss, P. L., & Smith, P. (1994). Risk and protective factors for alcohol use among pregnant African-American, Hispanic, and white adolescents: The influence of peers, sexual partners, family members, and mentors. *Addictive Behaviors*, *19*(5), 555–564.

Rosenbalum, E., & Kandel, D. B. (1990, August). Early onset of adolescent sexual behavior and drug involvement. *Journal of Marriage and the Family*, 783–798.

Rubin, R. H., Billingsley, A., & Caldwell, C. H. (1994). The role of the black church in working with adolescents. *Adolescence*, *29*(114), 251–266.

Rubington, E., & Weinberg, M. S. (1989). *The study of social problems: Six perspectives*. New York: Oxford University Press.

Rutter, M. (1987). Psychosocial resilience and protective mechanisms. *American Journal of Orthopsychiatry*, *37*, 317–331.

Rutter, M. (Ed.). (1988). *Studies of psychosocial risk: The power of longitudinal data*. Cambridge, England: Cambridge University Press.

Saari, C. (1986). *Clinical social work treatment: How does it work?* New York: Gardner Press.

Saari, C. (1991). *The creation of meaning in social work*. New York: The Guilford Press.

Saleebey, D. (Ed.) (1992). *Strengths perspective in social work practice* (2nd ed.). New York: Longman.

Sameroff, A. J., & Seifer, R. (1990). Early contributors to developmental risk. In J. Rolf, A. S. Masten, D. Cicchetti, K. H. Neuchterlein, & S. Weintraub (Eds.), *Risk and protective factors in the development of psychopathology* (pp. 52–66). Cambridge, England: Cambridge University Press.

Sampson, R. J., Raudenbush, S., & Earls, F. (1997). Neighborhoods and violent crime: A multilevel study of collective efficacy. *Science, 227,* 918–924.

Santrock, J. W. (1998). *Adalescence* (7th ed.). Boston: McGraw-Hill.

Sarah Vaughn, the divine one. (1991, July). *American Masters.* Public Broadcasting Station.

Sawicki, M. (1997). *Body, text, and science.* Dordrecht: Kluwer Academic Publishers.

Schaefer, J. A., & Moos, R. A. (1992). Life crises and personal growth. In B. N. Carpenter (Ed.), *Personal coping: Theory, research, and application* (pp. 149–170). Westport, CT: Praeger.

Schon, D. A. (1996). Reflective inquiry in social work practice. In P. McHess & E. J. Mullen (Eds.), *Practitioner-researcher partnerships* (pp. 31–55). Washington, DC: NASW Press.

Schulenberg, J., Maggs, J. L., & Hurrelmann, K. (Eds.) (1997). *Health risks and developmental transitions during adolescence.* New York: Cambridge University Press.

Selman, R. (1980). *The growth of interpersonal understanding.* New York: Academic Press.

Seltz, J. (2000, May 28). Teen brains are different. *The Boston Sunday Globe,* pp. E1, E5.

Shange, N. (1985). *Betsey Brown: A novel.* New York: St. Martin's Press.

Smitherman-Donaldson, G. (1977). *Talkin and testifyin.* Boston, MA: Houghton Mifflin.

Smith, C. (1997). Factors associated with early sexual activity among urban adolescents. *Social Work, 4*(241), 334–347.

Souljah, Sister (1994). *No respect.* New York: Times Books.

Spencer, M. B. (1982). Personal and group identity of black children: An alternative synthesis. *Psychology Monographs, 106,* 59–84.

Spencer, M. B. (1985). Cultural cognition and social cognition as identity correlates of black children's personal-social development. In M. B. Spencer, G. K. Brookins, & W. R. Allen (Eds.), *Beginnings: The social and affective development of black children* (pp. 215–230). Hillside, NJ: Lawrence Erlbaum Associates.

Spencer, M. B. (1995). Old issues and new theorizing about African-American youth: A phenomenological variant of ecological systems theory. In R. L. Taylor (Ed.), *African-American youth: Their social and economic status in the United States* (pp. 37–70). Westport, CT: Praeger.

Stack, C. (1974). *All our kin.* New York: Harper and Row.

Stack, C., & Burton, L. (1993). Kinscripts. *Journal of Comparative Family Studies, XXIV*(2), 157–170.

Staples, R., & Johnson, L. B. (1993). *Black families at the crossroads: Challenges and prospects.* San Francisco: Jossey-Bass Publishers.

Stattin, H., & Magnusson, D. (1990). *Paths through life, Vol. 2: Pubertal maturation in female development.* Hillside, NJ: Erlbaum.

Stein, St. (1964). *On the problem of empathy.* The Hague: M. Nijhoff.

Steinberg, L. (1990). Autonomy, conflict, and harmony in the family relationship. In S. Feldman & G. R. Elliott (Eds.), *At the threshold* (pp. 253–276). Cambridge, MA: Harvard University Press.

Sterk, C.E. (1999). *Fastlines: Women who use crack cocaine.* Philadelphia, Temple University Press.

Stern, D. (1977). *The first relationship: Mother and infant.* Cambridge, MA: Harvard University Press.

Stern, D. (1985). *The interpersonal world of the infant: A view from psychoanalysis and developmental psychology.* New York: Basic Books.

Sternberg, R. J. (1986). A triangular theory of love. *Psychological Review, 93*(2), 119–135.

Sternberg, R. J. (1988). Triangulating love. In R. J. Sternberg & M. Barnes (Eds.), *The psychology of love* (pp. 119–138). New Haven, CT: Yale University Press.

Stevens, J. W. (1993). The negotiation of adulthood status among a group of African-American lower class pregnant and nonpregnant female adolescents. *Dissertation Abstracts International, 54*(05), 1953–A (University Microfilms No. 9326183).

Stevens, J. W. (1994). Adolescent development and adolescent pregnancy among late age African-American female adolescents. *Child & Adolescent Social Work Journal, 11*, 433–454.

Stevens, J. W. (1995–96). Adolescent status negotiation among poor urban African-American pregnant and nonpregnant late age adolescent females. *The Journal of Applied Social Sciences, 20*(1), 39–50.

Stevens, J.W. (1996). Childbearing among unwed African American adolescents: A critique of theories. *Affilia, 11*(3), 278–302.

Stevens, J. W. (1997a). African American female adolescent identity development: A three dimensional perspective. *Child Welfare Journal, LXXVI*(1), 145–172.

Stevens, J. W. (1997b). Opportunity, outlook, and coping in poor urban African American late-age female adolescent contraceptors. *Smith College Studies in Social Work, 67*(3) 456–475.

Stevens, J. W. (1998a, May–June). A question of values in social work practice: Working with the strengths of black adolescent females. *Families in Society: The Journal of Contemporary Human Services,* 288–296.

Stevens, J. W. (1998b). Early coital behavior and substance use among African American female adolescents. *African American Research Perspectives, 4*(1), 35–39.

Stevens, J. W. (1999). Creating collaborative partnerships: Clinical intervention research in an inner-city middle school. *Social Work in Education, 21*(3), 151–162.

Stolorow, R. D., & Atwood, G. E. (1992). *Contexts of being: Intersubjective foundations of psychological life.* Hillside, NJ: The Analytic Press.

Sue, D. W., & Sue, D. (1990). *Counseling the culturally different: theory and practice.* New York: John Wiley.

Surrey, J. (1991). The "self in relation": A theory of women's development. In J. V. Jordan, A. G. Kaplan, J. B. Miller, I. P. Stiver, & J. L. Surrey (Eds.), *Women's growth in connection.* (pp. 51–66) New York: The Guilford Press.

Tajfel, H. (1978). *Differentiation between social groups.* San Diego, CA: Academic Press.

Tanner, J. M. (1962). *Growth at adolescence* (2nd ed.). Oxford: Blackwell Science, Ltd.

Taylor, J. M., Gilligan, C., & Sullivan, A. M. (1995). *Between voice and silence.* Cambridge, MA: Harvard University Press.

Taylor, R. D. (1996). Adolescents' perceptions of kinship support and family management practices: Association with adolescent adjustment in African American families. *Developmental Psychology, 32*, 687–695.

Taylor, R. D. (1997). The effects of economic and social stressors on parenting and adolescent adjustment in African-American families. In R. D. Taylor & M. C. Wang (Eds.), *Social and emotional adjustment and family relations in ethnic minority families* (pp. 35–52). Mahwah, NJ: Erlbaum.

Tolman, D. L. (1994). Doing desire: Adolescent girls' struggles for/with sexuality. *Gender & Society, 8,* 324–342.

Tolman, D. L., & Szalacha, L. A. (1999). Dimensions of desire: Bridging qualitative and quantitative methods in a study of female sexuality. *Psychology of Women Quarterly, 23,* 7–39.

Trebay, G. (1997, August 3). Style: Bound for glory. *The New York Times Magazine,* p. 43.

Tsui, P., & Schultz, G. (1995). Failure of rapport: Why psychotherapeutic engagement fails in the treatment of Asian clients. *American Journal of Orthopsychiatry, 55*(4), 561–569.

Udry, J. R., & Billy, J. (1987). Initiation of coitus in early adolescence. *American Sociological Review, 52,* 841–855.

Vaillant, G. E. (1993). *The wisdom of the ego.* Cambridge, MA: Harvard University Press.

Van Gennep, A. (1960). *The rites of passage.* Chicago: University of Chicago Press.

Vygotsky, L. S. (1978). *Mind in society.* Cambridge, MA: Harvard University Press.

Walker, A. (1983). *In search of our mothers' gardens: Womanist praise.* San Diego: Harcourt Brace Jovanovich.

Wallace, J. M. (1999). Explaining race differences in adolescent and young adult drug use: The role of racialized social systems. In M. R. De La Rosa, B. Segal, & R. Lopez (Eds.), *Drugs and society: Conducting drug abuse research with minority populations: Advances and issues* (pp. 21–36). New York: The Haworth Press, Inc.

Ward, J. V. (1991). A belief in self far greater than anyone's disbelief: Cultivating resistance among African-American female adolescents. In C. Gilligan, A. G. Rogers, & D. L. Tolman (Eds.), *Women, girls, and psychotherapy: Reframing resistance* (pp. 87–103). New York: The Haworth Press, Inc.

Washington, J. M. (1994). *Conversations with God: Two centuries of prayers by African Americans.* New York: Harpers/Collins.

Way, N. (1995). "Can't you see the courage, the strength that I have?" Listening to urban adolescent girls speak about their relationships. *Psychology of Women Quarterly, 19,* 107–128.

Werner, E. E., & Smith, R. S. (1982). *Vulnerable but invincible.* New York: McGraw-Hill.

West, C. (1993). *Race matters.* Boston: Beacon Press.

White, S., White, G. (1998). *Stylin': African American expressive culture from its beginnings to the zoot suit.* Ithaca: Cornell University Press.

Williams, C. W. (1991). *Black teenage mothers: Pregnancy and child rearing from their perspective.* Lexington, MA: Lexington Books.

Williams, L. F. (1995). Epistemology. In *Encyclopedia of Social Work.* (19th ed., pp. 872–883).

Williams, T. M., & Kornblum, W. (1985). *Growing up poor.* Lexington, MA: Lexington Books.

Williams, T. M. & Kornblum, W. (1994). *The uptown kids.* New York: G. P. Putnam's Sons.

Willie, Charles V. (1988). *A new look at black families* (3rd ed.). Dix Hills, NY. General Hall.

Wilson, Julius W. (1987). *The truly disadvantaged.* Chicago: The University of Chicago Press.

Wilson, W. J. (1996). *When work disappears.* New York: Alfred A. Knopf.

Wines, M. (2000, April 24). Heroin carries AIDS to a region in Siberia. *New York Times,* pp. A1, A8.

Wong, P. T. P., & Fry, P. S. (1998). *The human quest for meaning.* Mahwah, NJ: Lawrence Erlbaum Associates.

Worguh, G. S. (1980). *From magic to metaphor.* New York: Paulist Press.

INDEX

Family (*continued*)
  father-daughter relationship and, 74, 110,
    127, 128–29, 131
  female-headed, 75, 110
  kin-scriptions and, 61, 72–73, 74, 104, 142,
    187
  migration effects on, 87n.1
  mother-daughter relationship and, 61, 74–82,
    100, 127–28, 131–32, 155–56
  racial/ethnic/sex gender role commitment
    and, 61–64, 66, 70–81, 100
  resilience and, 73, 101–2, 104, 127
  role model formulation and, 100–104, 116,
    155–56
  self-esteem and, 55
  separation from, 83
  socially invested, 158
  therapeutic intervention and, 168, 169, 177,
    178n.2
  See also Kinship networks; Parents/parenthood
Family types
  defended, 103–4, 116, 142, 158
  extended, 73, 124
  nuclear, 72, 124–25
Fashion, 43, 52, 54, 70
Fathers
  expectant, 133–34
  nonbiological, 110, 127, 129, 131
  relationships with daughters, 74, 110, 127,
    128–29, 131
Feedback, interactive, 95, 96, 115
Feiring, C., 135
Feldman, S. S., 25, 89
Female-headed households, 75, 110
Feminist movement, 91
Feminist theory, 15, 16–17, 83, 110
Field slaves, 87n.2
Fitzgerald, Ella, ix
Fitzgerald, F. Scott, 57–58n.1
Flirting, 144
Folkman, S., 146
Folk songs and tales, 31
Fordham, S., 126, 127, 128, 131–32, 166
Formal operational thought, 64–65, 106, 115,
    120
Franklin, Benjamin, 87n.2
Franklin, D. L., 87n.1
Freel, M. A., 23
Freud, Anna, xiv, 14
Freud, Sigmund, 16
Friendships, 109–10, 111, 139, 142. *See also* Peer
    groups
Frontal lobe, 120
Fry, Christine, 57–58n.1
Fry, P. S., 121–22
Fukuyama, F., 41

Gaming enterprises, 103, 118n.2
Gangs, xvii, 76
  girl, 107–8
Gangsta rap music, 6, 26
Gender
  adolescent development and, 13, 16–17, 19
  as childrearing factor, 131–32
  developmental domains and, 28, 61–86
  in Erikson's identity theory, 27
  role model formulation and, 91, 96
  See also Daughters; Males;
    Pregnancy/motherhood

Gender role. *See* Racial, ethnic, and sex gender
    role commitment
"Generalized other," 164
Gibson, Althea, 85
Giddings, P., 114
Gilligan, C., xiv
Girl gangs, 107–8
Givens, Maxine, 46–47, 48–49
Goals, 177
God, xv–xvi, 51
Godfather films, 92
Goffman, E., 98
Gordon, S., xxiii–xxivn.1
Gourse, L., ix
Greenspan, S. I., 167, 168
Grewal, G., 69, 88n.6
Grier, W. H., 113
Growing Up: Learning to Make Choices
    (GULTMC), 5, 31–32, 37, 70, 71,
    74–80, 84, 92–93, 101, 104–5, 107–9,
    112, 116, 118nn.3, 4, 123–24, 127–29,
    131, 132, 138–40, 142, 144–46, 147n.3,
    151, 153, 157–59, 163–66, 168–70, 175,
    176, 183, 184
  study overview, xx–xxi
Grubb, W. N., 149
Guilt, 84
GULTMC. *See* Growing Up: Learning to Make
    Choices
Gutierrez, L. M., 173

Habermas, Jürgen, 51
Hair, concerns about, 112, 113
Halberstam, D., 6
Hall, Edward T., xviii–xix, 33, 48, 179
Hall, G. Stanley, xiv, 14, 182
Hamer, Fannie Lou, 4–5
Hardiness, 9, 72, 165, 177, 179
Hare Self-Esteem Scale, xxi
Harris, J. R., 115
Hauser S. T., 163
Helms Racial Identity Attitude Scale, xxi
Henderson, Fletcher, 57–58n.1
Higher education, 148–49, 182
  historical black institutions, 42, 69
Hill, Lauryn, 43
Hine, T., 148
Hip hop culture, 6, 43, 52, 54
Historical black universities, 42, 69
Historical dislocation, 88n.3
Honey, Hush (Dancer), 114
Hoodlum (film), 118n.2
Hope, 177
Hopelessness, 33, 182, 183, 184
Households
  establishment of, 150
  female-headed, 75, 110
House slaves, 87n.2
Howard University, 69
Human service organizations, 166
Humor, 31
Hunter, Alberta, 57–58n.1
Husserl, Edmund, 44, 50
Hyper-Research (computer program), xxi

Identity
  adolescent development of, xiii, 19, 21, 25–27,
    89
  beauty concerns and, 111–15

Maturity (*continued*)
  developmental tasks of, 89
  reproductive, 17, 24, 77, 122, 126, 182
  self-efficacy as key to, 18
  social, 24, 122, 135, 149
McKusik, L., 146
McMahon, A., 163
Mead, G. H., 51, 178n.1
Meaning making, 15, 48, 49, 115, 158
  identity and, 22–24
  peer relationships and, 109, 111
  personal, 121–22
  processes of, 187
  Spencer's view of, xii, xviii
Meaning synthesis, 82, 85, 115
  adulthood preparation and, 180
  definition of, 187
  group sessions as venue for, 171
  of media images, 92–93
  mother-daughter relationship and, 78, 79, 100
  social identity and, 64, 65, 68, 69
Meaning systems, xv, 22, 38, 89
Media, 56, 115, 117
  black creativity and, 43
  "generalized other" and, 178n.1
  influence on role model formulation, 91–97
Mediation
  in person-process context, 38
  of risk, xiii, xiv, 33, 44, 99
Meenaghan, T. M., 33
Membership norms, 56, 189
Menarche, 122, 126
Mentoring, 115–16, 159
Merton, R. K., 39–40
Migration, impact of, 87n.1, 102
Military schools, 69
Misfortune, resilience and, 7
Mississippi Freedom Democratic Party, 5
Mobility. *See* Opportunity mobility; Social mobility
Moral agency, 90, 97–100, 150, 151, 159
Moral alienation, 64–65
Moral career, 98, 187
Morality, definition of, 187. *See also* Ethics
Moral sensibility, 18
Moral strength, 3
Moratorium, adolescence as, 14, 26
Morrison, Toni, 30, 32, 69, 88n.6, 99
Mother-daughter relationship, 61, 74–82, 131–32
  adulthood preparation and, 155–56
  meaning synthesis and, 78, 79, 100
  puberty and, 76, 127–28
Motherhood, adolescent. *See* Pregnancy/motherhood
Mother wit, 66, 189
Motivated acts of meaning, 53, 54, 187–88
Motivation, 50
Movies, 43, 95–96
MTV (cable network), 96
Multiculturalism, 62, 175
Murray, Albert, 3, 30, 32, 33, 57–58n.1, 87n.2
Music, xv, 6, 26, 43, 66
  jazz/blues idiom, xix, 30–31, 32, 50, 57–58n.1, 159, 181
  recording industry, 88n.5
Music videos, 88n.5, 96
Mutual aid societies, 4
Mutuality, 16, 17, 44, 90

Mutual recognition. *See* Recognition

National Association of Social Work (NASW), xii
Nation of Islam, 68–69
Natural helping networks, 41–42, 188
Negative identity, 33, 82
Negotiation, 38, 49
  of adulthood status, 152–56, 159
  definition of, 188
Neighborhoods, 38, 71, 78, 145, 184
Nested contexts, 24, 34, 72, 118n.1
  Bronfenbrenner's theory of, xviii, 34, 37, 118n.1, 164, 178n.1, 180
  case illustration, 18, 23, 31, 35–36, 40, 115
  definition of, 188
  recognition within, 18
  role model formulation and, 28, 96, 100, 102
New Negro, 43
Nonbiological fathers, 110, 127, 129, 131
No Respect (Souljah), 74
Norm-modeling actions, 56–57, 188
Norm-modeling behaviors, 57
Norms, 49, 56–57
  proximal and distal, 40–41
  self-generated, 56, 57–58n.1
  social, 150, 159, 181
Nouwen, H., 88n.3
Nuclear family, 72, 124–25
Nurturance, 111
  by adult males, 110, 127
  care protective sensibility and, 90, 92, 102
  dating/mate selection issues, 128
  See also Care/caring

Oedipal conflicts, 15, 16
Ogbu, John U., xxivn.3, 166
Opportunity mobility, 39, 148–60, 165, 182
  adulthood readiness/status negotiation and, 152–56, 159
  definition of, 188
  as development domain, xiii, xvii, 28–29
  social investment and, 156–59, 160
Oppression, 173, 185
  internalization of, 82–83
Oral sex, 141
Orange, D. M., 22–23, 48, 49
Ostrom, C. W., 23
Other, 164
Outcomes, resilience and, 7

Palombo, J., 22
PANSI. *See* Pregnancy Adulthood Negotiation of Status Inventory
Parents/parenthood, 150, 184
  adolescent, 40, 76, 77, 99, 126, 133–34, 149, 154
  adolescents' view of, 65
  courtship and, 125
  dating/mate selection concerns, 126–29, 131–32
  father-daughter relationship, 74, 110, 127, 128–29, 131
  mother-daughter relationship, 61, 74–82, 100, 127–28, 131–32, 155–56
  nonbiological fathers, 110, 127, 129, 131
  psychodynamic theory and, 72
  therapeutic intervention role of, 168, 169, 177
Parks, Rosa, 3, 4